IMAGES
of America

Historic Cultural Landscapes of Oklahoma

ON THE COVER: This is a stunning view of the formal garden at the Philbrook Museum of Art that attracts visitors to stroll through while visiting the museum. (Courtesy Villa Philbrook.)

IMAGES
of America

Historic Cultural Landscapes of Oklahoma

Dr. Charles L.W. Leider

ARCADIA
PUBLISHING

Copyright © 2018 by Dr. Charles L.W. Leider
ISBN 978-1-4671-2992-3

Published by Arcadia Publishing
Charleston, South Carolina

Printed in the United States of America

Library of Congress Control Number: 2018958882

For all general information, please contact Arcadia Publishing:
Telephone 843-853-2070
Fax 843-853-0044
E-mail sales@arcadiapublishing.com
For customer service and orders:
Toll-Free 1-888-313-2665

Visit us on the Internet at www.arcadiapublishing.com

This book is dedicated to the former landscape architecture students and others at Oklahoma State University whose names and drawings are listed in the introduction for each project.

Contents

ACKNOWLEDGMENTS

I wish to thank Kirk A. Jewel, president of the Oklahoma State University Foundation, for sponsoring the publication of my research work on the historic cultural landscapes of Oklahoma. In addition, I wish to thank my wife, Yuvone, and my two sons, Chuck and Steve Leider, for their support and encouragement to publish this work—especially Steve, who worked with me on two of the historic landscapes, Villa Philbrook and 101 Ranch. In addition, I wish to thank two Oklahoma State University faculty members, Dr. Williams Bryans of the Department of History and Prof. Nigel Jones of the School of Architecture, for their review of student work.

All the images used in this book, unless otherwise noted, are from the Library of Congress's Historic American Landscape Survey (HALS) collection (memory.loc.gov/ammem/collections/habs_haer/).

Introduction

Cultural landscapes are settings that human beings have created in the natural world. They reveal fundamental ties between people and the land––ties based on our need to grow food, give form to our settlements, meet requirements for recreation, and find suitable places to bury our dead. Cultural landscapes are intertwined patterns of things both natural and constructed—plants and fences, watercourses, and buildings. They range from formal gardens to cattle ranches and from cemeteries and pilgrimage routes to village squares. They are special places—expressions of human manipulation of and adaptation to the land and the environment. As the recognition of cultural landscapes has expanded nationally and internationally, landscape inventories are increasingly being initiated by federal, state, and local governments and private nonprofit organizations. These inventories involve a variety of professionals, such as landscape architects, historians, biologists, and geographers. These efforts, although varied in scope, all serve the same purpose: to document the qualities and attributes of a cultural landscape that make it significant and worth preserving.

Historic landscapes are an important part of the world's cultural heritage. Studying cultural landscapes provides an opportunity to understand history through examples of built work showing how people related to their natural environment, provided housing, developed an economy, socialized, and created these spaces we can still experience today. Historic cultural landscapes are recognized by international, national, and local organizations. At an international level, the United Nations Educational, Scientific, and Cultural Organization (UNESCO), through its World Heritage Program and its International Committee on Monuments and Sites (ICOMOS), identifies and recognizes significant cultural landscapes. The International Federation of Landscape Architects (IFLA), through its Cultural Landscape Committee, has worked with ICOMOS to create a common definition for both organizations of historic cultural landscapes. A UNESCO World Heritage Site is a place (such as a forest, mountain, lake, desert, monument, building, complex, or a city) that is listed by UNESCO because of its special cultural or physical significance. The list is maintained by the International World Heritage Program, administered by the UNESCO World Heritage Committee.

World Cultural Heritage Organizations

The World Heritage Program catalogues, names, and conserves sites of outstanding cultural or natural importance to the common heritage of humanity. Under certain conditions, listed sites can obtain funds from the World Heritage Fund. The program was founded with the Convention Concerning the Protection of World Cultural and Natural Heritage, which was adopted by the General Conference of UNESCO on November 16, 1972. Since then, 186 state parties have ratified the convention. As of 2010, 911 sites are listed: 704 cultural, 181 natural, and 26 mixed properties in 187 states party to the convention. Italy is home to the greatest number of World Heritage Sites. UNESCO references each World Heritage Site with an identification number, but new inscriptions often include previous sites now listed as part of larger descriptions. As a result, the identification numbers exceed 1,200 even though there are fewer on the list. Each World Heritage Site is the property of the state in whose territory the site is located, but it is considered to be in the interest of the international community to preserve each site.

Since the adoption of the World Heritage Convention by UNESCO in November 1972, the identification and protection of cultural and natural heritage sites considered to be of outstanding universal value to humanity have been achieved through the UNESCO World Heritage List. The World Heritage List contains the world's premier cultural landscapes. In 1992, the World Heritage Committee adopted the concept of cultural landscapes on the UNESCO World Heritage List, and since then, the committee has inscribed almost 100 such landscapes. The World Heritage Committee adopted three main categories of cultural landscapes:

1) Clearly defined: a landscape designed and created at a point in history, often in a recognized style or applying known principles, such as Versailles in France, Kew Gardens in the United Kingdom, and Muskauer Park in Germany and Poland.
2) Evolved:
2a) Evolved Relict: a place of former habitation and landscape imprint.
2b) Evolved Continuing: a place where people live today and continue to interact with and change the cultural landscape, such as Viñales Valley in Cuba and the Puszta pastoral landscape of Hortobágy National Park in Hungary.
3) Associative: a landscape that may not have been transformed by humanity but exhibits religious, artistic, or cultural associations important to society, such as Tongariro National Park in New Zealand and Uluru–Kata Tjuta National Park in Australia.

Countries that are members of ICOMOS work with the World Heritage Program. ICOMOS fosters heritage conservation and historic preservation at the national and international levels through education and training, international exchanges of people and information, technical assistance, documentation, advocacy, and other activities consistent with the goals of ICOMOS and through collaboration with other organizations. In the United States, this organization is known as US/ICOMOS.

Cultural Heritage Organizations in the United States

The National Park Service Heritage Documentation Program website (www.nps.gov/) provides detailed guidelines for producing landscape architectural measured drawings, large-format photography, and written history reports according to standards defined by the Historic American Buildings Survey (HABS), the Historic American Engineering Record (HAER), and the Historic American Landscape Survey (HALS).

In addition to the World Heritage List criteria, HALS, the cultural landscape foundation in the United States, has identified four recognized types of historic cultural landscapes. Only one of these types, historic designed landscapes, is the purview of the landscape architect.

1) Historic Designed Landscapes: landscapes that were consciously designed or laid out by a landscape architect, master gardener, architect, or horticulturist according to design principles or an amateur gardener working in a recognized style or tradition.
2) Vernacular Landscapes: landscapes that evolved through use by the people whose activities or occupancy shaped that landscape. Through social or cultural attitudes of an individual, family, or community, the landscape reflects the physical, biological, and cultural character of those everyday lives.
3) Historic Sites: landscapes significant for their association with a historic event, activity, or person.
4) Ethnographic Landscapes: landscapes containing a variety of natural and cultural resources that the associated people define as heritage resources.

Historic Cultural Landscapes in Oklahoma

In 1987, the American Society of Landscape Architects (ASLA), in an effort to promote the preservation of historic landscapes, requested each of its chapters in the United States to conduct an inventory of historic designed landscapes using the National Register of Historic Places guideline of 50 years old as historic. To undertake a statewide survey of historic designed landscapes, the Oklahoma chapter (OK/ASLA) designated a historic preservation chairperson. Members of OK/ASLA, along with the public, were invited to nominate significant historic designed landscapes in Oklahoma. As a result, 47 historic landscapes were nominated (see appendix), which included predominately designed landscapes but also historic sites, vernacular landscapes, and ethnographic landscapes. Since the 1987 survey, additional significant historic landscapes, such as the 101 Ranch and the Ardenum at McAlester, have been recorded with HALS.

Using the ASLA survey form, Oklahoma State University (OSU) landscape architecture students in a recreation planning course visited each site and completed the survey form. Additionally, the students conducted a literature search on each site. Following the survey and literature search, an information file was established for each landscape. The individual file included information such as the survey form, photographs of the site, maps, history, news articles, and any National Register of Historic Places nominations. After the inventory was completed, the definitions from the National Register Bulletin 18 of the US National Park Service were applied to identify and classify each of the designed historic landscapes as to type. In Oklahoma, estates constituted the largest category, followed by parks.

Fifteen different types of designed landscapes are identified in Bulletin 18:

- small residential grounds
- estates or plantation grounds
- arboreta, botanical, and display gardens
- zoological gardens and parks
- churchyards and cemeteries
- monuments and memorial grounds
- plaza, squares, green malls, or other public spaces
- city planning and institutional grounds
- subdivisions and planned communities or resorts
- commercial and industrial grounds
- parks and campgrounds
- grounds designed or developed for outdoor recreation or sports activities
- fairgrounds and exhibition grounds
- parkways, drives, and trails
- bodies of water and fountains

After the completion of the survey, an analysis was conducted of each site. The analysis used criteria to determine the significance of each site based on design integrity, general property considerations, and plant material. Additional criteria to evaluate the site for design integrity included consideration of identifiable components such as encroachment on the original site, the quality of the original design, the setting for the property, materials used, quality of workmanship, and the ambience, feeling, or atmosphere of the site. The criteria used to evaluate the general considerations of the site included historic character, irrevocable changes that have taken place, original property boundaries, site grading and drainage, site furnishings, architectural features, circulation systems, and the condition of the site. Criteria to evaluate the plant material included identification of the original plant species used in the plan, their current condition, new plant material installed, and invasive plant materials found on the site. The above criteria were created to evaluate and rank the significance of the sites. The ranked information was used in choosing sites for individual case studies. The results of the survey, analysis, and recommendations were published as the Statewide Plan for Oklahoma Historic Designed Landscapes in 1988 and presented to OK/ASLA Chapter, the Oklahoma State Historic Preservation Office, and the Oklahoma Department of Tourism and Recreation. The report recommended that the Department of Tourism and Recreation prepare a brochure on sites to be visited for distribution through its visitors centers throughout the state to give citizens and tourists an opportunity to visit these historic landscapes.

Using information from the ranking list, individual case studies were selected by students through special topics courses offered in the OSU Landscape Architecture Program. The individual case studies were prepared using HABS and now HALS guidelines, literature, and methods for recording and documenting historic landscapes through interpretive and measured drawings. The drawings typically show the footprints of buildings on the site and the facade of the major structure; all the minor structures related to the landscape, such as arbors, gazebos, fences, walls, and retaining walls; and other related elements. Before the site survey for a case study was undertaken, a thorough literature search focusing on the historical development of the site was undertaken. The literature searches typically produced historic photographs, drawings, and the history of the site. If an original landscape site plan existed, it was used to locate the remaining plant material of the original design. After the research was completed, an overall measured "as-built" site plan with topography and sections through the site was prepared. Woody plant material was also shown on the as-built drawing, along with a plant list. Additional measured as-built drawings were prepared on landscape features such as retaining walls, patios, pools, fountains, walls, and fences. Two of the hand-drawn case studies in ink on plastic film, for Thomas Berry Estate in Stillwater and Villa Philbrook in Tulsa, won HABS Honorable Mention in the National Charles E. Peterson Prize Competition for university design programs. OSU was the only landscape architecture program in the United States to enter and win recognition in the competition. All drawings under HALS are now developed digitally in AutoCad, like the Oklahoma City Civic Center case study, in contrast to earlier hand drawings prepared for the 101 Ranch and Villa Philbrook case studies.

The Oklahoma City Civic Center is an example of a case study of a designed landscape for a mall that documents how a conceptual plan—designed in the mid-1920s by Hare & Hare of Kansas City, the oldest surviving landscape architecture firm in the country after the Olmsted firm—evolved over the years before being built during the Great Depression in the mid-1930s. Because of the flat site, the conceptual site plans did not contain any topographic information. To achieve greater clarity, no plant material was shown on the concept plan. To interpret the site, an overall plan was created to measure and document the as-built areas, as shown in the drawing of the Municipal Building, which terminates the mall on the east end. The Music Hall, one of the major buildings on the site, terminates the west end of the mall.

Drawings of vernacular landscapes came about as a result of a request to the OSU Landscape Architecture Program from the National Park Service to document, through measured and interpreted drawings, the headquarters site of the 101 Ranch near Ponca City, an endangered national landmark due to erosion of the site by the South Fork River. The 100,000-acre ranch was one of the largest in the United States. The case study is an example of a vernacular landscape, because the owners were involved in shaping the landscape as opposed to having it designed by a landscape architect. The headquarters site, at its highest level of development in 1929, was chosen as the study area. Very few of the original buildings remained due to the financial collapse of the ranch in 1929 and the subsequent loss of buildings due to a bankruptcy liquidation sale, fires, and natural disasters. All remaining buildings and the foundations of previous buildings were measured. Since the entire site had been neglected and could not be inspected or surveyed to determine the location of the former buildings due to overgrown weeds and brush, an aerial photograph taken in the early 1930s was used to re-create the footprints of buildings and the circulation system at the headquarters site in 1929. Using infrared photography, the building footprints and drives that existed on the site in 1929 were located and shown on the site plan. Historic photographs found in the Western History Museum at the University of Oklahoma, the State Historical Museum in Oklahoma City, and the Glass Negative Shop in Ponca City provided further information on the appearance of the site and buildings so they could be re-created to scale, showing the elevations of barns, service buildings, and the White House (the ranch house) as they existed in 1929.

Villa Philbrook, a Tulsa estate listed in the National Register of Historic Places, is an example of a case study documenting a designed landscape that demonstrated interdisciplinary collaboration between two prominent Kansas City offices—Hare & Hare and Edward B. Delk, an architectural office. After the site plan with topography was created, two sections were made through the site to show elevation change between the front and rear yards. The front yard of the villa was level, while the rear had a long slope to a creek at the rear property line. This accommodated formal gardens with a cascading water feature, copied after the Villa Lante, a notable Italian Renaissance garden, and a rock garden and pond terminated by the tempietto. Recording and documenting all the garden structures, such as the tempietto, summerhouse, and fountain, with measured and interpretive drawings were very important to understanding the renovation of the site.

One

Estates

Villa Philbrook, Tulsa
Type of Project: Landscape Plan
Designers: Hare & Hare, Landscape Architects; Edward B. Delk, Architect; both, Kansas City, Missouri
Landscape Contracting Company: Thomas Landscape & Nursery Date: 1926
Renovation Designer: Howell & VanCuren, Landscape Architects Renovated: 2004

The 1920s were a flamboyant period in the United States, and in Oklahoma, wealthy oilmen such as Waite Phillips were building lavish estates. Born in Bartlesville, Oklahoma, he moved to Tulsa in 1918 and established the Phillips Petroleum Company. Waite Phillips purchased 64 acres for the Philbrook Estate in several parcels between 1921 and 1926, when Phillips commissioned architect Edward B. Delk and landscape architect Herbert Hare of Hare & Hare to design the estate. Hare chose to model the cascade after Villa Lante, an Italian Renaissance design with a naturalistic landscape. Delk designed the house and the architectural elements, including the south terrace, tempietto, and garden house, in the Italian Renaissance villa style. Hare was responsible for the overall site design and circulation system, as well as the formal garden and the rock garden. Construction was done by the Long Construction Company of Kansas City, general contracting by Henry Lohman of Tulsa, and landscape installation by Phillip Thomas and C. Burton Fox, superintendent of Thomas Landscape & Nursery of Tulsa. The final cost of the villa was $1,190,245, which included the cost of the land at $31,176 and $128,694 for landscape materials. The Phillips family resided in this 72-room villa from the date of its completion in 1927 until 1938, when Waite Phillips donated the property to the City of Tulsa to be a center for the arts.

Today, the Philbrook Museum is known for its outstanding medieval art collection. The most recent renovations to the gardens were completed in 2004, after this case study was completed. Work included extending the garden to the summerhouse on the south, needed re-engineering to the creek on the west side of the property, and connecting trails with gardens paths and increasing handicap accessibility.

Study Director: Dr. Charles L. Leider, Landscape Architecture Program
Faculty Advisors: Dr. William Bryans, Department of History, and Prof. Nigel Jones, School of Architecture
Study Team Members: David Holland, team leader; Stephen F. Leider, Charlene Collins, Kyle Clayton, Michael Harris, Todd Hodges, Scott Hundley, Dennis Kennedy, Hunter Pittman, Leo Sheck, Michael Schwegman, and Jeffrey Suiter

Sources:
Hare & Hare archives, University of Missouri, Kansas City
Villa Philbrook records

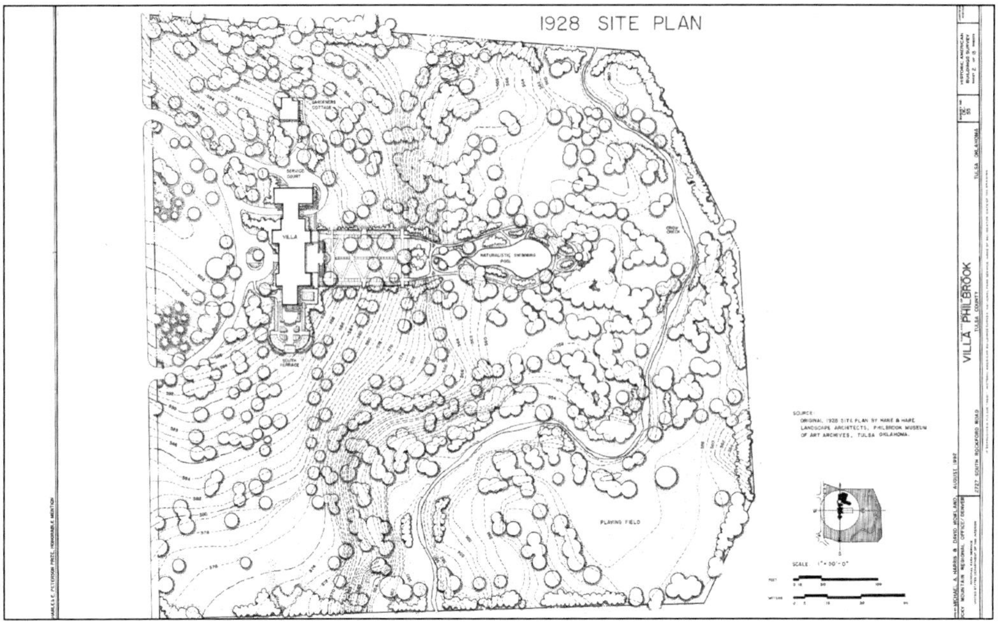

This project represented the first major joint collaboration between an architect and a landscape architect in Tulsa. The villa was on the crest of the slope in the center of the site ,with a deep 200-foot setback from the Rockford Avenue. The villa is sited on a slight slope to the street and a moderate slope to the rear yard through a heavily wooded site to Crow Creek. The entrance to the villa is off Rockford Avenue near the intersection of Twenty-Eighth Street with a wide U-shaped driveway to the front door and a circular driveway to the service area, garage, and gardener's residence. Terraces and the formal gardens are on the east and south sides of the villa, with informal walkways throughout the site.

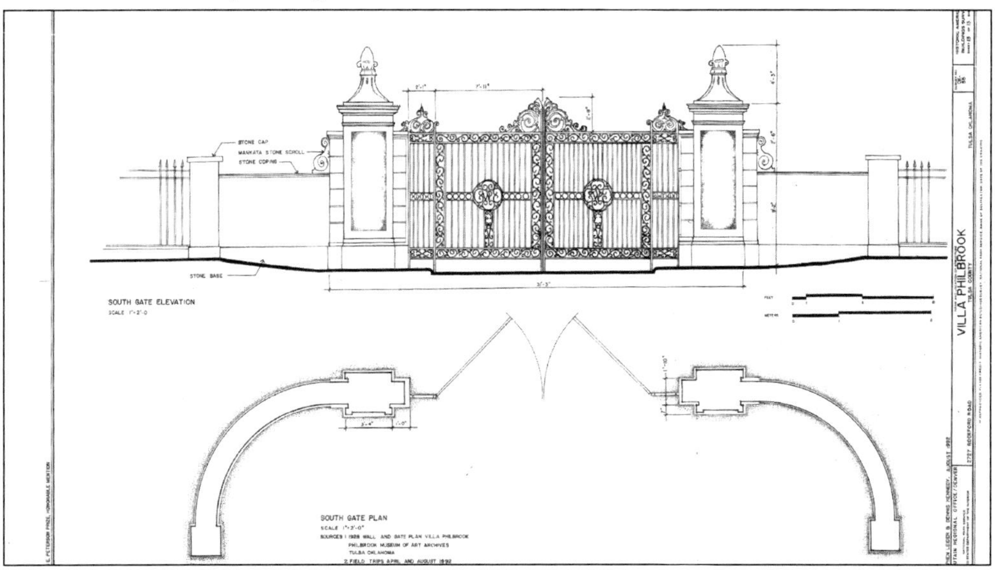

The 1992 as-built measured drawings of the gate in plan and elevation form show the wrought iron entrance gate on Rockford Avenue with the Phillips logo at the top of the gate. The gate is support by two 10-foot masonry columns, a semicircular wall with two smaller six-foot columns, and wrought iron fencing along the front yard on Rockford Avenue.

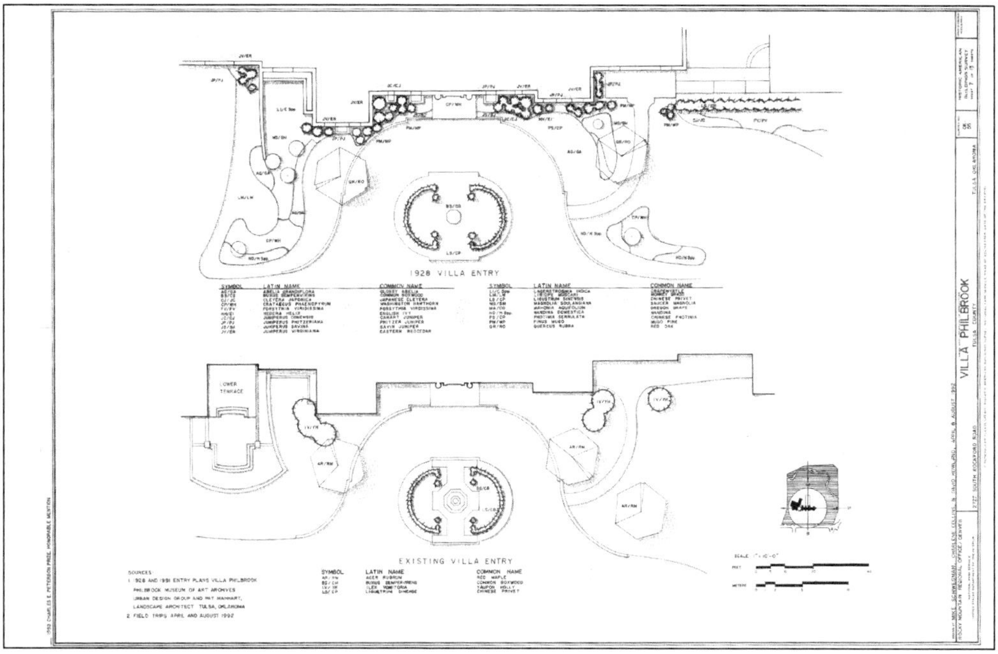

As-built measured drawings from 1928 and 1992 of plans and plant lists are compared. The 1928 flat U-shaped entrance drive shows no change in 1992. The location and choice of plant material around the entrance in 1928 has been simplified to use a smaller number of plants in 1992.

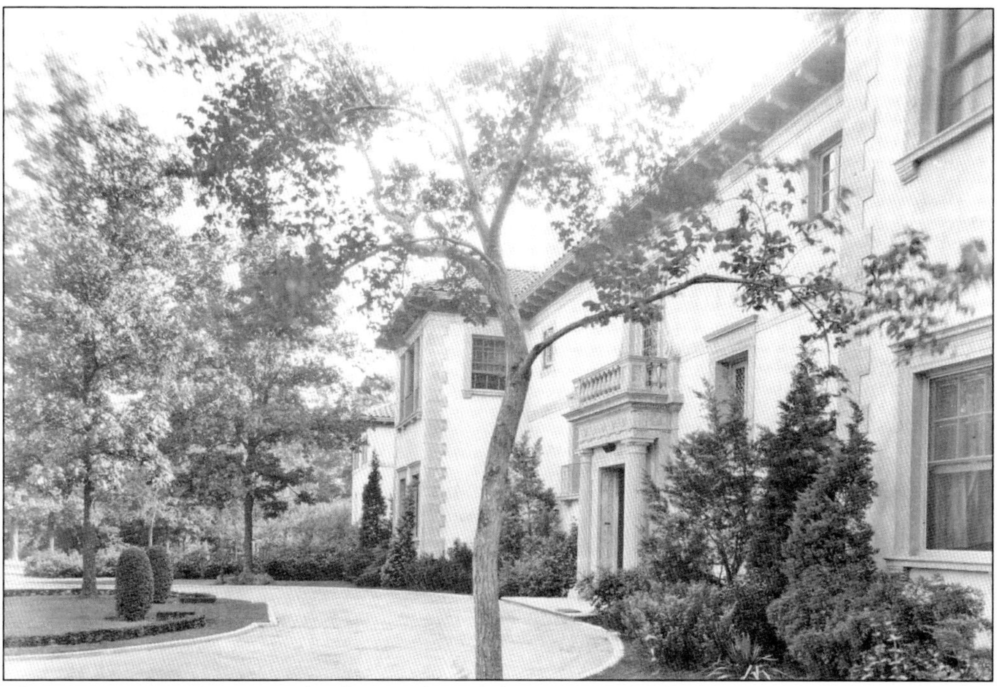

The view in 1928 shows a wide, flat, U-shaped driveway to the front door of the villa. The view also shows a formal symmetrical planting arrangement. Vertical evergreen shrubs are used to accent the entrance to the door of the villa. Low hedges with stone curbing are used to highlight the driveway. Shade trees are placed along the driveway. (Courtesy Waite Phillips Collection.)

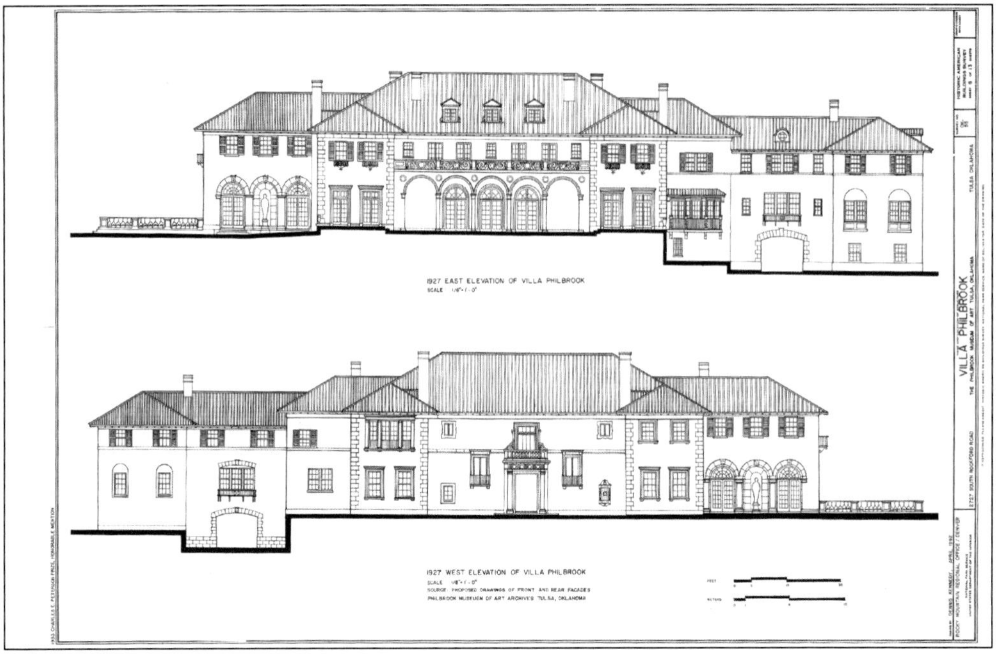

The as-built measured drawings in 1992 show the front and rear elevations of the villa with a sloping tile roof, stucco walls, and a rear walk-out basement from 1928. The front elevation of the villa on Rockford Avenue is two-story structure. The rear elevation, facing the garden, is a two- to three-story structure. The elevations show the opening for a ground-level service drive through the villa.

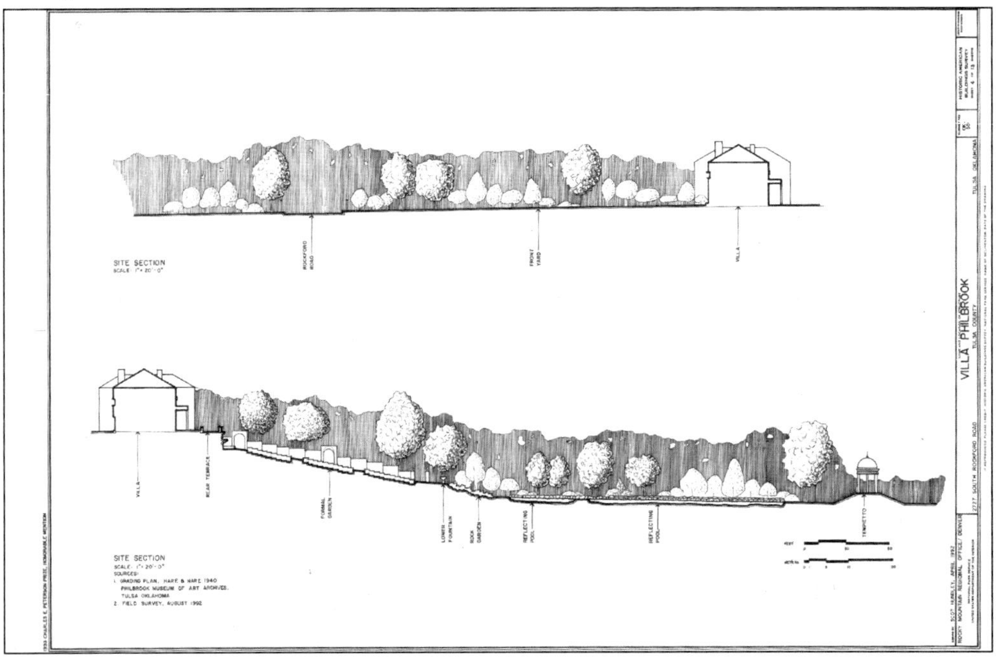

The as-built measured drawings in 1992 show profiles of the front and rear yards of the Villa Philbrook, with the front yard sloping gradually to Rockford Avenue and rear yard with a steeper slope to Crow Creek.

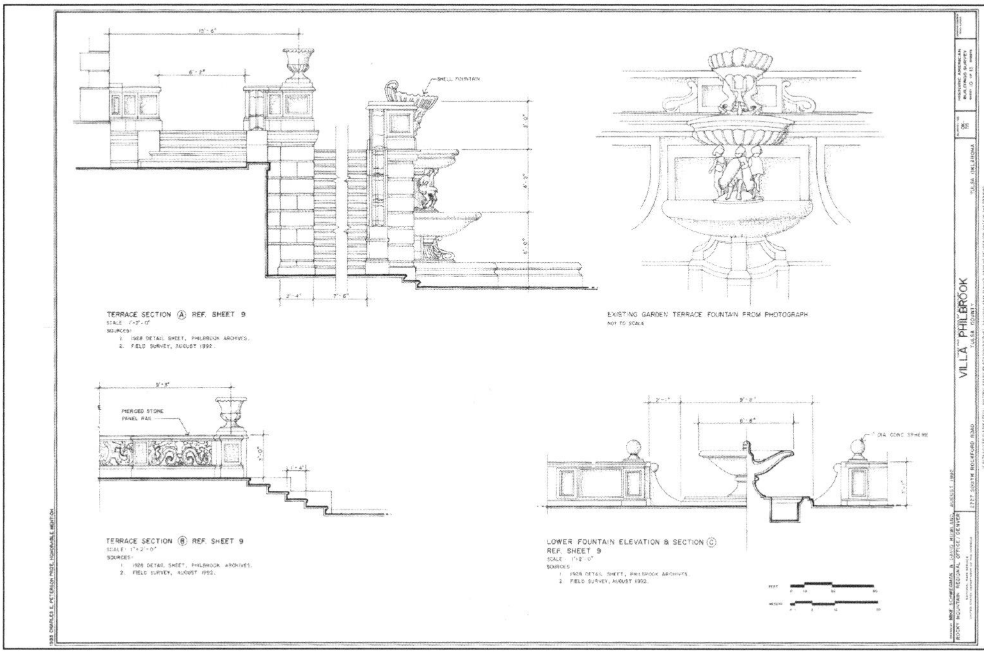

The as-built measured drawings in 1992 show details used in the construction of the rear terrace with elevations and sections for steps, balustrades, fountains, and urns. The design details were modeled after Villa Lante near Florence. The rear terrace provides access from the first floor of the villa to the formal gardens. (Courtesy Philbrook Museum of Art.)

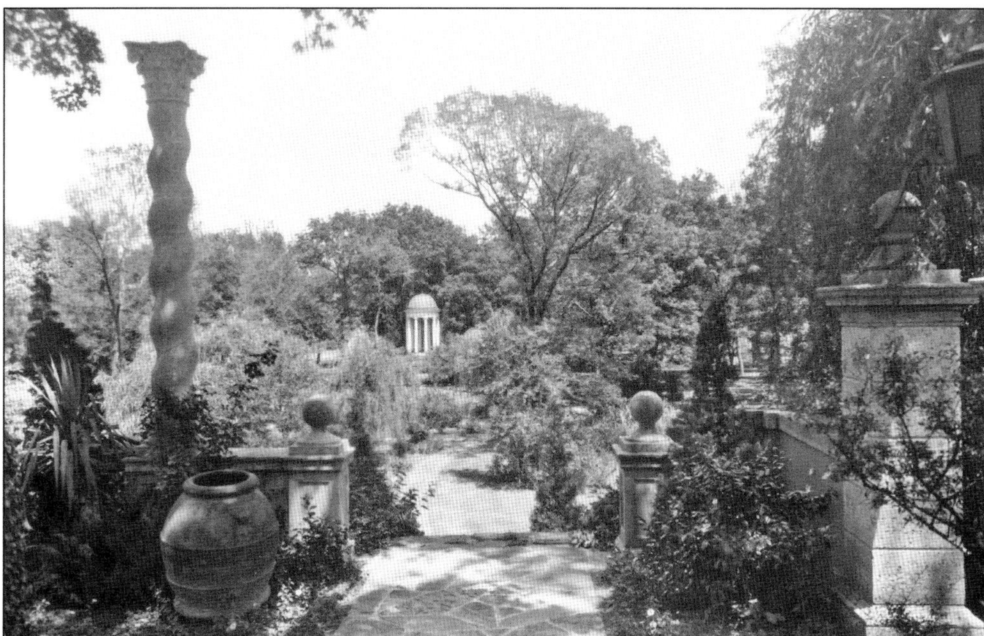

This 1928 view shows the tempietto from the walkway on the right side terrace to the formal gardens below the terrace. The walkway provides access to the formal garden, rock garden, swimming pool, and the tempietto. The walkway continues beyond the tempietto to provide access to the rest of the site. (Courtesy Waite Phillips Collection.)

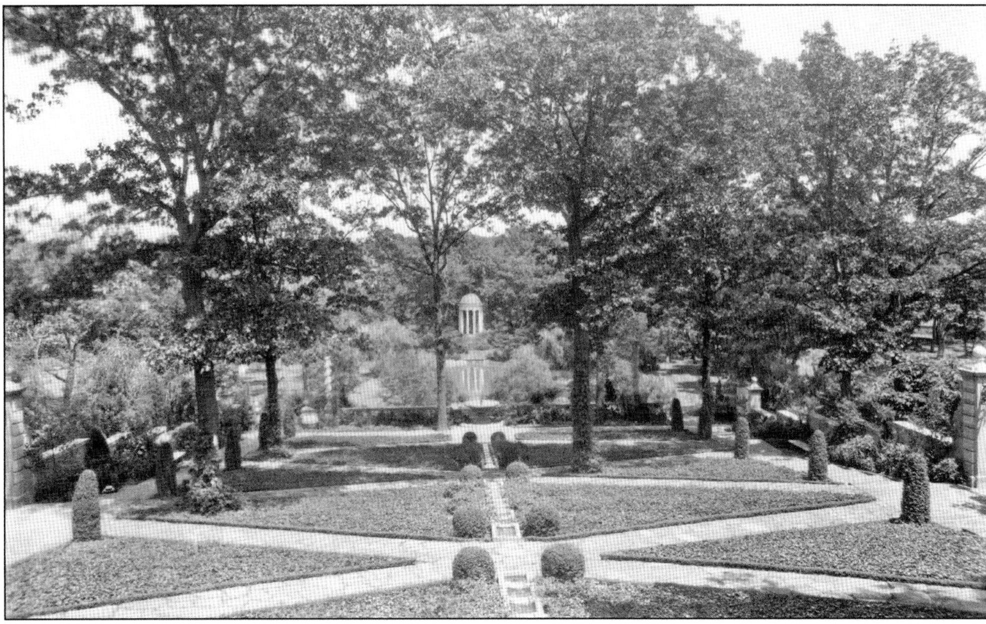

This 1928 view of the tempietto and the formal Italian Renaissance garden is on a central axis from the rear terrace of the villa to the tempietto. The runnel, modeled after the water feature at Villa Lante, is used as the principal water feature and is on the axis in the formal garden. The formal garden is highlighted by globe- and column-shaped evergreens. The several existing trees were retained in the formal garden when it was built. (Courtesy Waite Phillips Collection.)

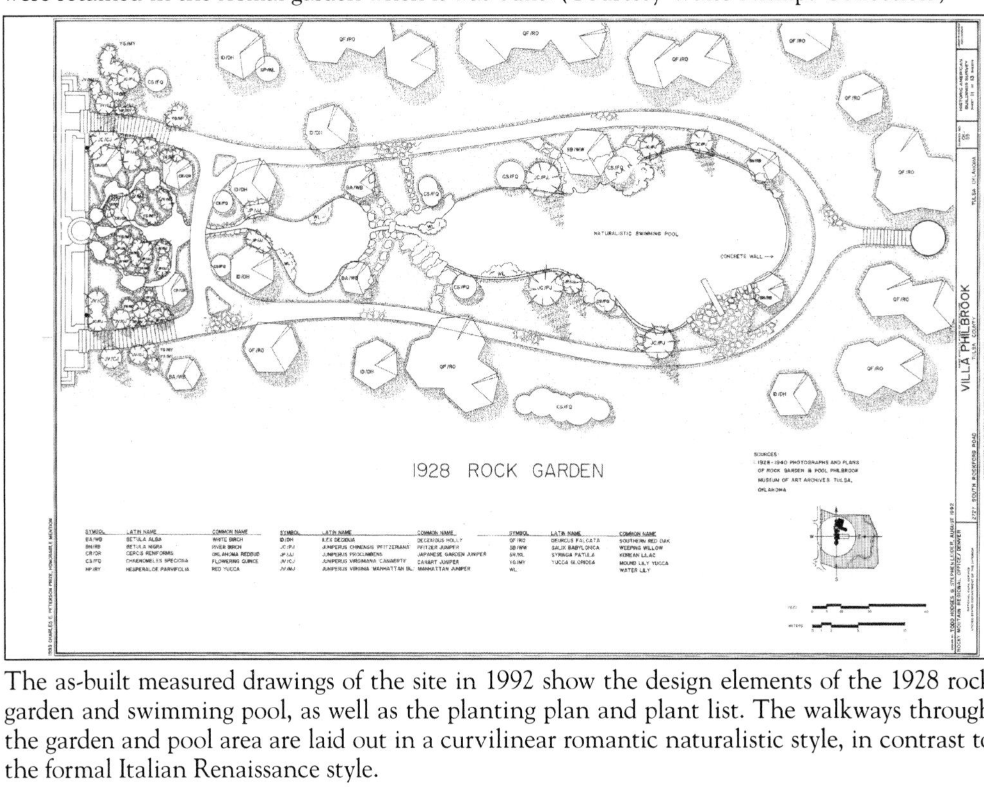

The as-built measured drawings of the site in 1992 show the design elements of the 1928 rock garden and swimming pool, as well as the planting plan and plant list. The walkways through the garden and pool area are laid out in a curvilinear romantic naturalistic style, in contrast to the formal Italian Renaissance style.

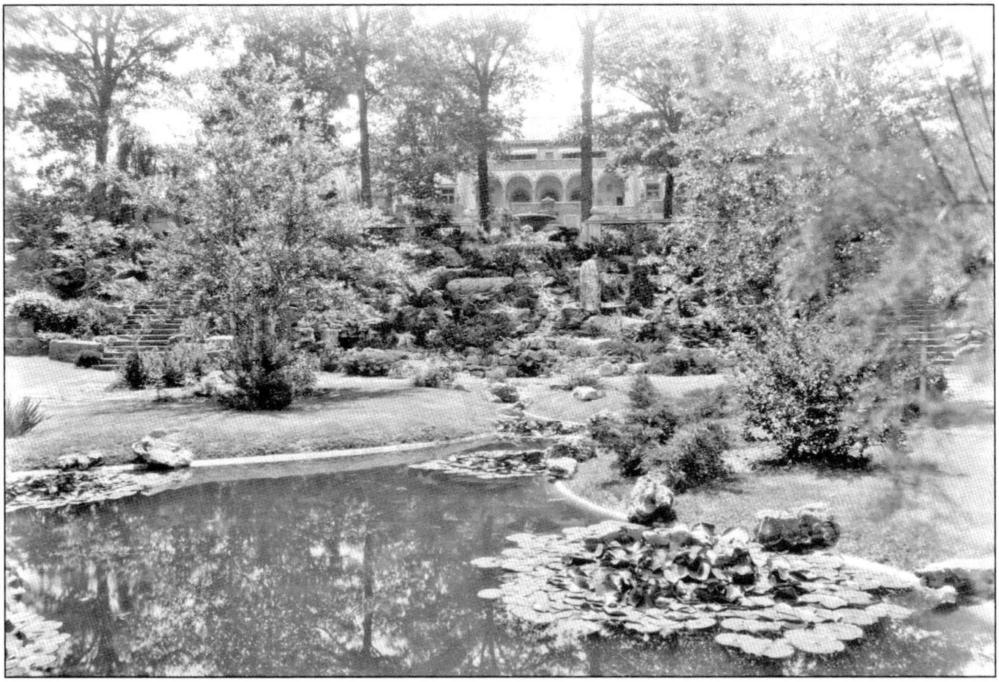

A 1930s view of the pool and rock garden shows the villa in the background. The pool was original designed to be used for swimming but was later converted to a lily pond. (Courtesy Waite Phillips Collection.)

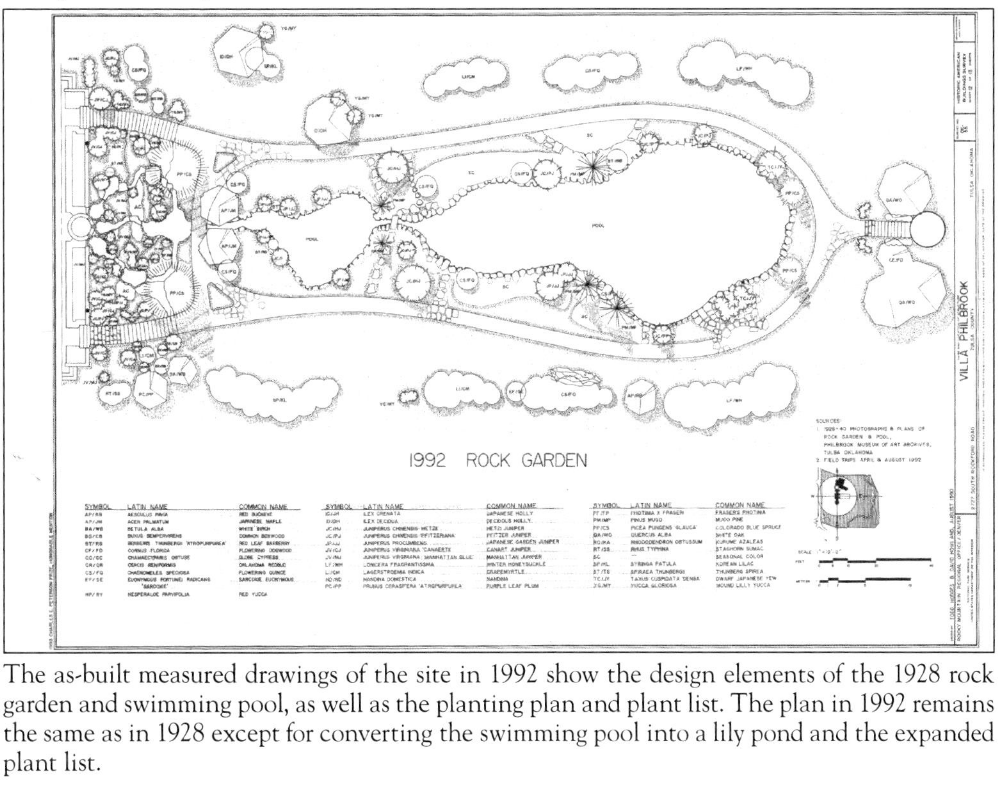

The as-built measured drawings of the site in 1992 show the design elements of the 1928 rock garden and swimming pool, as well as the planting plan and plant list. The plan in 1992 remains the same as in 1928 except for converting the swimming pool into a lily pond and the expanded plant list.

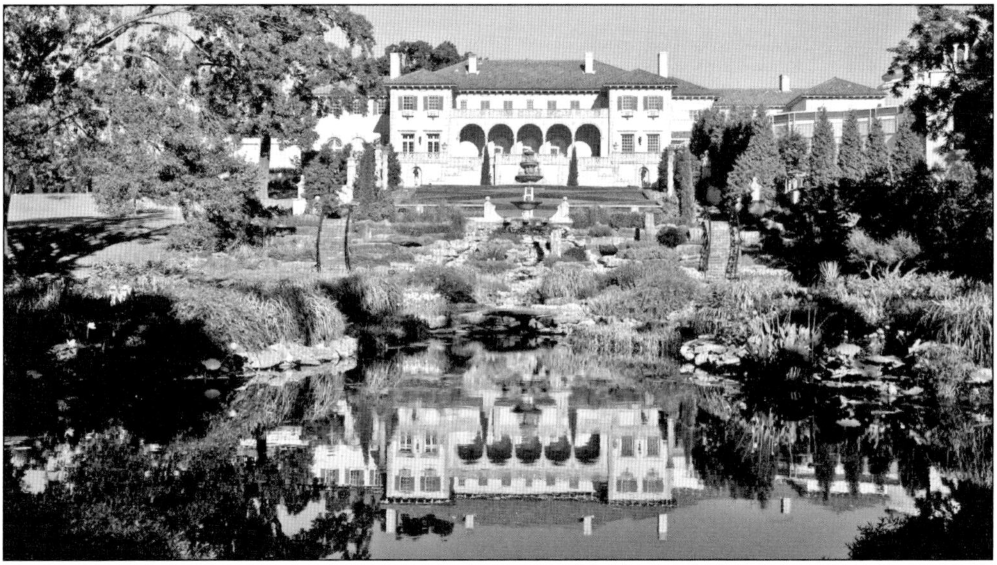

A 2018 view from the tempietto of the garden pool, rock garden, formal garden, and villa shows how they were built. The view illustrates the contrast between the informal and formal garden design styles. The addition on the left side of the villa was screened with vertical evergreens. The right side of the garden was left partially screened but opens up to the natural area of the site. (Courtesy Philbrook Museum of Art.)

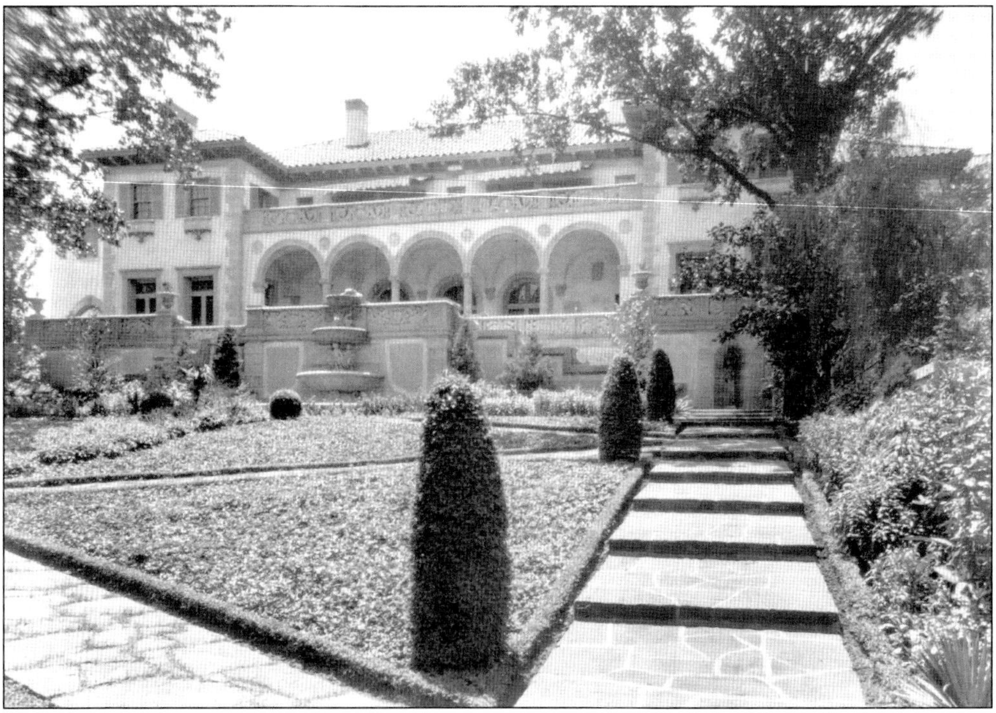

A 1928 view of the villa from the stone walkway on the left corner of the formal Italian garden focuses on the fountain on the wall of the terrace, showing how it was built. Column- and globe-shaped evergreen plants accent the of the formal garden and were used to reflect its Renaissance design character. (Courtesy Waite Phillips Collection.)

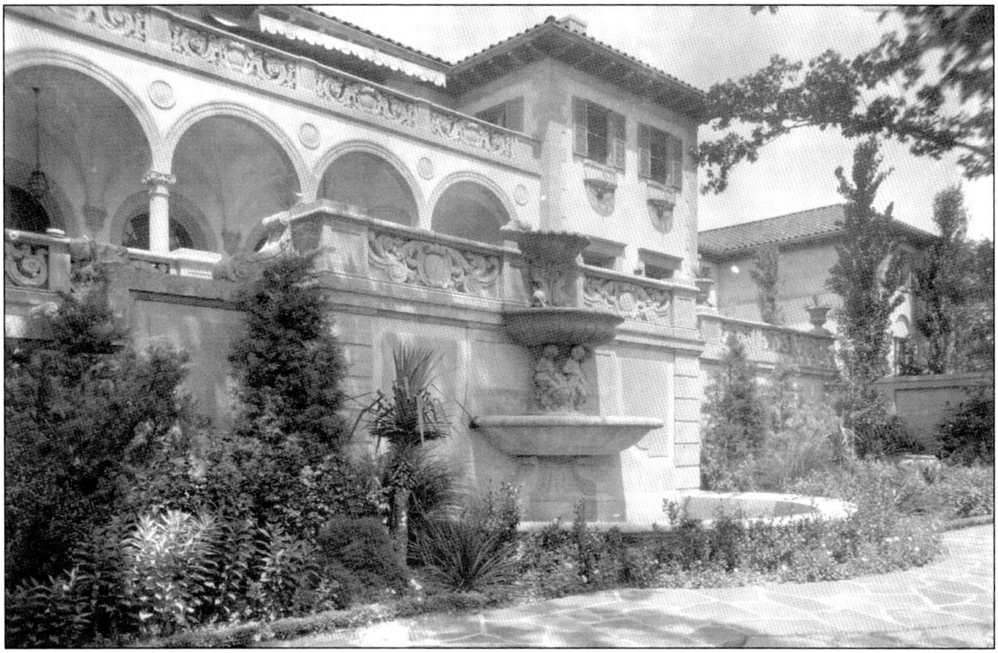

A 1928 view shows the fountain on the retaining wall for the terrace at the rear of the villa, designed in the Italian Renaissance style by Edward B. Delk of Kansas City. A planting bed between the wall and the stone-paved walkway softens the view of the wall. (Courtesy Waite Phillips Collection.)

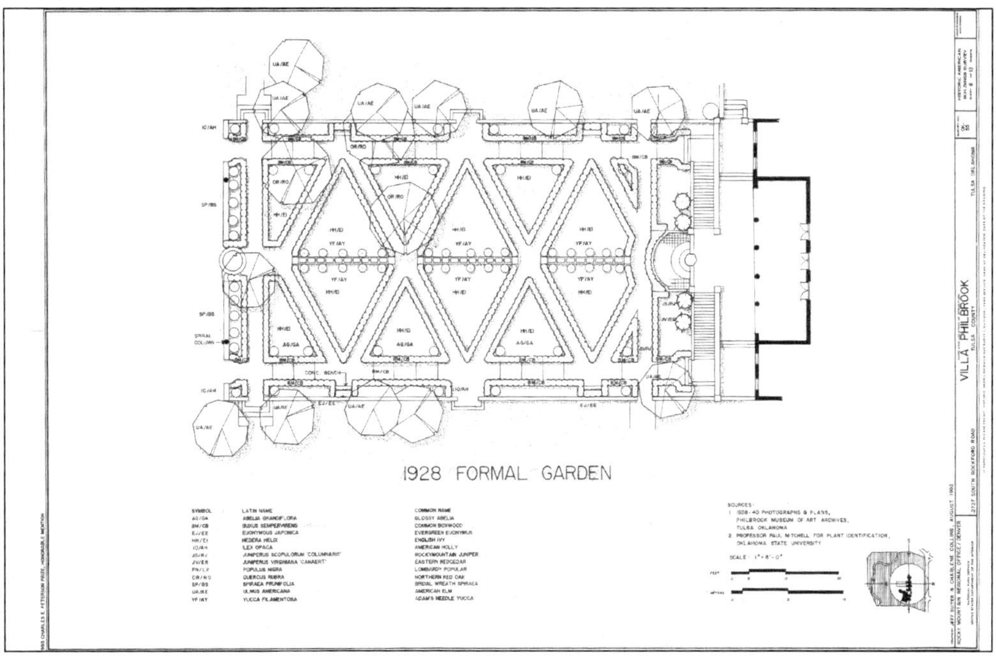

The 1928 drawing of the site shows the formal Italian Renaissance design style for the garden as well as the planting plan and plant list, which were created by Hare & Hare, landscape architects from Kansas City. Even though it is out of character for a formal garden, several existing shade trees were retained in the garden.

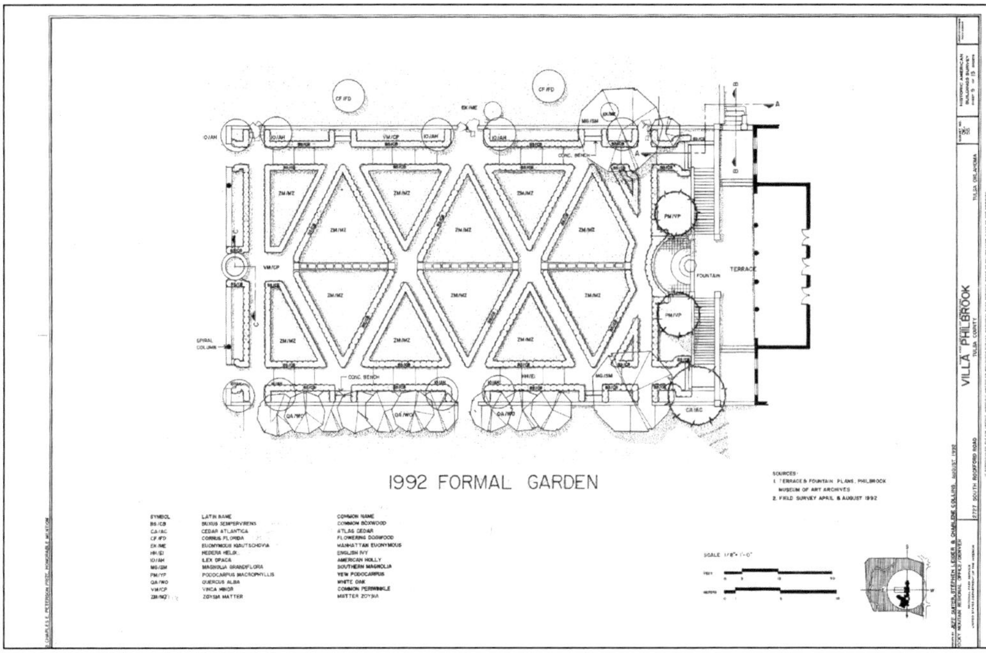

The as-built measured drawings of the site in 1992 show the design elements of the 1928 formal Italian Renaissance–style garden as well as the planting plan and plant list, which were retained with minor modifications except for shrubs along the runnel and the shade trees, which were removed.

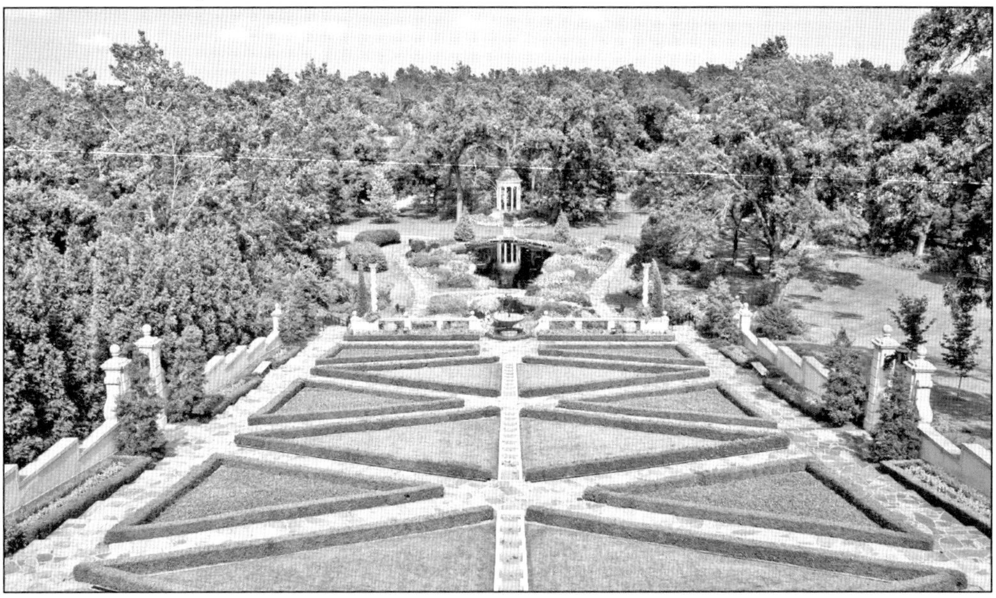

This full view shows the renovated Italian Renaissance formal garden, rock garden, pool, and the area around the tempietto as designed by landscape architects Howell & VanCuren and installed under the supervision of landscape contractor James Lemon, both from Tulsa. Overgrown shrubs and trees throughout the site were removed and replaced with an evergreen screen on the left, conical evergreens at the entrances to the garden, and low-growing hedges to highlight the walks and beds. All the original stone pavers were removed, marked, and reinstalled. (Courtesy Waite Phillips Collection.)

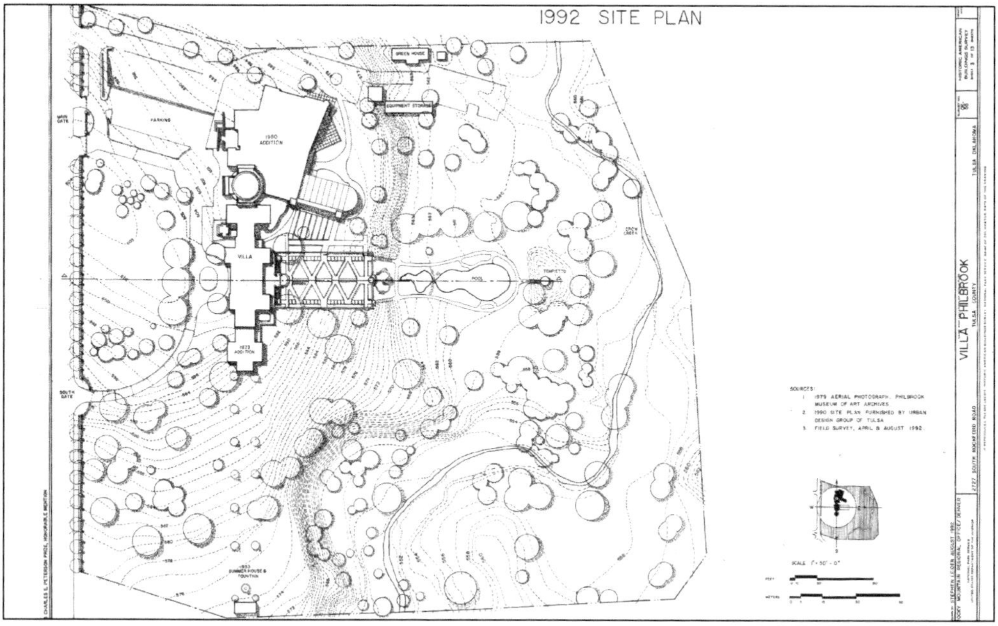

The 1992 as-built measured site plan shows a reduction of the pre-1928 site from 64 acres to 23 acres through the creation of the Rockridge Park residential development. The Phillips family lived in the villa for approximately 11 years. Waite Phillips donated the property in 1931 to the City of Tulsa to be used as an art museum. In 1990 and 1992, an addition was made to the north side of the villa along with an adjoining parking garage. The front yard, the south yard with the summerhouse, and the rear garden of the original site of the villa remained intact in 1992.

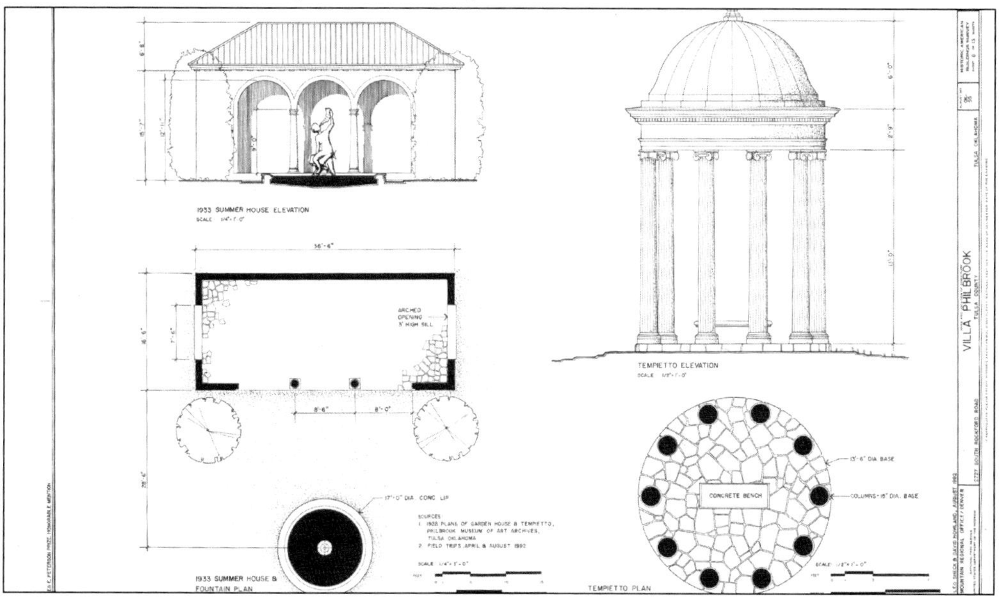

The 1992 as-built measured drawings of the summerhouse and tempietto show that the floor plans and elevations of each structure, designed in the Italian Renaissance style by Edward B. Delk, remain intact. A pool with a sculpture is located in front of summerhouse on an axis with the south side of the villa. The tempietto is on the east side of the villa on an axis from the terrace through the formal garden, rock garden, and pool to a 10-foot mount.

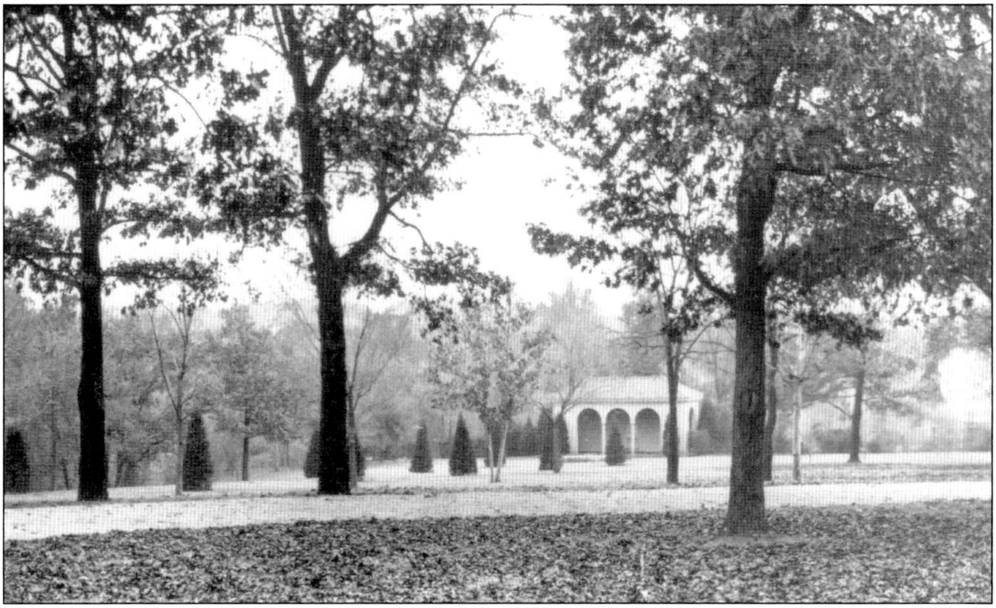

This view of the summerhouse was taken across the lawn from the south side of the villa. Two separate rows of conical evergreens define the view from the villa to the summerhouse. (Courtesy Philbrook Museum of Art.)

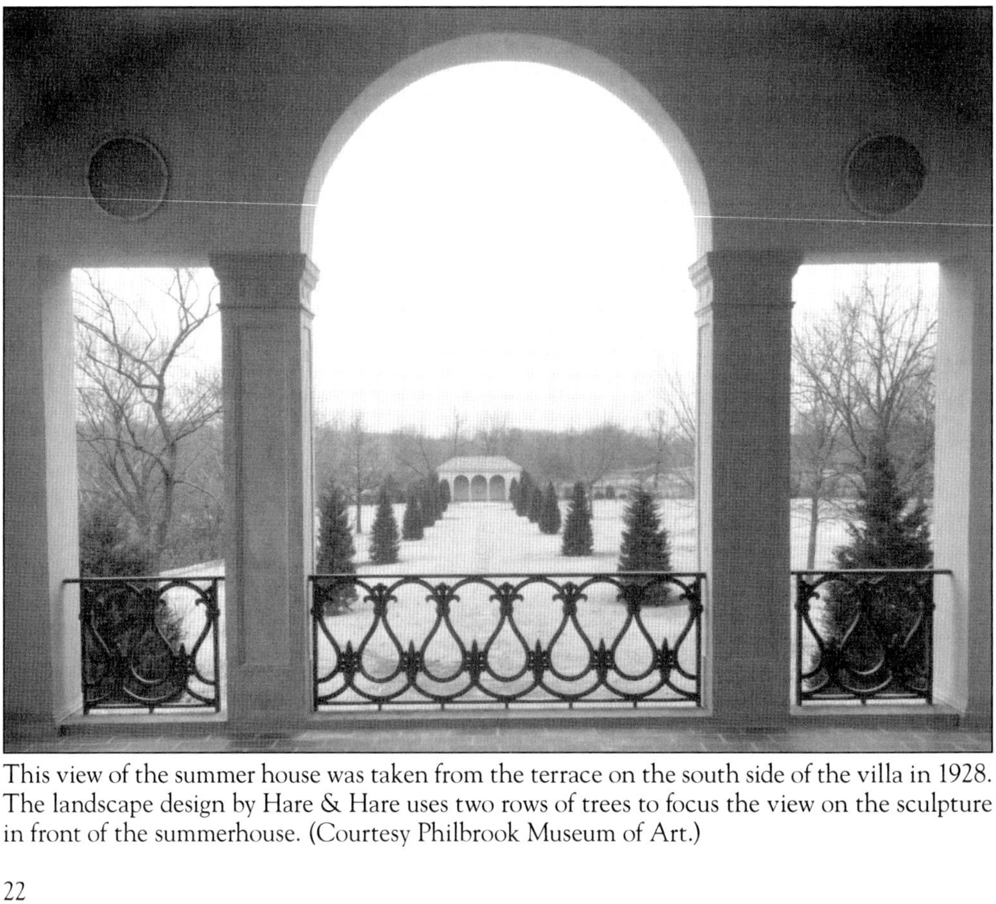

This view of the summer house was taken from the terrace on the south side of the villa in 1928. The landscape design by Hare & Hare uses two rows of trees to focus the view on the sculpture in front of the summerhouse. (Courtesy Philbrook Museum of Art.)

Frank Phillips Mansion, Bartlesville
Type of Project: Residential Design
Designer: Frank Phillips — Date: c. 1924
Renovation Design: Randy Weatherly, Landscape Architect — Date: c. 1980

When oil baron Frank Phillips built his first home at 1107 South Cherokee Avenue in Bartlesville, it was a lonely mansion on an oil-soaked prairie. Phillips had the streets around his house paved and streetlights installed. The Greek Revival home was decorated with Filipino mahogany, and the grounds were planted in American elms and red cedars. Gracious living was set to begin.

He built a garden shed and greenhouse for his wife, Jane, who loved arrangements of freshly cut flowers next to her damask-covered walls.

Jane died in 1948 and Frank in 1950. Granddaughter Elizabeth Jane deeded the property to the Oklahoma Historical Society (OHS) in 1973. While the interior of the mansion, arrayed with the Phillipses' furniture, looked as remarkable as it did in 1930, the landscape had aged.

A jungle of trees and shrubs had taken over the south lawn ,obscuring the view of the house, and Dutch elm disease had struck many of the elms that once lined the avenue, further blighting the facade of the mansion. No landscape plan was found to use as a guide for the restoration. Numerous photographs had been taken of the mansion over the years, although none were dated. Luckily, the remodeling of the house in 1930s produced changes, so many of the photographs could be divided into pre- and post-remodeling. Complicating the task was the fact that Phillips did not stick with one landscape style over the years. Just as he was diversifying his business, he was also diversifying his yard. At times, the yard resembled a woodland, while at others, it was a more formal, spacious park. Luckily, a photograph of the landscape from before 1930 was found, and the landscape was restored in 1990.

The plan left in place some very old trees, including a "huge, ancient redbud" and arborvitaes grown together as one tree, according to Randy Weatherly, consulting landscape architect. The plan added a pair of green ashes on either side of the front door and next to them two weeping mulberries. These plantings matched an old photograph exactly. Avenue trees on the parkway between the street and the sidewalk were replaced with a graceful row of young elms. Flowerbeds were planted with periwinkles and lantana, while a string trellis was hung for the hyacinth bean vine. Disease-resistant lacebark elms replaced the American elms because of the continuing threat of Dutch elm disease. New plantings of redbuds were of the improved Oklahoma variety.

Study Director: Dr. Charles L. Leider, Landscape Architecture Program
Faculty Advisors: Dr. William Bryans, Department of History, Prof. Nigel Jones, School of Architecture
Study Team Members: Richard Coleman, team leader; Larry Vinson

Source:
National Register of Historic Places

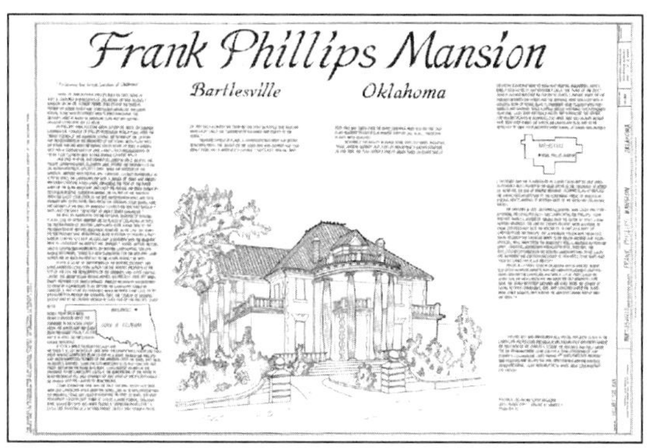

The 1992 poster of the Frank Phillips Mansion gives the history of the Greek Revival estate during the Beaux-Arts movement, with maps showing the location of the mansion within Oklahoma and Bartlesville. The mansion is at 1107 South Cherokee Avenue, at the corner of Eleventh Street.

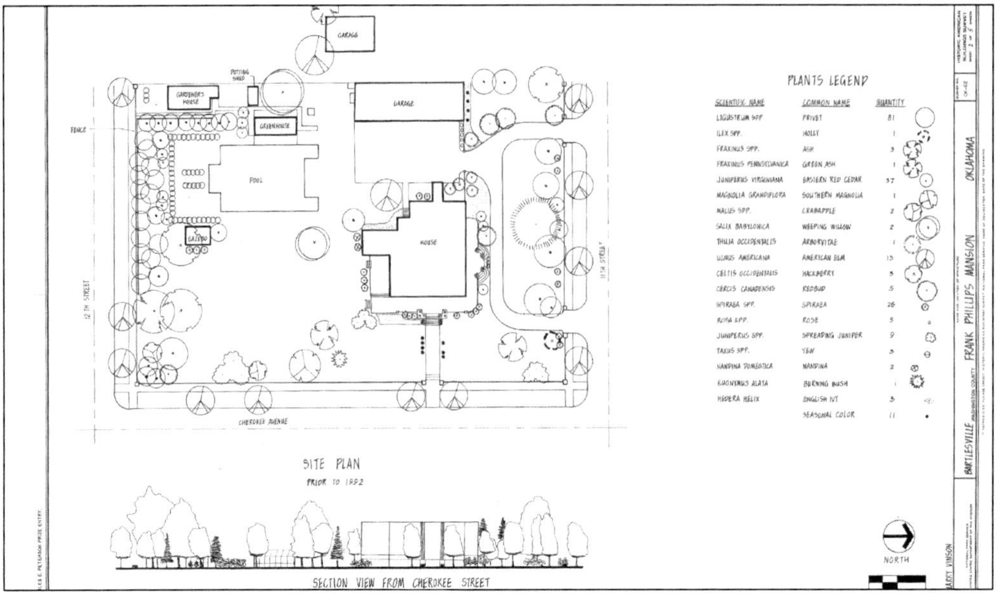

A site and landscape restoration plan was prepared based on the site's highest level of development. The year chosen was 1930, based on a review of historic photographs by local landscape architect Randy Weatherly. The planting plan was prepared by Weatherly in the garden style based on Frank Phillips's love of a mixture of plants. The site plan retained the original vehicular circulation system off Eleventh Street, which included a U-shaped driveway to the side entrance to the mansion and access to the carriage house in the backyard. In addition to the carriage house, the rear yard also contains a greenhouse, gardener's house, potting shed, swimming pool, change house, and storage building.

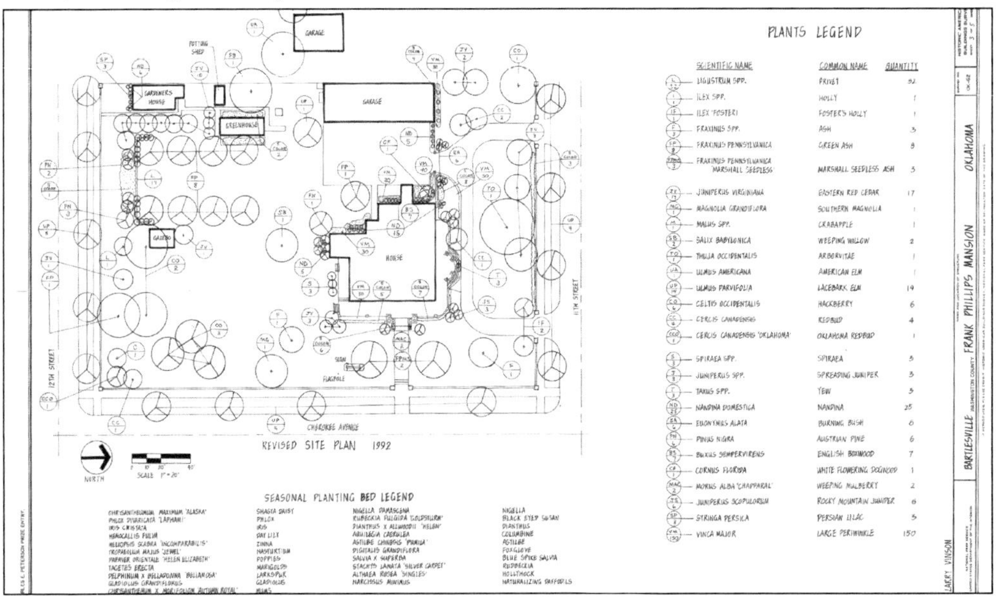

The as-built measured drawing of 1992 found the original site to be intact. The majority of the 1930 restoration plan was still in place, with the exception of the swimming pool, which had been removed. The carriage house was converted into a garage. The other structures retained included a greenhouse, gardener's house, gazebo, and storage building.

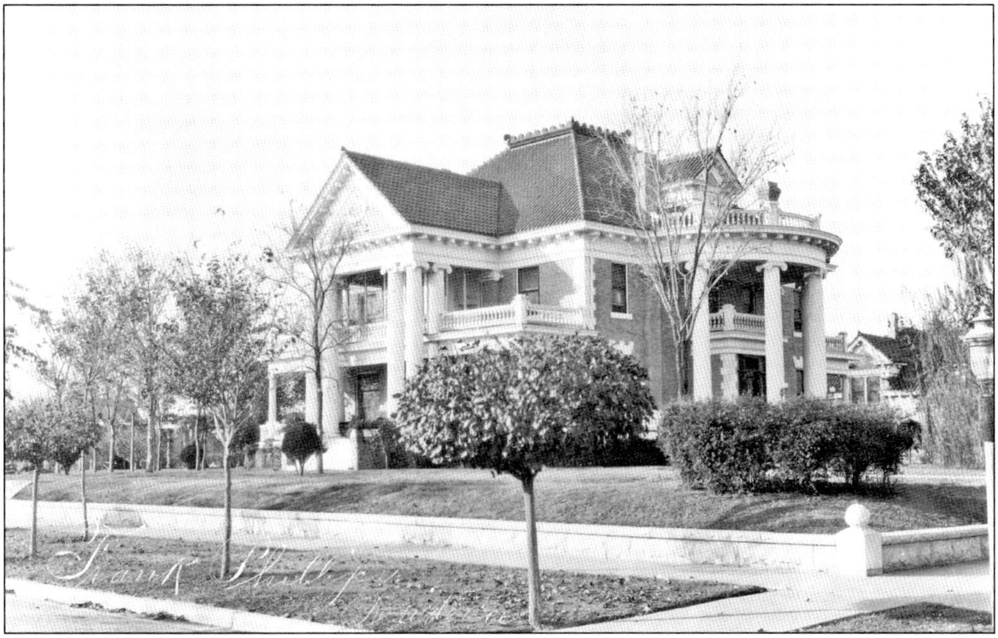

A 2018 view shows the Frank Phillips Mansion, a Greek Revival three-story brick building with a red tile roof on the corner of Cherokee Avenue and Eleventh Street. A low retaining wall and steps have been retained, as shown in the 1930 restoration plan by landscape architect Randy Weatherly. (Courtesy Bartlesville Area History Museum.)

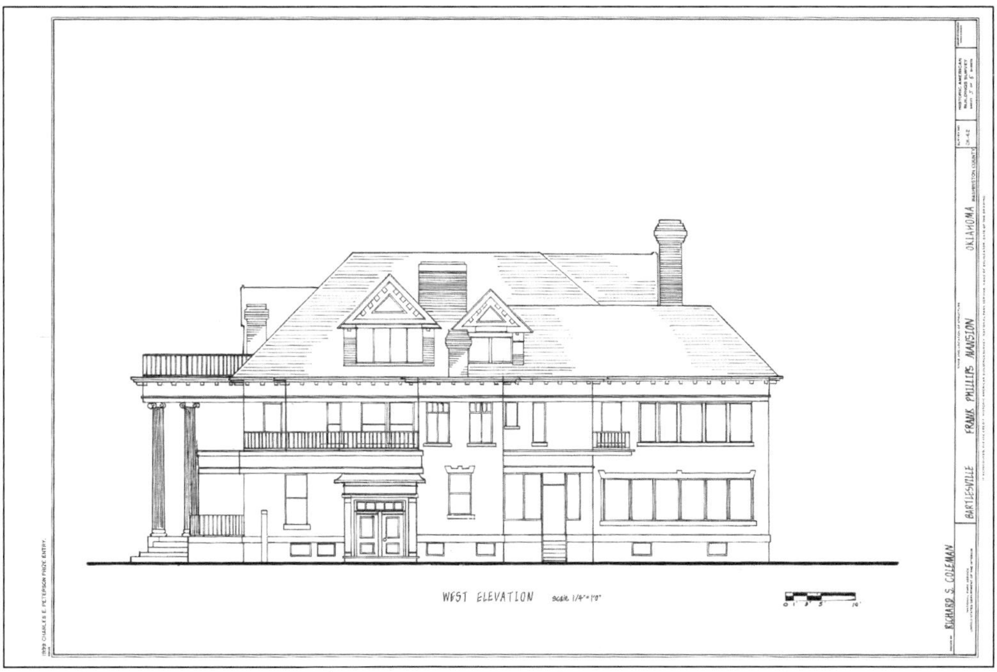

The as-built measured drawing from 1992 of the west elevation shows a Greek Revival three-story mansion with a high basement. The mansion remains unchanged from its initial construction. The second floor has two balconies on the outside wall. The third floor has two dormers with large windows.

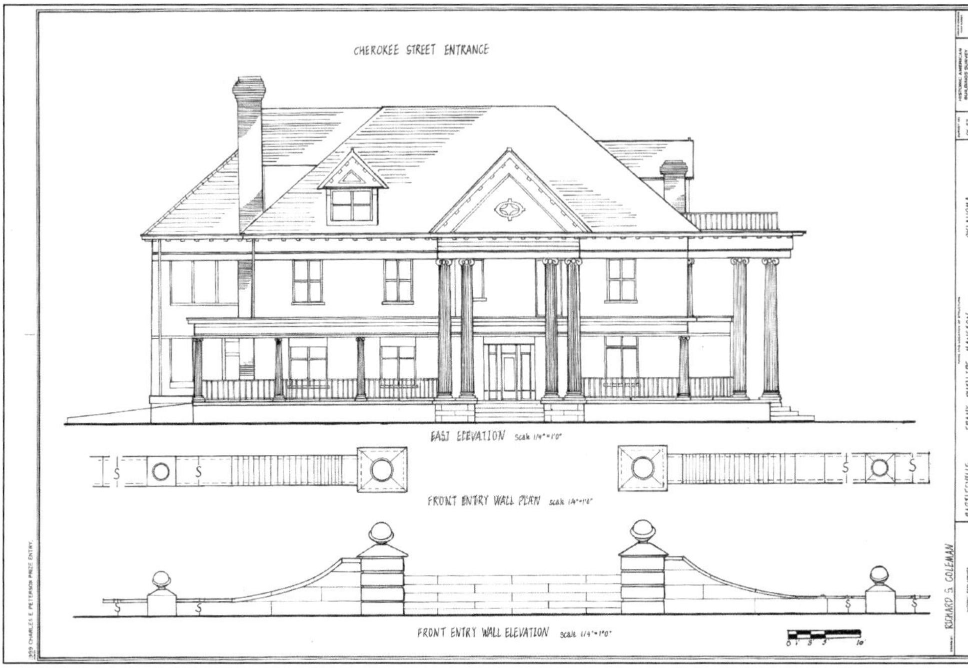

The as-built measured drawing from 1992 of the front or east elevation shows the mansion with a plan and elevation of the front retaining wall along the property line on Cherokee Avenue. The 1992 drawing shows there have been no changes from the 1930 restoration plan.

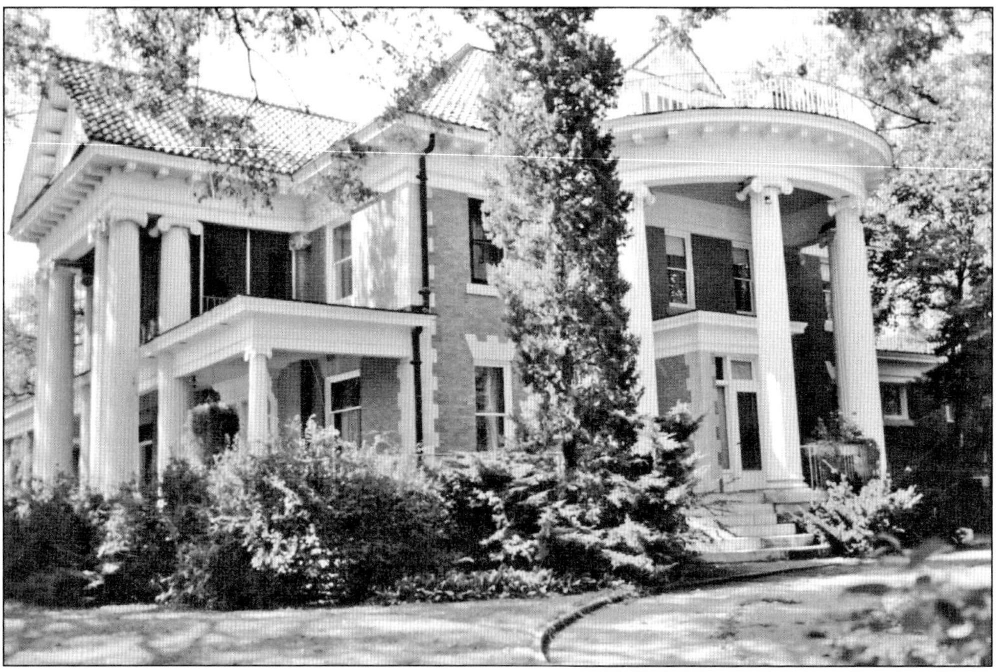

A close-up view shows the Frank Phillips Mansion at the corner of Cherokee Avenue and Eleventh Street in 2008. The mansion remains intact as originally built. The landscape has been restored by Randy Weatherly, whose plan was based on 1930 photographs, taken when the mansion was at its highest level of development. (Courtesy Bartlesville Area History Museum.)

H.H. Champlin Estate, Enid
Type of Project: Residential Design
Designers: R.W. Shaw and Norris Wheller, Architects; unknown landscape designer
Date: 1939

The H.H. Champlin home in Enid is a two-and-one-half story limestone building designed in the Tudor Revival style. Located at 612 South Tyler Street near the intersection of US Highways 64 and 81, the building was started in 1936 and completed in 1939. The Champlin house is a landmark example of Tudor Revival residential architecture, a style popular in the United States from the 1890s through the 1930s.

The house was designed by R.W. Shaw and Norris Wheeler. Shaw also did the original site plan for the estate. For the landscape plan, the burr oaks that line the front were brought to Enid from the Marland Mansion in Ponca City. The buildings on the grounds include the 1939 house; a 1941 stone, metal, and glass greenhouse; and a 1948 wood-frame carport. The house is unaltered from its original appearance, but the landscaping has been altered from the original plan.

The Champlin home is in a neighborhood developed in the 1920s that consists of other, smaller examples of typical 1920s architecture. The house faces Champlin Park, which has existed since the 1930s and is now a city park. In 1992, the Champlin estate was nominated for the National Register of Historic Places. The house is currently owned by H.H. Champlin's grandson Joel Champlin, who is keeping the estate in its original form.

Study Director: Dr. Charles L. Leider, Landscape Architecture Program
Faculty Advisors: Dr. William Bryans, Department of History; Prof. Nigel Jones, School of Architecture
Study Team Member: Michael Whaley

Source:
Champlin family records

The poster gives the history of the H.H. Champlin Mansion with maps showing the relationship of the mansion to the Kisner Heights neighborhood and Enid. The sketch of the house shows a setback from the street of nearly 150 feet on a flat, U-shaped drive in front of the house and a side drive to the garage behind the house.

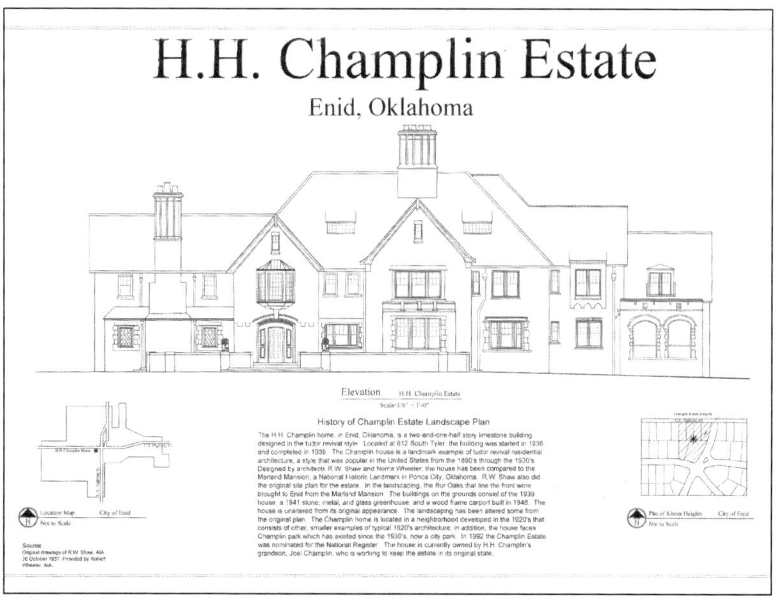

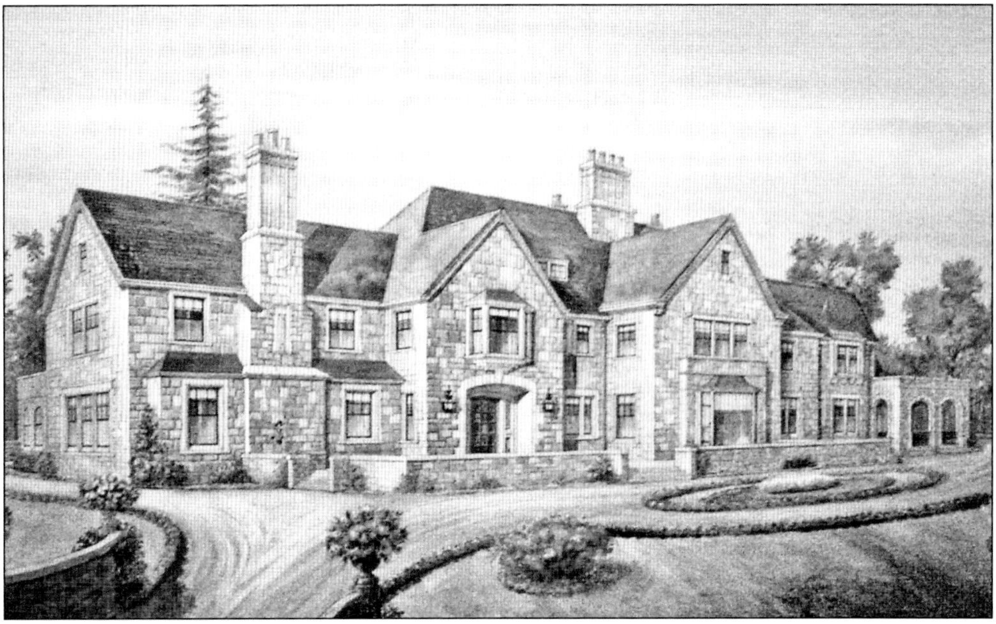

A rendering of the proposed mansion in 1930 was based on the design of architects R.W. Shaw and Norris Wheeler. H.H. Champlin accepted the proposed rendering of the house and the landscape for the site, and it was completed in 1939. (Courtesy Champlin Mansion.)

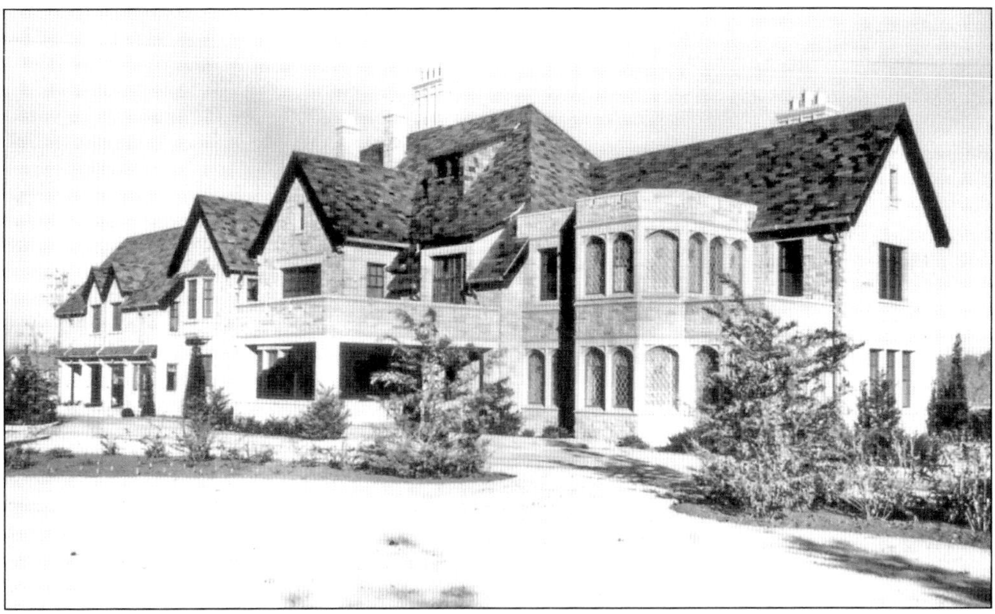

This view shows the two-story limestone-veneer frame house built in 1939 for H.H. Champlin. To maintain a year-round green color, various sized junipers were used to landscape the front of the house. (Courtesy Champlin Mansion.)

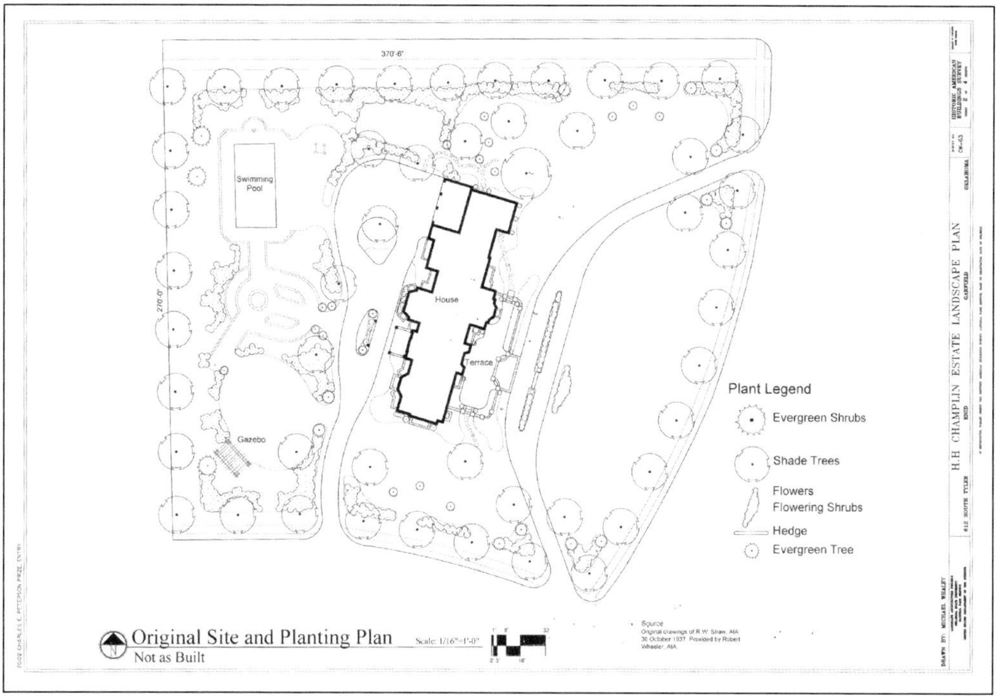

The as-built drawing shows the original 1930 site and planting plan designed by Norris Wheeler in an informal style with a broad, curvilinear, two-way driveway from Tyler Street to the front entrance of the house with a side driveway to the back to provide access to the garage and the rear yard. The planting plans show that shade trees and shrubs were planted around the perimeter of the property enclosing the backyard and at the corners of the mansion while leaving the front yard open.

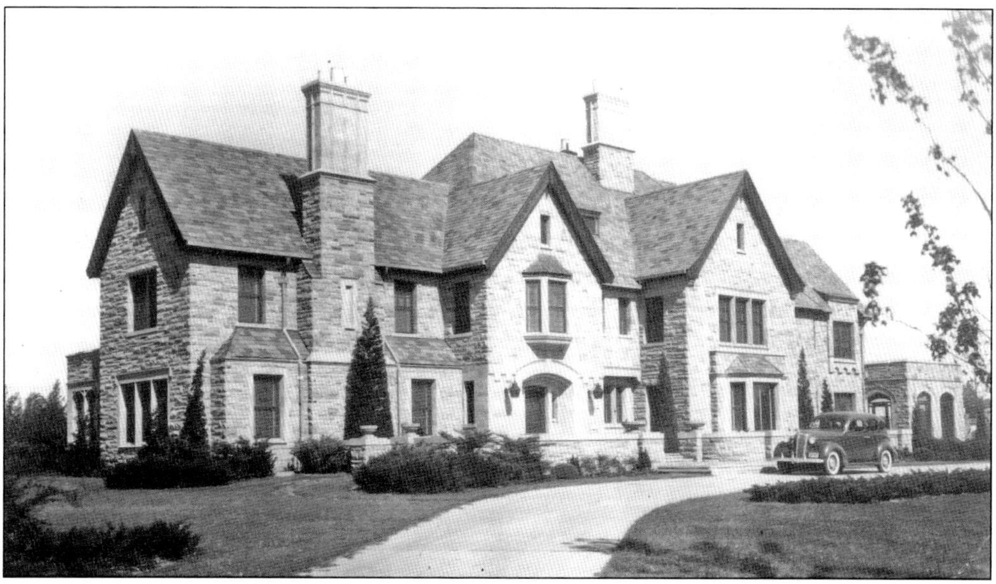

This view shows the H.H. Champlin Mansion a few years after it was completed and the landscape was installed. The house reflects various design elements of the Tudor Revival style in the use of chimneys, window bump-outs, and arched window frames. (Courtesy Champlin Mansion.)

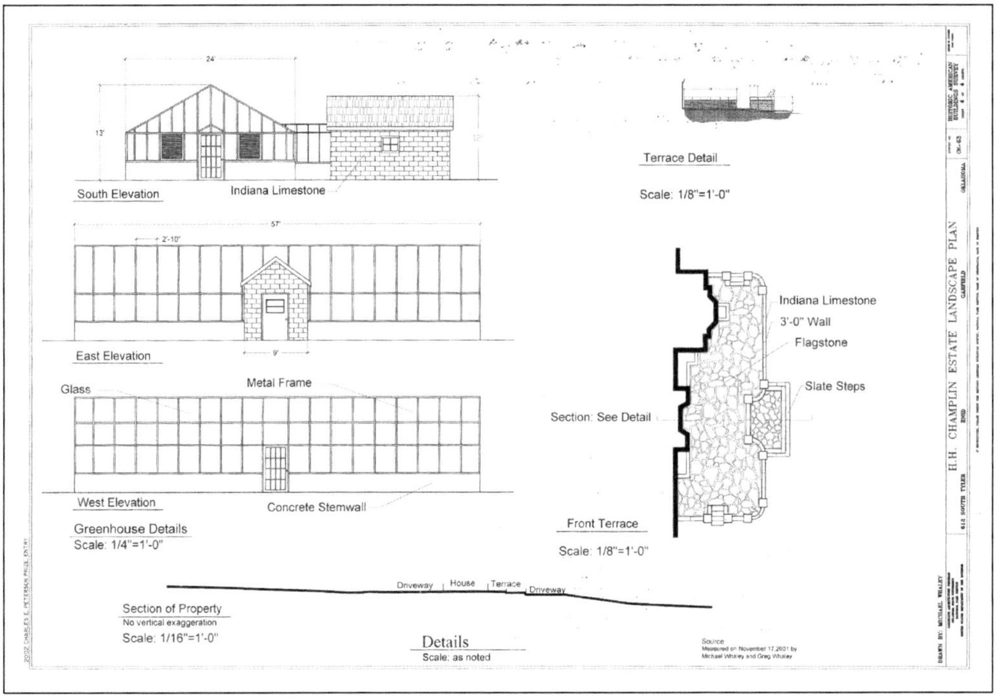

The as-built measured drawings of 2002 show the plan and elevation of the greenhouse, a plan of the front terrace, and a profile of the site showing it sloping toward Tyler Street. The full glass greenhouse has a limestone entrance that serves as a workspace and a space for supplies and storage. A four-foot terrace wall in front of the mansion was constructed of Indiana limestone to match the mansion. The floor of the terrace used flagstone paving. Steps to the terrace have slate covers. (Courtesy Champlin Mansion.)

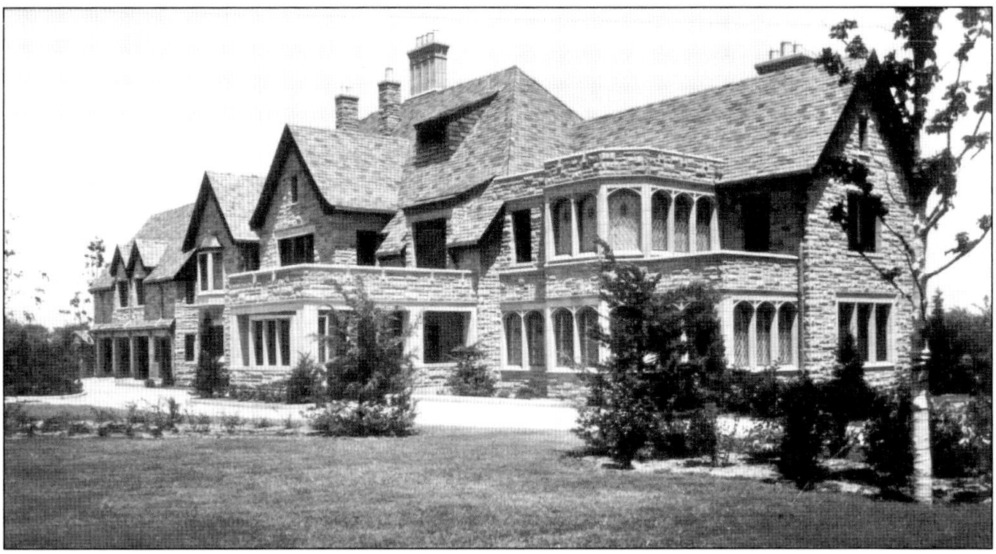

A rear view shows the H.H. Champlin Mansion as it appeared in the 1940s. The driveway to the garage was built as planned next to the mansion, separating it from the back lawn. The landscape plan shows the early growth of the vegetation, with conical junipers used as accent plants. (Courtesy Champlin Mansion.)

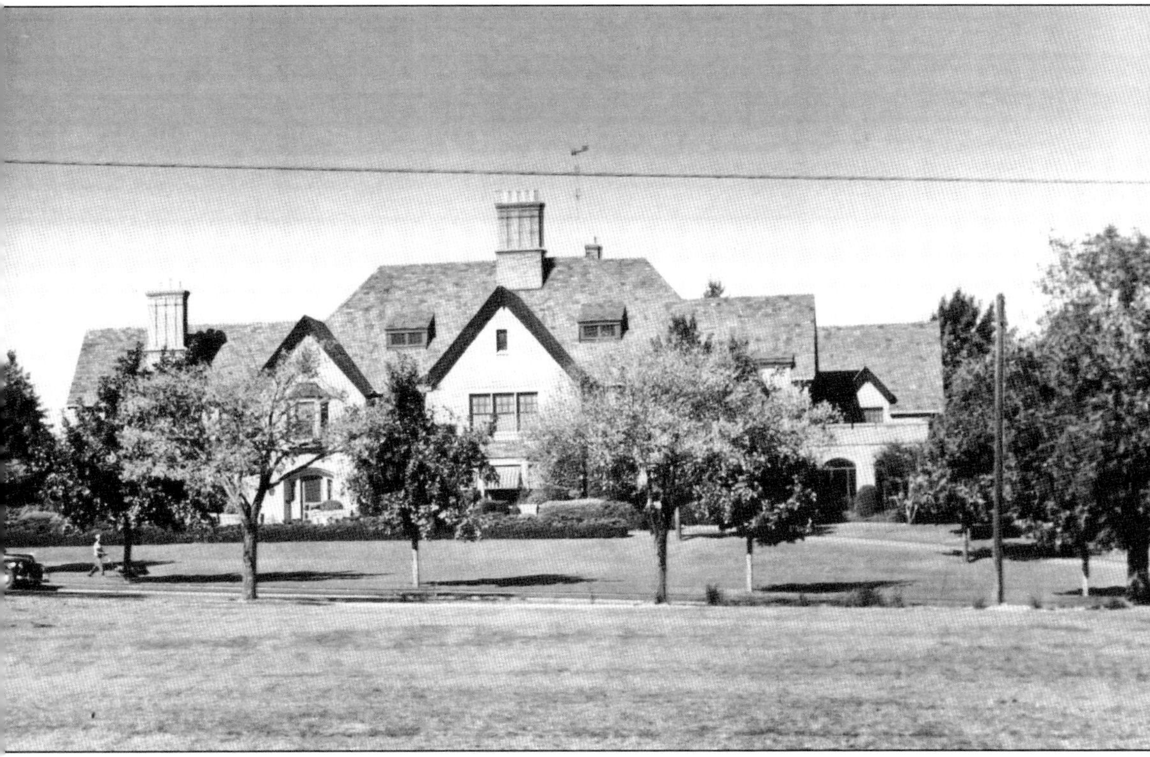

This view shows the mansion as it appeared in the 1950s from the park across the street. The more mature vegetation enhances the site. Low-growing evergreen shrubs screen the driveway and the foundation from the street. Trees along the street block a full view of the mansion. (Courtesy Champlin Mansion.)

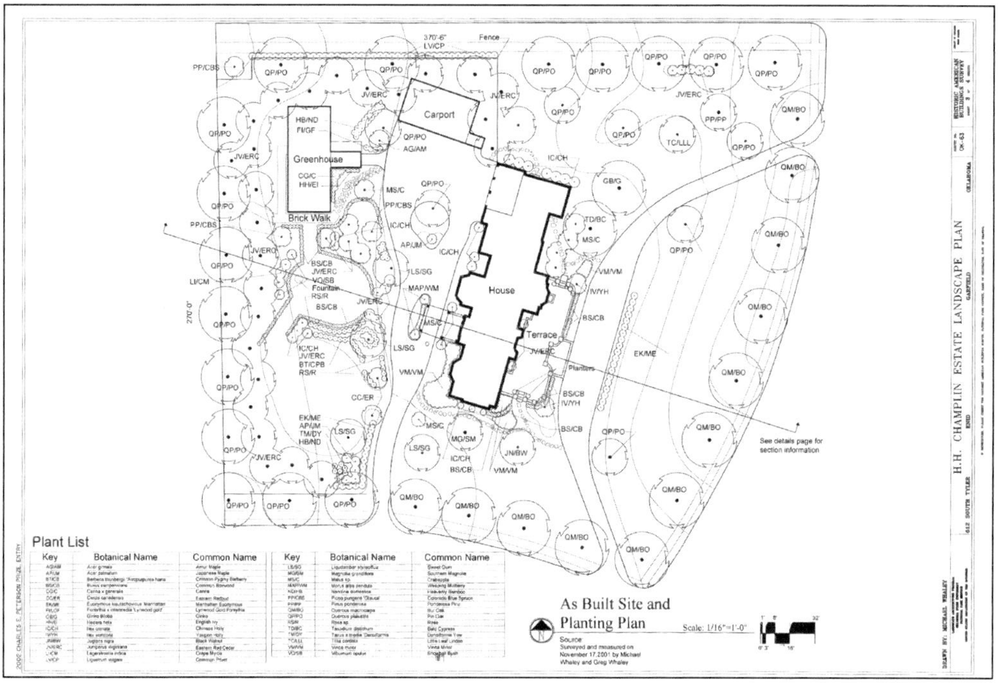

The 2002 measured site and planting plan shows the 1939 flat, U-shaped driveway in front of the house has been retained. The driveway to the back of the house has been expanded with a turnaround circle and a carport. The swimming pool has been removed and replaced with a greenhouse. The vegetation in the background of the property has matured, with large shade trees and tall shrubs enclosing the side and back yards.

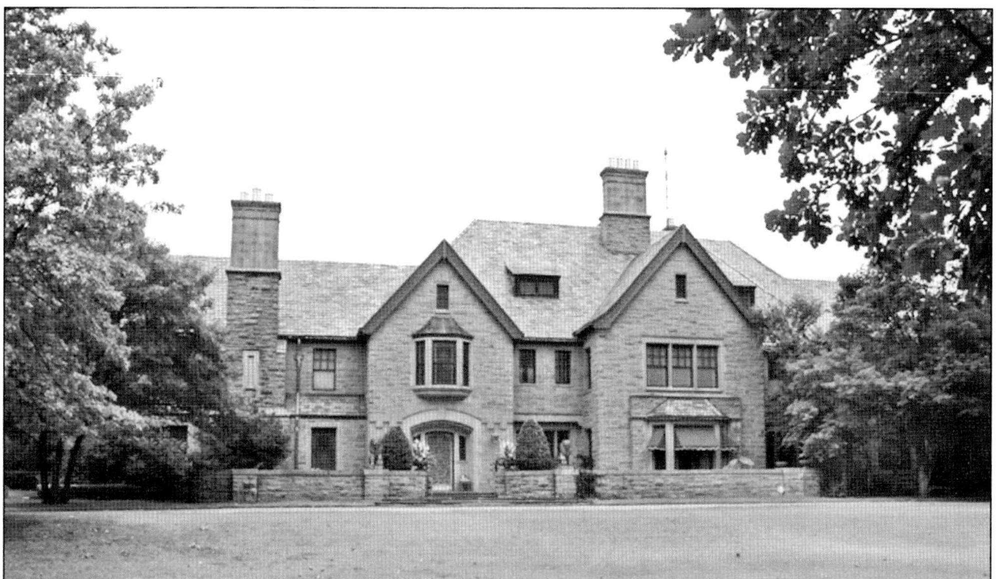

A view shows the mansion as it appeared in the 1960s from Tyler Street. The landscape plan has created a wide view shed to the front of the mansion, showing the four-foot retaining wall for the terrace across the front of the mansion. The mansion is framed by mature trees from the street. The entrance to the mansion is accented by conical evergreens. (Courtesy Champlin Mansion.)

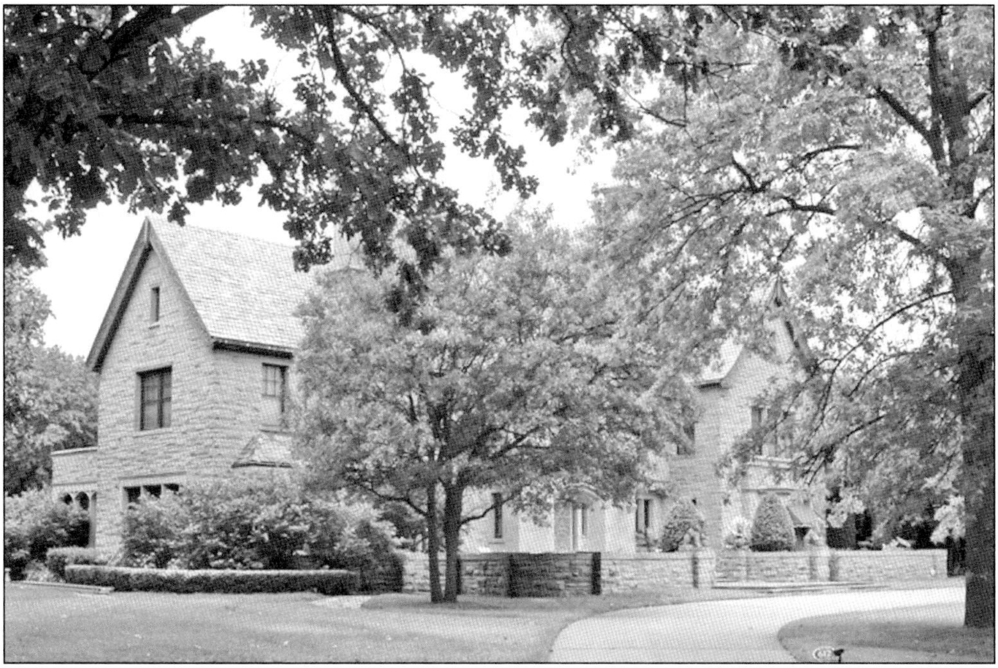

This view of the mansion was taken from the tree-shaded entrance drive in the 1960s and shows the retaining wall for the terrace along the full length of the front of the mansion. Shrubs were used to soften the corner of the mansion. Evergreen shrubs along the side of the mansion and conical evergreens at the entrance provide green color year-round. (Courtesy Champlin Mansion.)

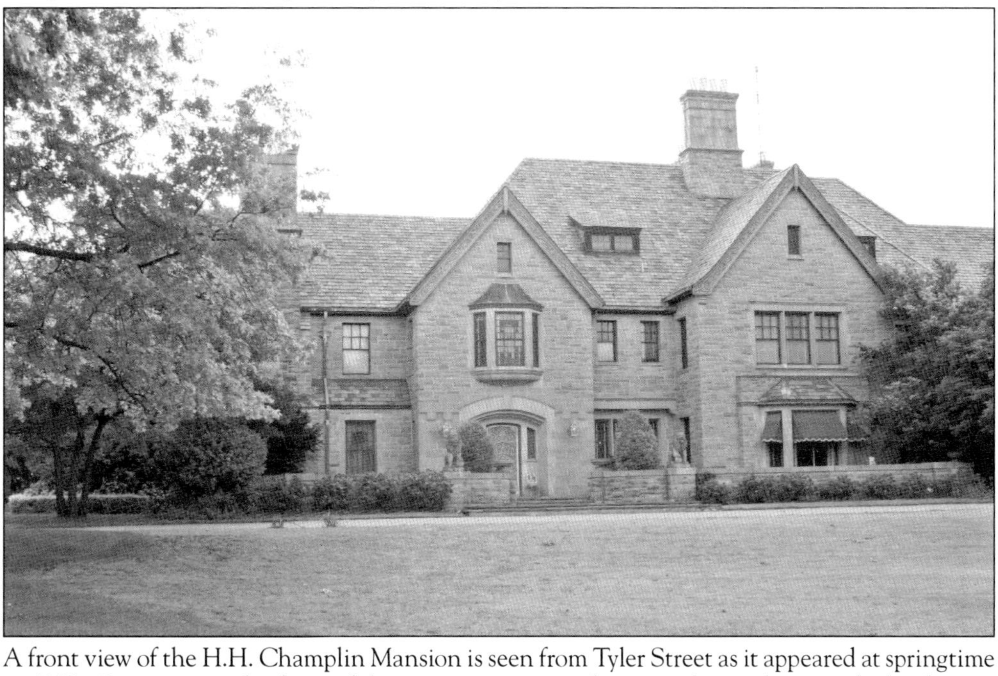

A front view of the H.H. Champlin Mansion is seen from Tyler Street as it appeared at springtime in 1970s. Roses across the front of the mansion were used to introduce color into the landscape. Rose-colored window awnings were used to shade the principal windows and complement the color of the roses. (Courtesy Champlin Mansion.)

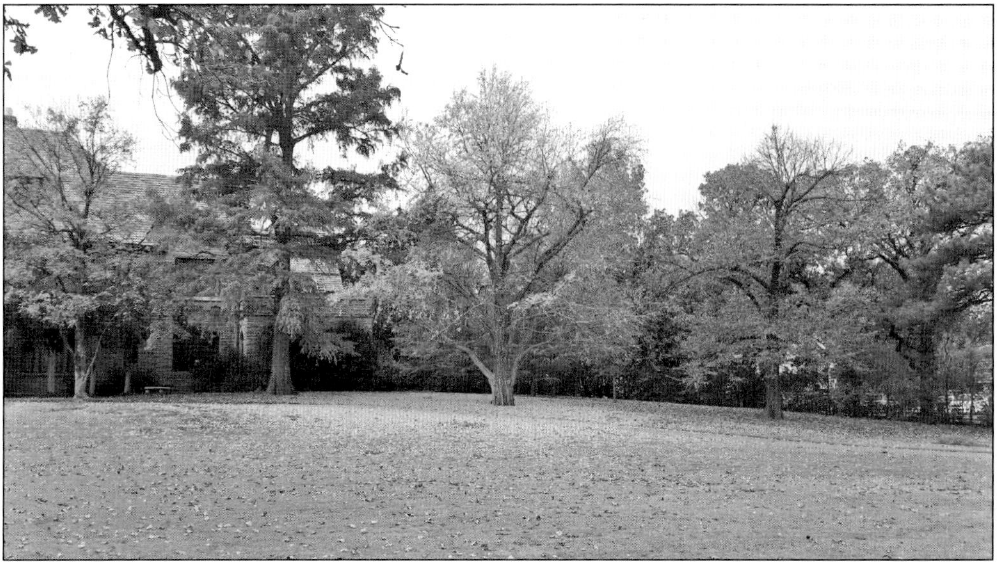

A corner view of the front yard of the estate shows the landscape in the autumn in the 1980s. The view shows how the trees and shrubs have matured in the informal landscape designed by Shaw and Wheeler. The landscape also shows the use of an evergreen background screen planting on the property line with free-standing shade and evergreen trees on the lawn. (Courtesy Cherokee Strip Regional Heritage Center.)

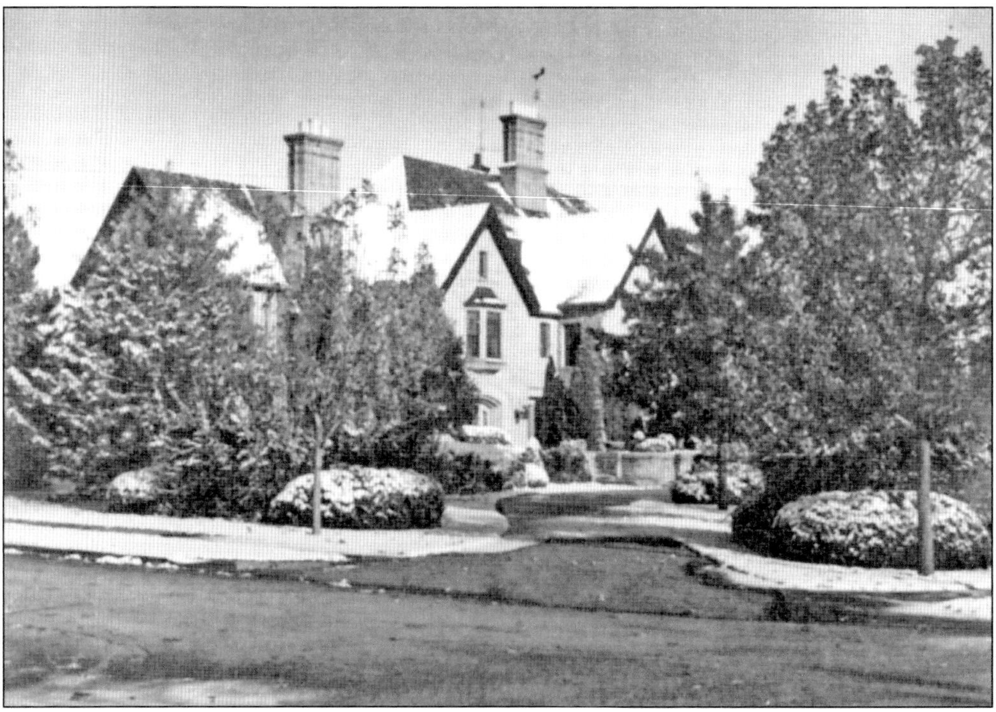

This 2014 view shows the mansion in the wintertime. The driveway from Tyler Street has been embellished with the addition of evergreen shrub beds and trees to create a more private setting for the mansion. The landscape design is maintained in the informal style established by Shaw and Wheeler. (Courtesy Champlin Mansion.)

HARWELDEN ESTATE, TULSA
Type of Project: Residential Design
Designer: Unknown Date 1926
Renovation Design: Joe Braun of Jacob Braun Company, Landscape Architects Date: c. 1980

Harwelden was originally the home of Earl Palmer and Mary Harwell. *Harwelden* is a Welsh term meaning "place from which the Harwells came," and the name was given to the house in 1967 by the Arts and Humanities Council of Tulsa. It reflects the history of Harwell's family, who came to the United States from Wales. The home was completed in 1926 and has 30 rooms, four levels, and seven fireplaces. Of note are the main-floor rooms and stairway, which are decorated with hand-carved wood. The carvings are based on the family's coat of arms, which consists of two shields, a lion, and a flower. The mansion's exterior boasts carved Indiana limestone, gargoyles, and a slate roof. Adjoining the landscaped grounds are a carriage house where the servants once lived and a goldfish pond that the Harwells' daughter, Margo, used as a pool.

The Harwells lived quietly but generously. They were very supportive of the University of Tulsa, and Earl Harwell was a founder of the Tulsa Boys Home. After his death in 1957, Mrs. Harwell continued the family's charitable contributions. Upon her death in 1967, she bequeathed Harwelden to the Arts and Humanities Council of Tulsa to provide a base for community arts organizations. The council restored the landscape after it acquired the property.

In 1978, Harwelden was one of five Tulsa landmarks to be placed in the National Register of Historic Places. In 1983, the Maple Ridge District, containing Harwelden, was placed in the National Register of Historic Districts.

The Arts and Humanities Council of Tulsa maintains Harwelden for public use. It serves as a location for private functions and many of the council's programs in arts education, literary arts, and arts advocacy.

Study Director: Dr. Charles L. Leider, Landscape Architecture Program
Faculty Advisors: Dr. William Bryans, Department of History; Prof. Nigel Jones, School of Architecture
Study Team Member: Michael Crumb

Sources:
Tulsa Arts and Humanities Council
The Jacob Braun Company, Tulsa

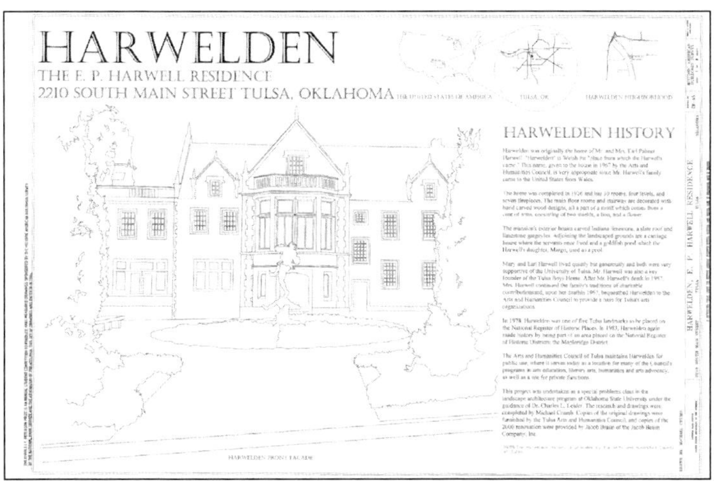

The poster gives the history of the Harwelden Estate and maps showing the estate's location in Tulsa at 2210 South Main Street. The sketch of the house shows a nearly 100-foot setback from the street on a broad U-shaped drive to the front of the house with a connection to the carriage house and access to Twenty-Second Street.

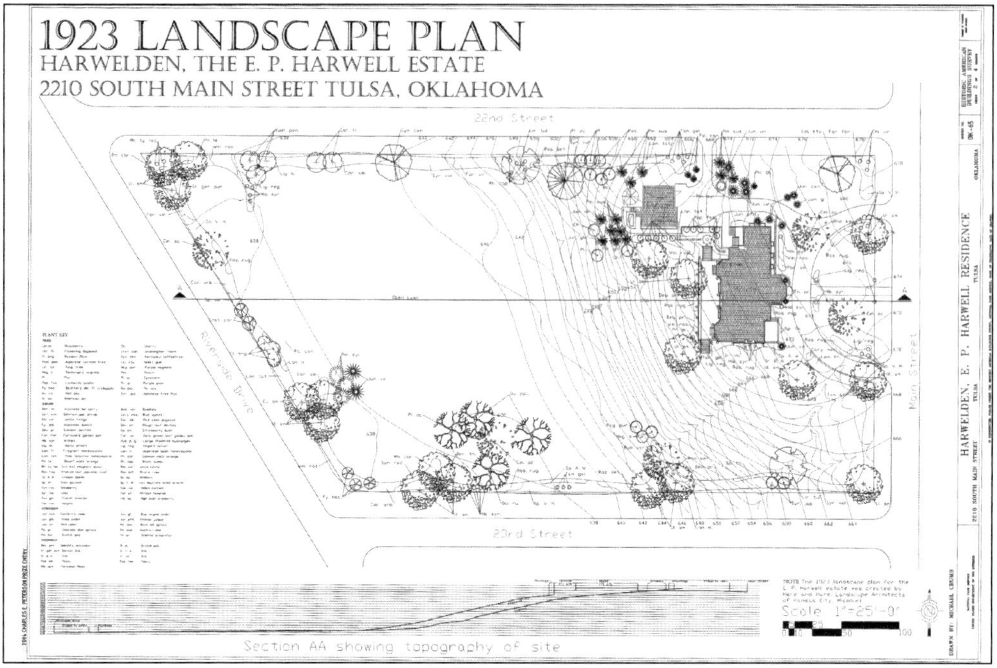

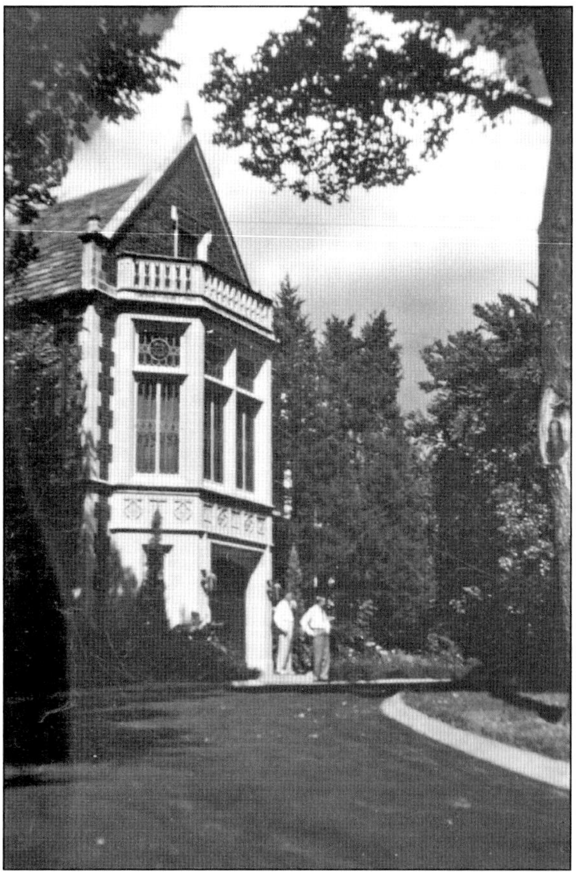

The house fronts on South Main Street near the corner of Twenty-Third Avenue. The side yard slopes to the adjoining Riverside Drive. A broad U-shaped driveway off Main Street provides access to the front of the house and the carriage house with a connection to Twenty-Second Street. A terrace for outdoor living was built on the back of the house with a connection to the carriage house. The landscape design was completed in an informal style that included a partial enclosure with trees on the open, sloping lawn to Riverside Drive. (Courtesy Caroline Owens Crain.)

This view of the front door was taken from the U-shaped driveway. The house was built in brick and trimmed with Indiana limestone. Balustrades, gargoyles, and other features trim the house in the English Tudor Renaissance style. Evergreen shrubs were planted around the entrance to provide year-round color. (Courtesy Caroline Owens Crain.)

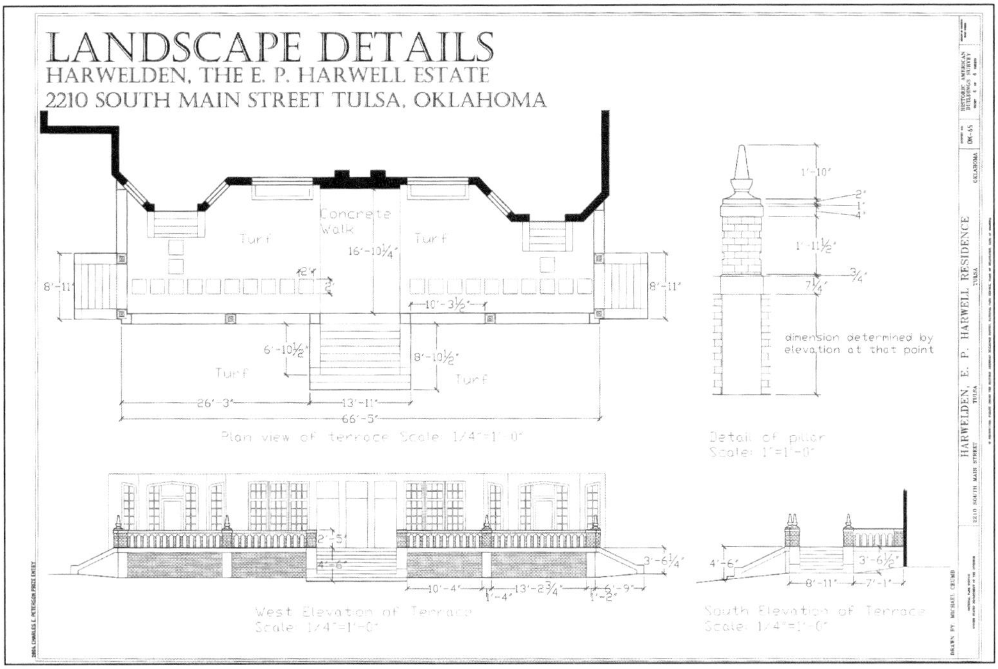

The as-built 2003 measured drawing shows the design details of the raised terrace, steps, and a balustrade used at the rear of the house in establishing connections to the lawn and carriage house. Trees flank either side of the raised terrace and show a full view of the formal garden on the open lawn.

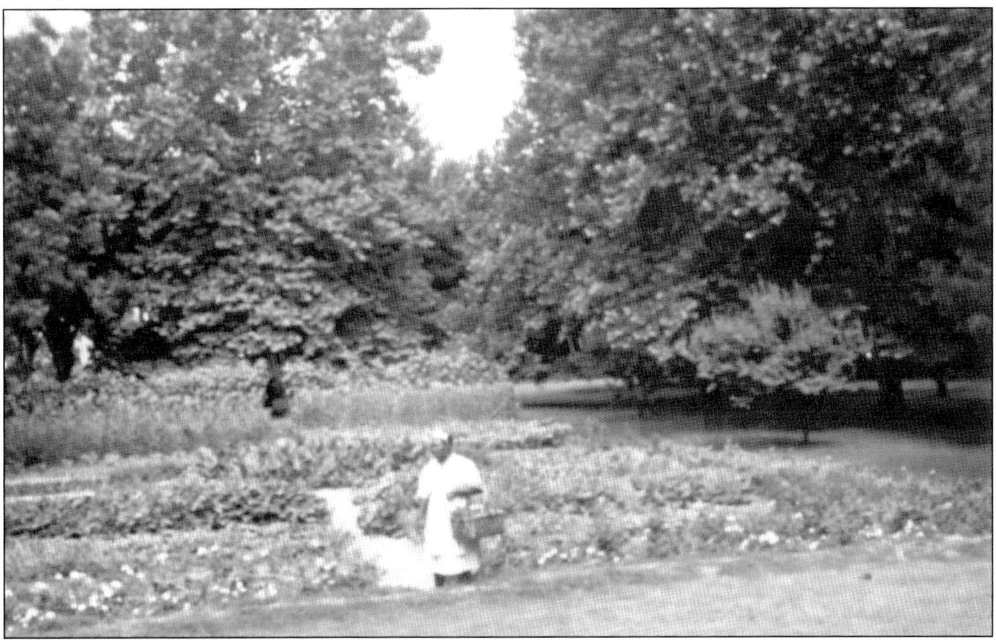

A close-up view from the 1930s shows the formal garden on the rear lawn of the Harwelden Estate. The garden is designed in the Italian Renaissance rectilinear style, with a fountain in a circular central bed for a focal point. The formal garden shows no relationship to the house or the informal landscape design. (Courtesy Caroline Owens Crain.)

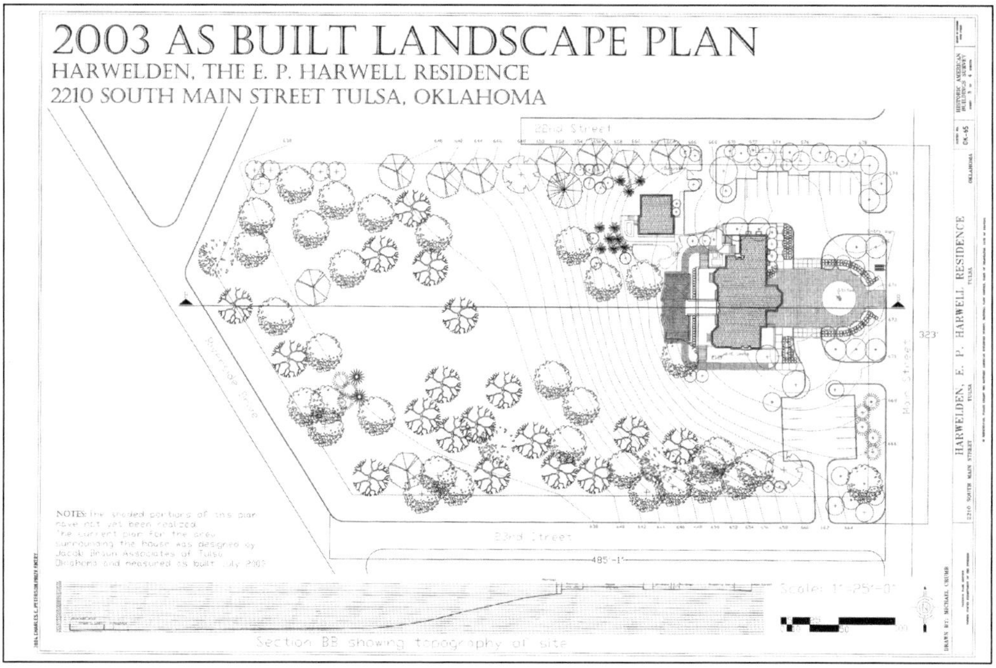

The as-built 2003 measured drawing shows the site and planting plan of the estate. In 1967, the estate was bequeathed by the Harwell family to the Arts and Humanities Council of Tulsa. The site was redesigned when the house was converted from a residence to an office for the council. The front yard was redesigned with two parking lots on each side of the entrance driveway to accommodate 12 parking spaces each. The walk to the front door was redesigned and widened. The formal garden in the rear yard was removed. The original open rear lawn was retained. In 1983, the property was listed in the National Register of Historic Places.

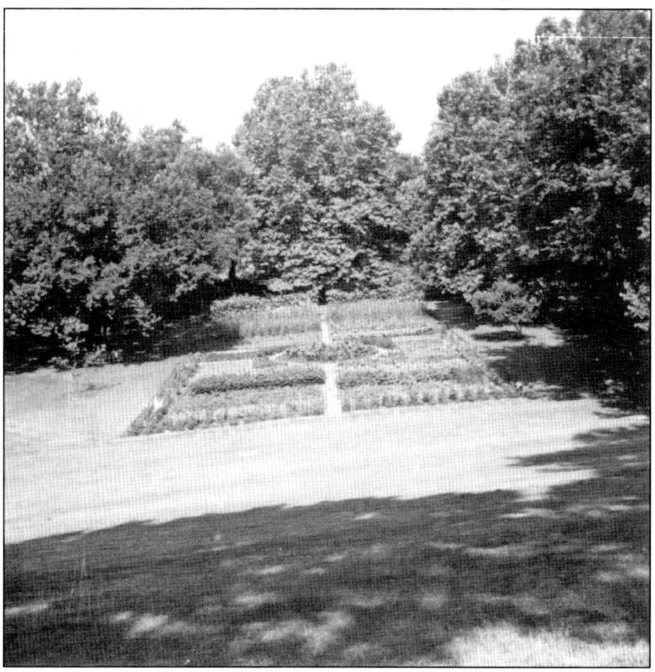

This view shows the formal garden in the rear yard in the 1930s as designed in the Italian Renaissance rectilinear style, with a circular central bed and fountain as its focal point. The garden shows no relationship to the house or the informal landscape design of the site. (Courtesy Caroline Owens Crain.)

Thomas N. Berry Estate, Stillwater

Type of Project: Residential Design
Designer: C. Burton Fox, Landscape Architect; J.K. Knoblock, Architect Date: 1927

The estate is an outstanding example of a collaborative design effort between an architect, J.K. Knoblock, and a landscape architect, Burton Fox, both of Tulsa. It was designed during Oklahoma's 1920s oil boom for Thomas N. Berry, a minor oil baron.

The landscape plan follows the Romantic style as illustrated by the great country houses of England. The house is a fine example of Colonial Revival architecture. The estate is named for the original owner of the house and founder of the company that now uses the house for its main headquarters.

Study Director: Dr. Charles L. Leider, Landscape Architecture Program
Faculty Advisors: Dr. William Bryans, Department of History; Prof. Nigel Jones, School of Architecture
Study Team Members: William Cole, team leader; Michael Egan; Joe Grubbs; Mitch Gwartney; Spencer Matheny; and Ernestine Mbrho

Source:
Thomas Berry Oil Company, Stillwater

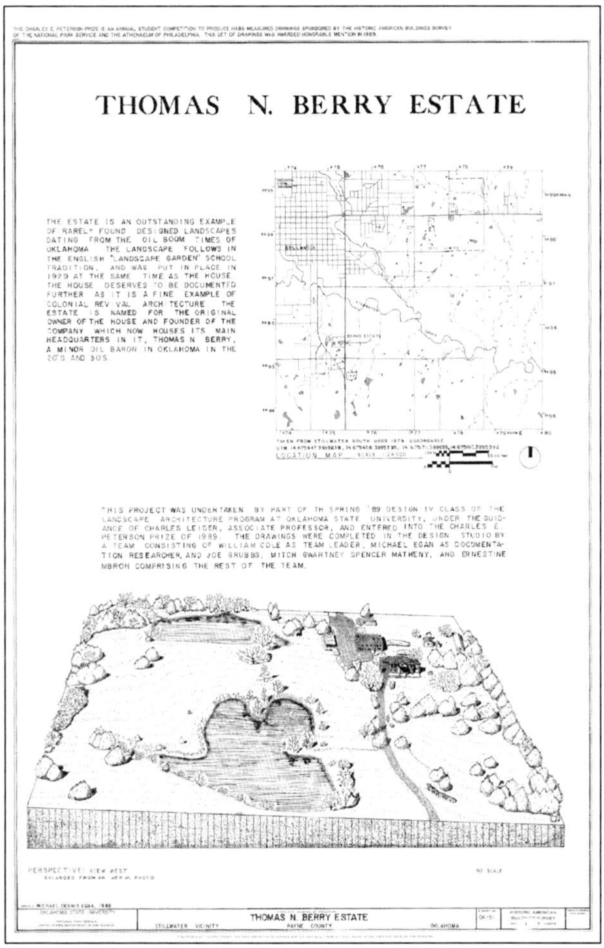

The poster gives the history of the Thomas N. Berry Estate and shows the location of the estate in the southeast portion of Stillwater, off South Perkins Road/ US Highway 177. The east-facing aerial sketch of the site shows that the mansion has a nearly 600-foot setback on a curvilinear drive from Perkins Road to the mansion and Main Street.

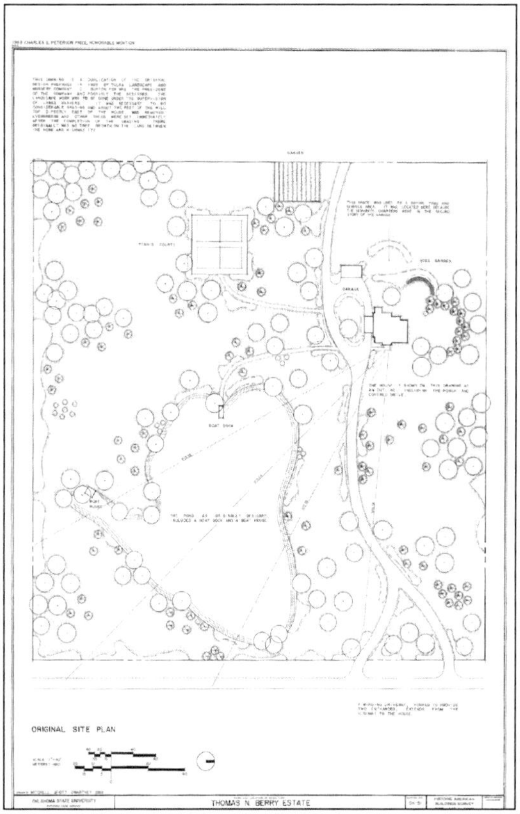

A drawing shows the overall site plan of the estate in 1927. The design represents the first example of a collaborative design effort in Stillwater between an architect, Fred Knoblock, and a landscape architect, Bertram Fox. Both had their offices in Tulsa. The site was designed in an informal landscape style, while the mansion was designed in the Beaux-Arts Colonial Revival style. The original site plan proposed the location of one pond on the front lawn on the west side of the drive and an open lawn the east side. To create year-round color in the landscape, and since there were no evergreen trees in the area, junipers (known as red cedars) were brought from the Cimarron River 20 miles away. The project was completed in 1929.

A close-up view of the side entrance to the mansion shows a walkway to the front entrance. The exterior design included Colonial Revival details. Bertram Fox created an informal landscape design with a great lawn in front of the mansion. (Courtesy Thomas N. Berry & Company.)

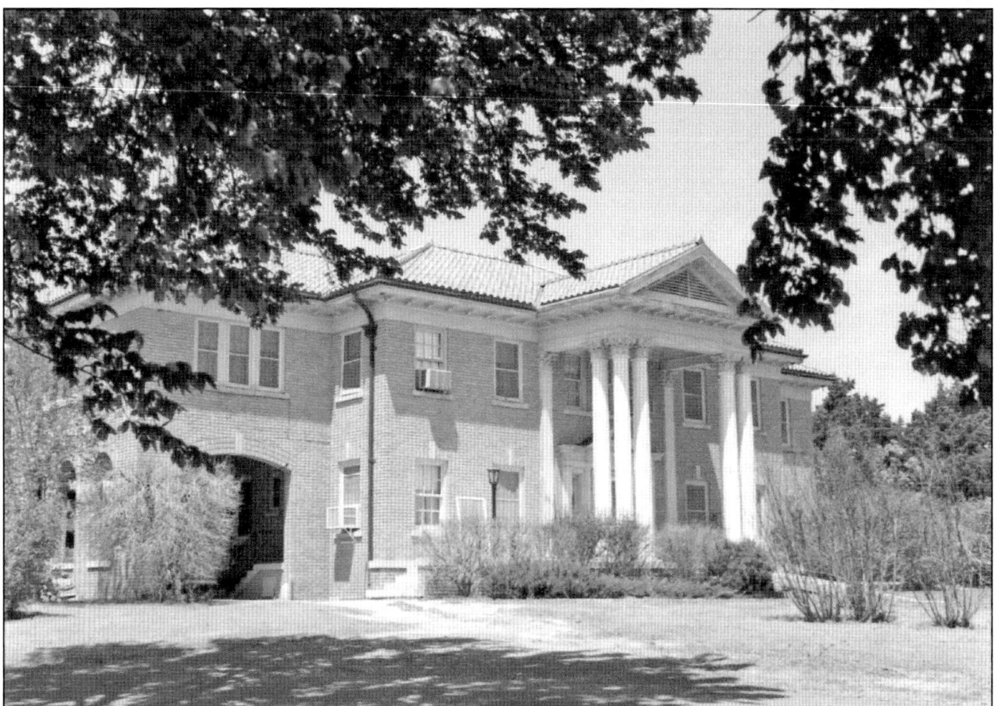

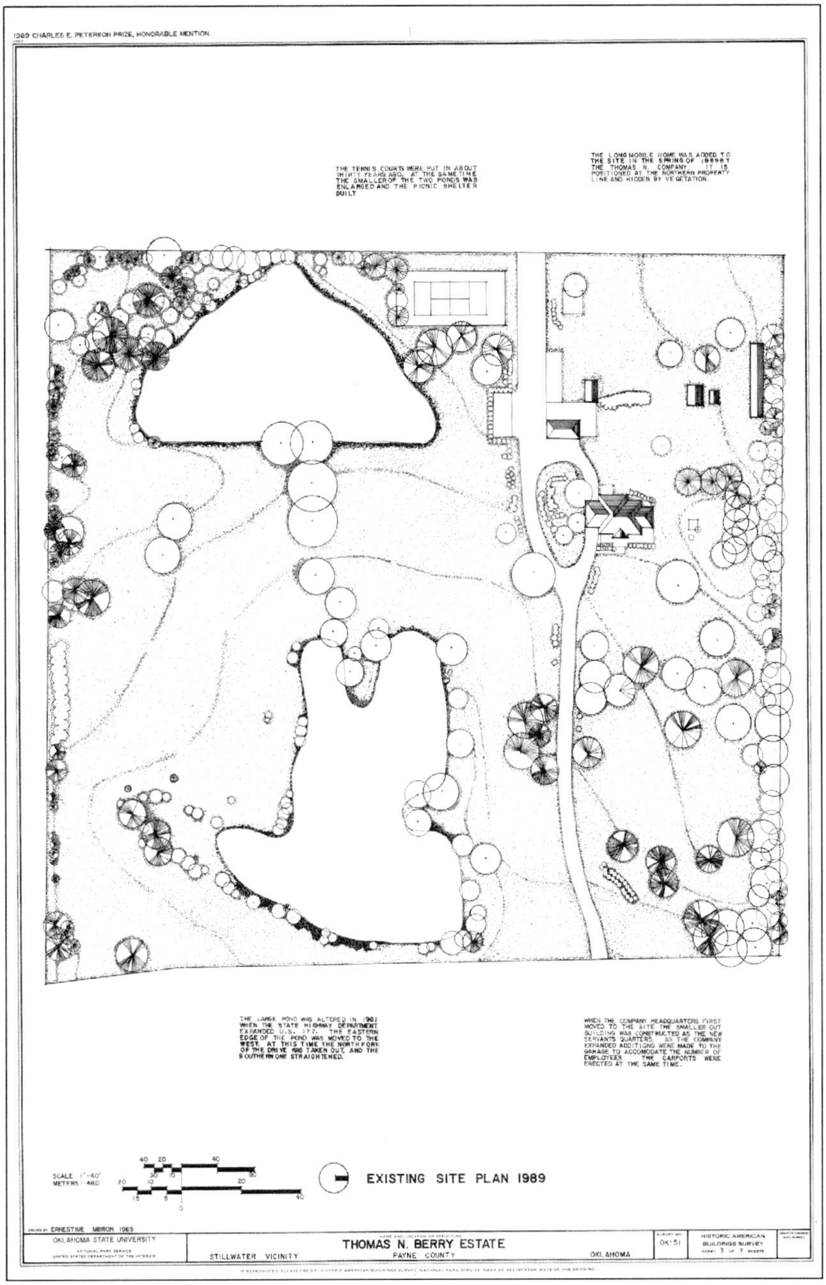

The as-built measured drawing of the site plan in 1989 shows differences with the original 1927 site plan. The 1989 site plan shows the location's two ponds, as compared to one pond proposed in the original 1927 site plan. The upper pond was built as a retaining pond while the larger, lower pond was being constructed. It was later decided to keep the two ponds. The site plan also shows that the location of the original mansion and carriage house have been unaltered since 1927, but a tennis court, sun shade structure for cars, and several small buildings near the garage have been added to the site. The original wye entrance road was eliminated when Perkins Road was widened. The sight lines to view the front portico of the house from Perkins Road and the driveway were not fully maintained and have been infilled with shrubs and trees.

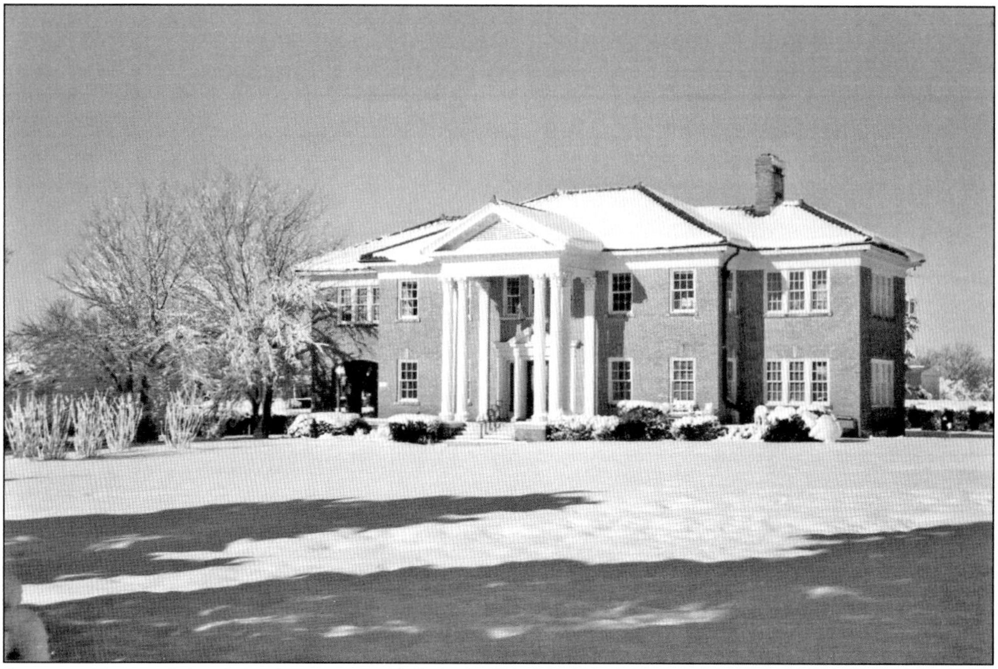

A winter scene provides a front view of the Thomas N. Berry Estate, designed by Fred Knoblock, which remains unchanged from 1928, when the mansion was completed. The landscape, designed by Bertram Fox, appears as originally planned. The view shows the extensive lawn in front of the mansion with vegetation around the house, which creates a suitable setting. Below is a close-up front view of the mansion in 2018. The landscape has been enhanced with an open lawn to view the mansion and evergreen foundation plantings to blend the house into the landscape. (Both, courtesy Thomas N. Berry & Company.)

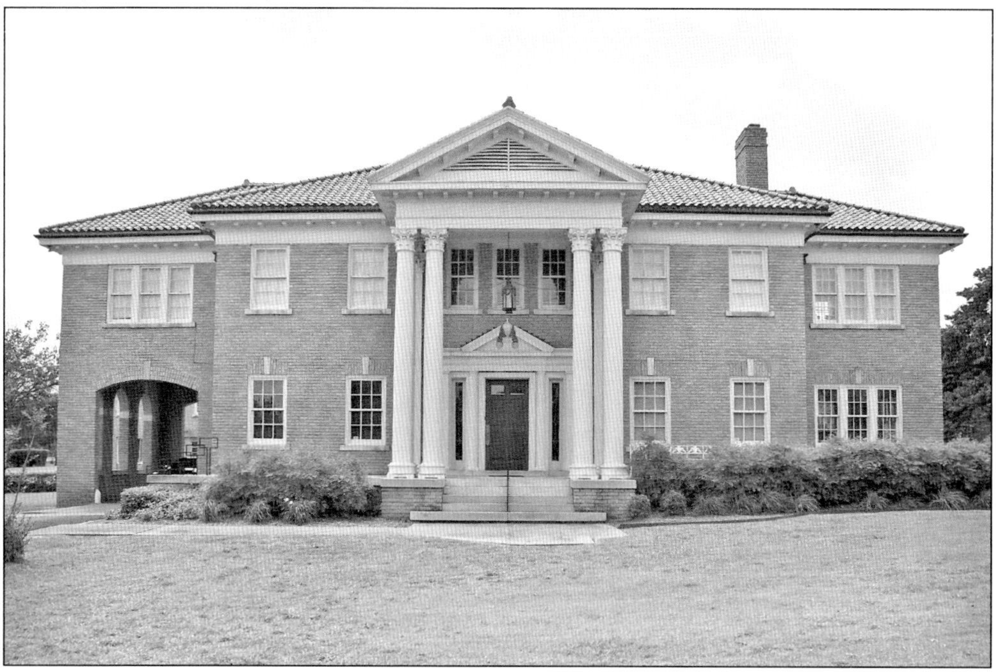

The as-built measured drawing of 1989 shows that the site plan and profile of the southeast portion of the estate have been unaltered since 1927. The curvilinear driveway runs through the center of the site, with the pond on the south of the driveway and the lawn on the north. The profile of the site shows the driveway on the crest of the slope.

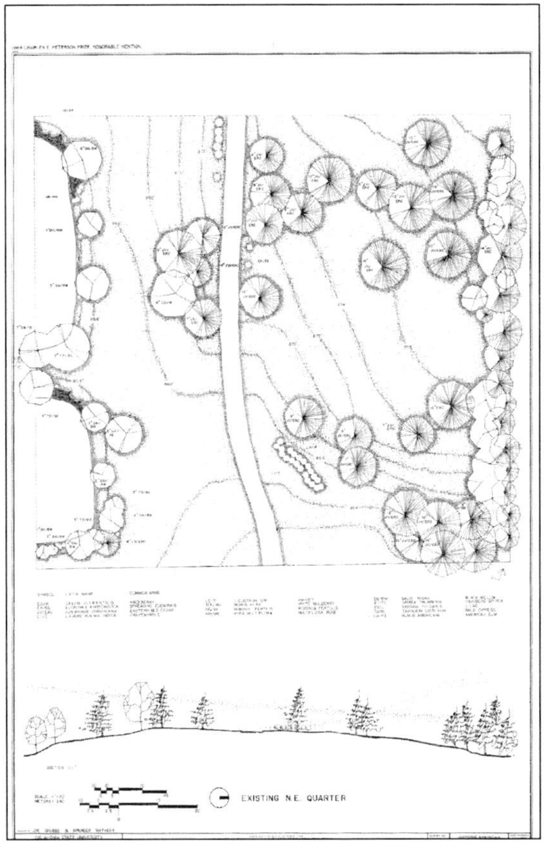

In a current view of the rear side of the mansion, the rear yard is a well-kept lawn with shade trees and a foundation planting to blend the house into the lawn, as advocated by Bertram Fox. (Courtesy Thomas N. Berry & Company.)

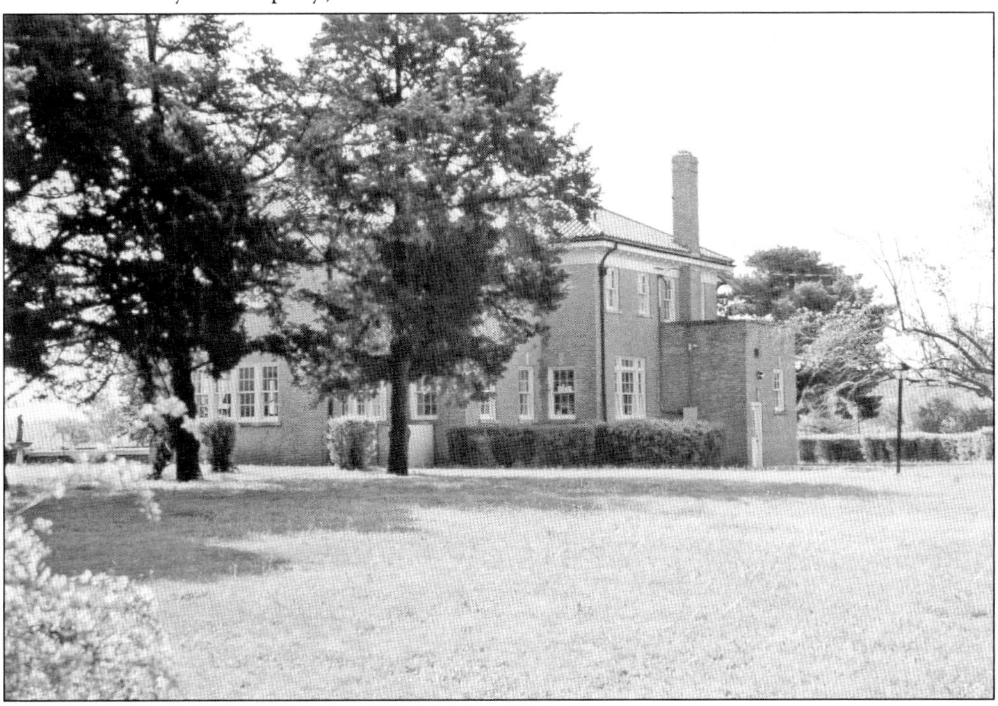

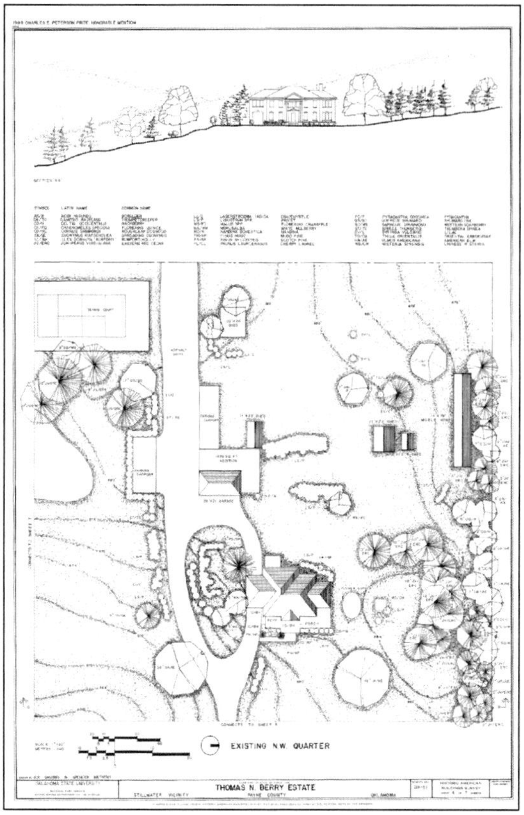

The as-built measured drawing of 1989 shows a detailed site and planting plan of the northwest portion of the estate. The drawing shows the location of the mansion, carriage house, sun shade for visitor parking, tennis court, and auxiliary buildings. The driveway continues west for around 600 feet to connect with Main Street and downtown Stillwater. The profile on the drawing shows the site slopes from the driveway to the pond.

A current view shows the carriage house after it was converted into an office for Thomas N. Berry & Company with a rear addition for the office and covered parking on the back side of the original building.

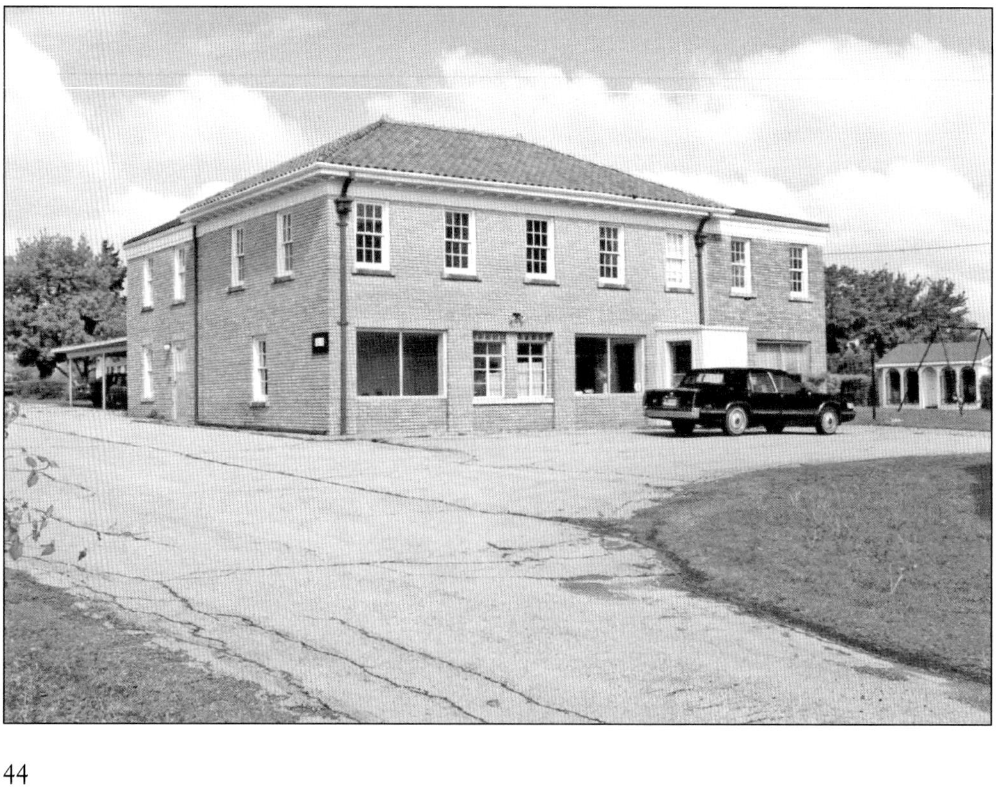

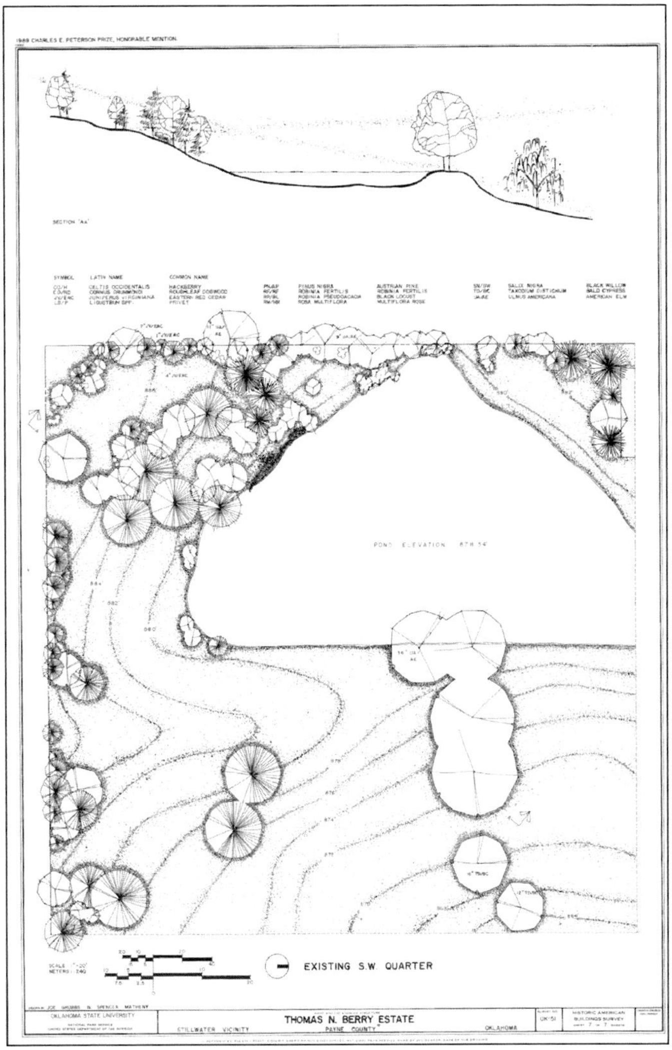

The as-built measured drawing of 1989 shows the southwest portion of the estate site and planting plan, and a profile of the upper pond. The setting of the pond is enhanced by clusters of trees and shrubs as envisioned by Bertram Fox. The profile shows the high point of the land sloping north toward the pond.

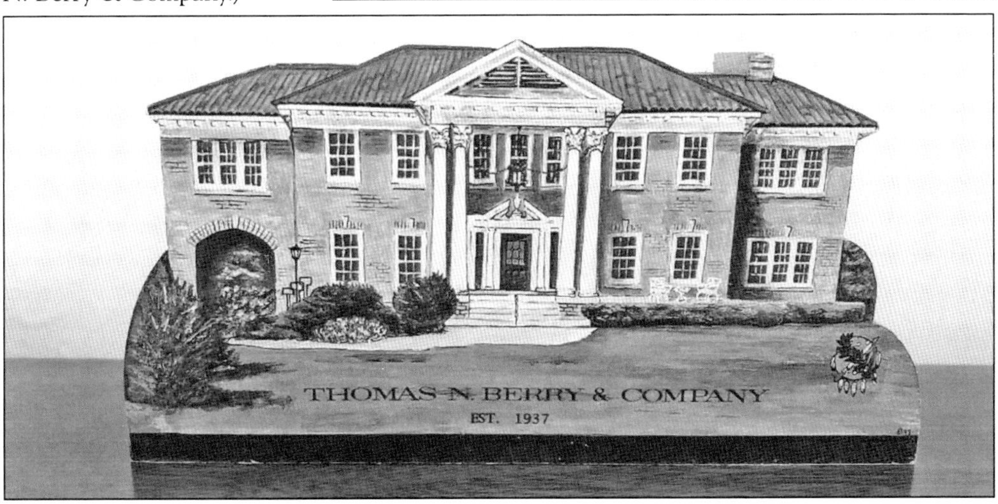

This woodcut of the mansion was commissioned on the 60th anniversary of Thomas N. Berry & Company to commemorate the company's founder. The woodcut also commemorates the first collaborative work in Stillwater of architect Fred Knoblock and landscape architect Bertram Fox. (Courtesy Thomas N. Berry & Company.)

E.W. Marland Mansion Estate, Ponca City

Type of Project: Residential Design
Designer: Henry Hatashita, Resident Landscape Designer, Ponca City; John Forsythe, Architect, New York
Date: 1928

The Marland Estate was built in 1928 as a dream of multimillionaire oilman and philanthropist E.W. Marland, his wife, and their two adopted children. The sprawling estate is a significant piece of Oklahoma's landscape architectural history. The magnificence of the landscape and buildings is the result of good design and the use of local building materials. The original site covered more than 2,500 acres of untouched land, converted into a majestic complex of botanical gardens, foxhunting, and polo grounds. The estate cost Marland $5.5 million to build. Henry Hatashita, a Japanese American resident landscape designer in Ponca City and graduate of Kansas State University, was commissioned to design and maintain the immense landscape of the Marland Estate. John Duncan Forsythe of New York was the architect of record who designed the estate.

Marland moved out of the mansion in 1931 during the Great Depression. He and his second wife, Lydie, lived there less than three years. After losing the company in a hostile takeover, to J.P. Morgan, he was unable to live in the mansion on a daily basis. The Marlands then lived in the artist studio and later in the chauffeur's quarters. The villa provided space for social events for the Marlands while E.W. served as the 10th governor of Oklahoma (1935–1939). He sold the mansion in 1941 to the Carmelite Religious Order for $66,000 for use as a seminary. The Carmelites sold the property in 1948 to the Order of the Felician Sisters for $50,000. The sisters constructed several buildings on the property that were used as a girls' high school, a chapel, a gymnasium, and a dormitory. The Felicians sold the estate to the City of Ponca City for $1.5 million. Today, the mansion is used as a museum, is listed in the National Register of Historical Places, and is designated a National Historic Landmark. The property is maintained by the City of Ponca City and the Marland Estate Foundation. The estate today consists of both original structures and one noncontributing structure. The original structures include the villa, influenced by the Davanzatti Palace in Florence, Italy, and designed by New York architect John Duncan Forsythe, the artist's studio, and Lydie's cottage, formerly known as the chauffeur's quarters.

Study Director: Dr. Charles L. Leider, Landscape Architecture Program
Faculty Advisors: William Bryans, Department of History; Prof. Nigel Jones, School of Architecture
Study Team Members: Michael Albert, team leader; Sean Rohrbacker; and Rebecca Bailey

Sources:
National Register of Historic Places
Marland Foundation Records
Copies of the original drawings were furnished by David Keithly, director of the E.W. Marland Mansion Estate.

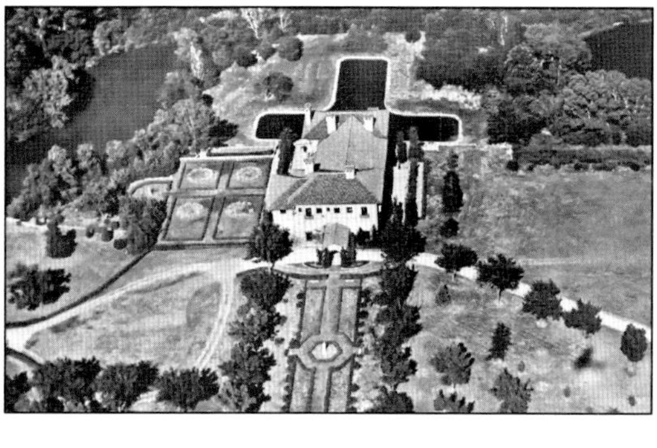

A 1928 aerial view of the front approach to the E.W. Marland Mansion Estate shows a blending of the formal Italian Renaissance garden style with an informal, naturalistic landscape design style. The formal gardens, pond, and mall of the Italian Renaissance style adjoin the informal curvilinear driveway and lakes in the woods in a harmonious way. (Courtesy E.W. Marland Estate Archives.)

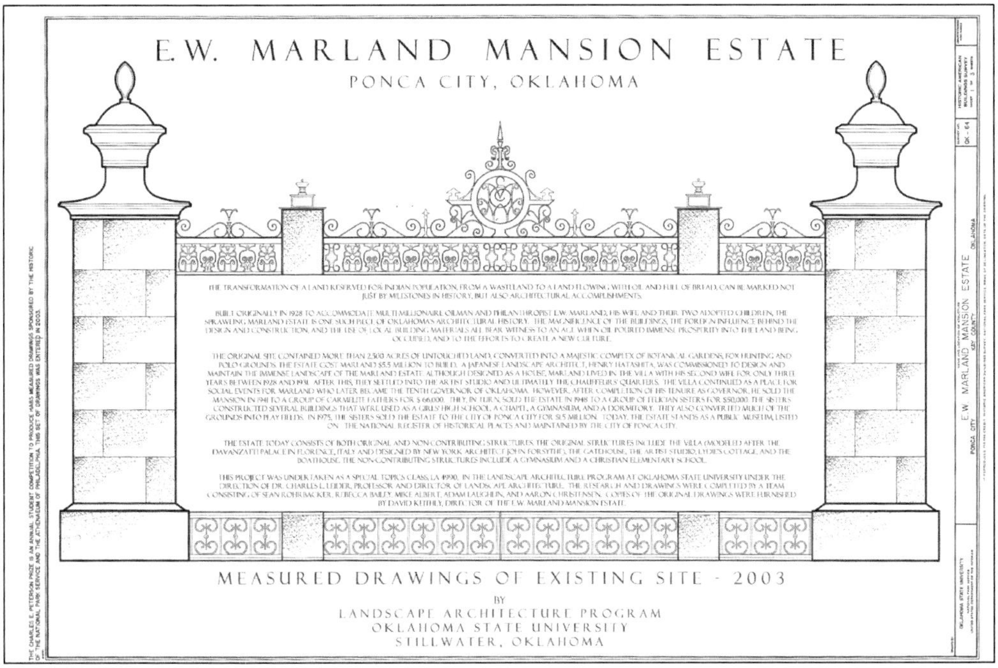

The poster of the E.W. Marland Mansion Estate entrance gate contains the history of the 2,500-acre estate, at the edge of Ponca City in 1928. The estate at one time included seven lakes, botanical gardens, a polo field, and a foxhunting area in addition to the mansion and related buildings. Henry Hatashita was also in charge of maintaining the site from 1928 to 1941, when the estate was sold. John Forsythe was the architect who designed the mansion, the artist studio, and other related buildings and collaborated with Henry Hatashita in designing the wall, fence, and wrought iron gates.

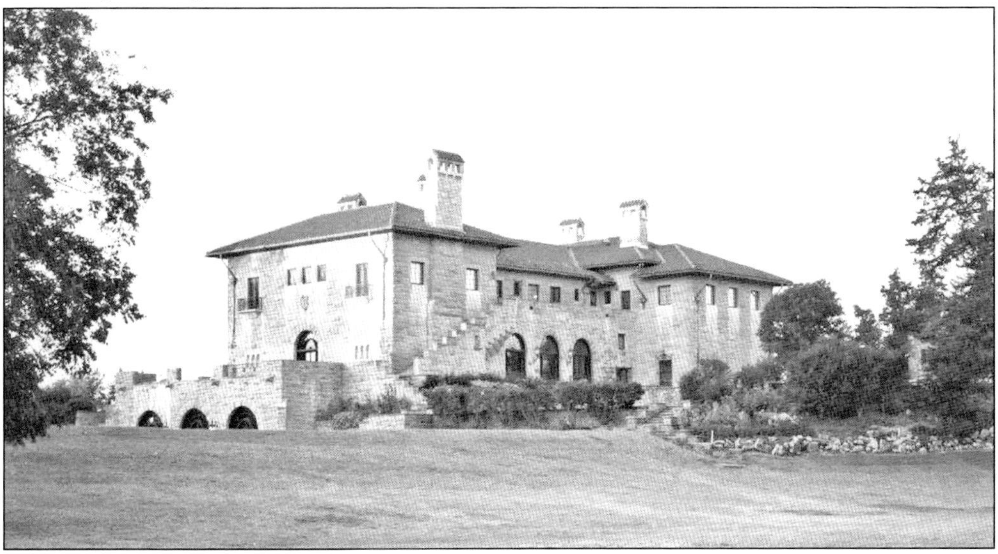

This view shows the mansion in the 2000s, after the pools had been filled and converted to a lawn. The estate was originally designed in the Beaux-Arts style, which combines the best design elements of past buildings and gardens. The mansion was designed by John Forsythe, a New York architect, in the Italian villa style in 1926. (Courtesy E.W. Marland Estate Archives.)

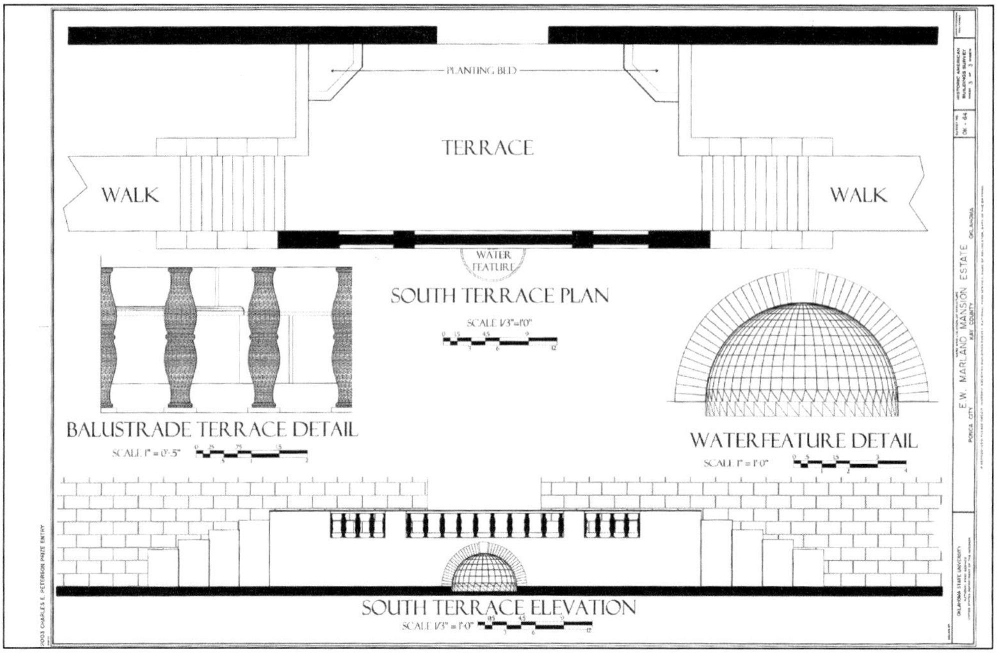

This drawing shows the as-built details of the terrace, stairway, walk, water feature, and balustrade of the mansion, which were modeled after the Davanzatti Palace. The details were designed and construction supervised by John Forsythe.

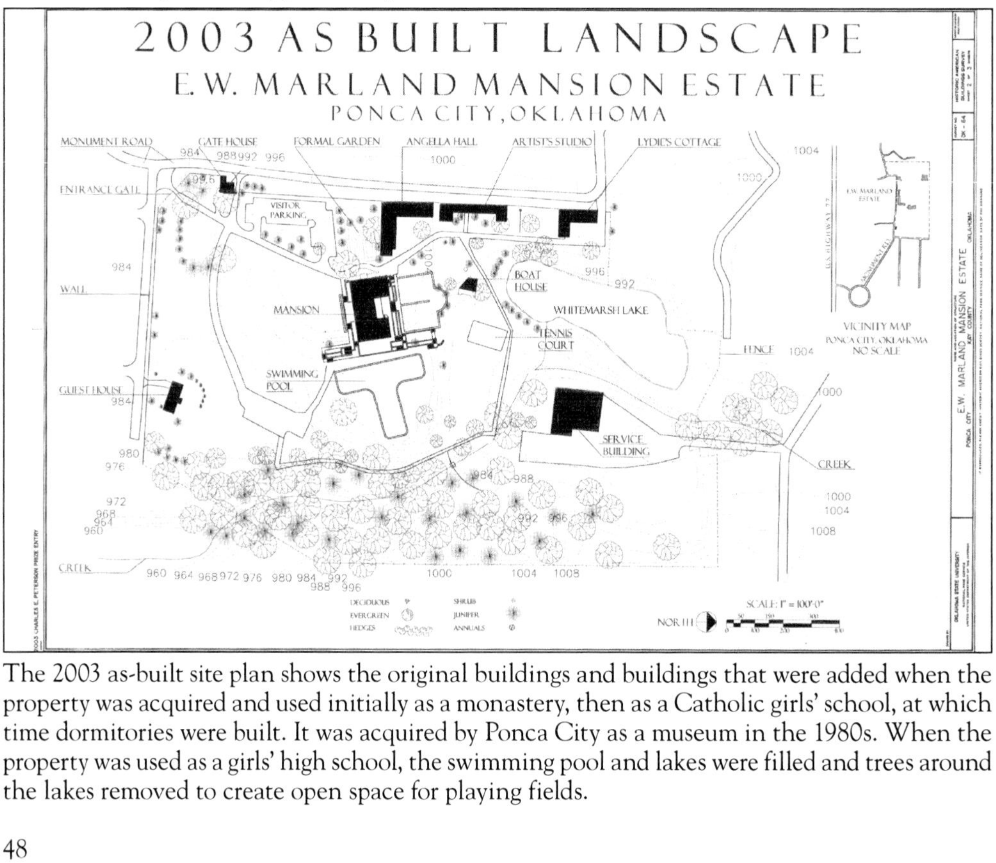

The 2003 as-built site plan shows the original buildings and buildings that were added when the property was acquired and used initially as a monastery, then as a Catholic girls' school, at which time dormitories were built. It was acquired by Ponca City as a museum in the 1980s. When the property was used as a girls' high school, the swimming pool and lakes were filled and trees around the lakes removed to create open space for playing fields.

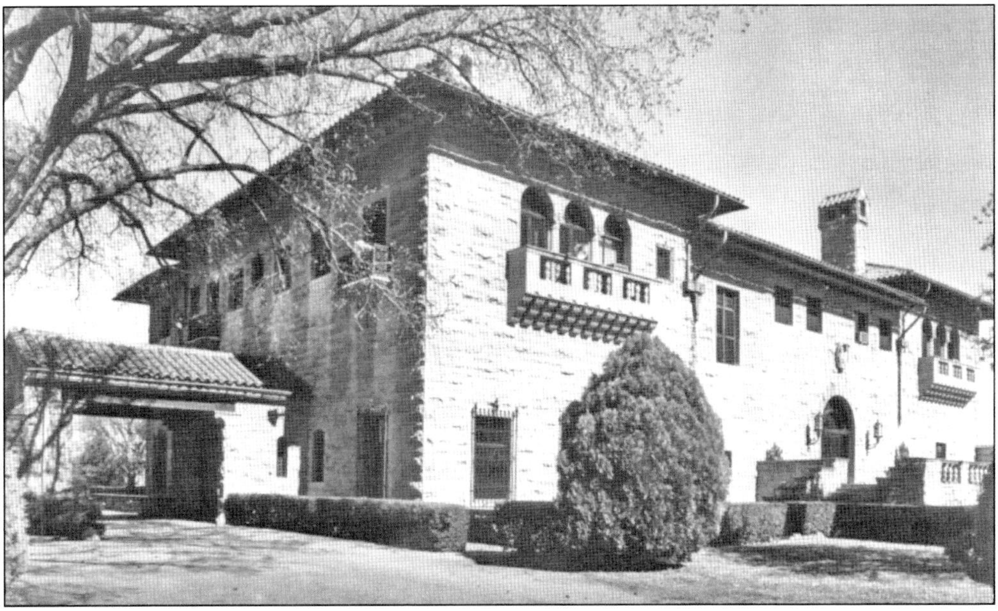

Above is a northeast view of the front entrance of the Marland Mansion Estate showing its limestone walls and red tile roof, with Italian Renaissance design features such as balconies, balustrades, and terraces designed by John Forsythe, a New York architect, in 1926. Henry Hatashita selected and maintained the plant material, like the trimmed evergreens at the entrance and throughout the estate. Below is another view of the northeast front entrance showing tourists visiting the mansion in early 1930s to see the work of Forsythe and Hatashita. (Both, courtesy E.W. Marland Estate Archives.)

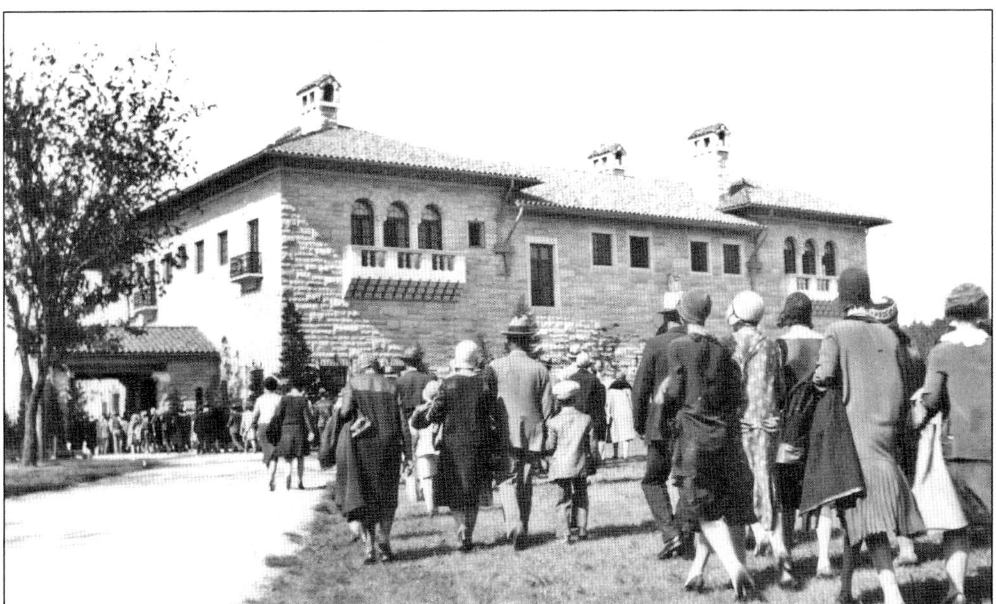

Overholser Mansion, Oklahoma City

Type of Project: Residential Design
Designer: W.S. Matthews, Architect, New York Date: 1904

The Overholser Mansion has been called "the product of an artist's eye." Conceived as a permanent residence that would need no future alterations, it has carried itself into the 21st century with undiminished dignity and untarnished beauty. It is unchanged on the outside, and the interior is much the same as when the mansion was opened in 1904.

Henry Overholser arrived in Oklahoma City in 1889 and was involved with nearly every aspect of the city's growth. He constructed over 35 buildings, including two opera houses, the US Courthouse, and the state fairgrounds. In 1901, Overholser purchased three lots north of Oklahoma City for his own home. W.S. Matthews, an architect trained at London's Kensington Academy, supervised the construction and furnishing of the three-story, French Château–style home.

The 11,000-plus-square-foot home and 4,000-square-foot carriage house were finished in 1903 with extravagant furnishings, stained-glass windows, and an interior of Antwerp oak. The mansion was a symbol of Oklahoma City's development and prosperity. The landscape around the Overholser mansion can be described as eclectic. Although the mansion never included an official landscape design, it has seen additions by a number of people over the years. After the mansion was built, a few trees were placed around the site. Over time, a foundation was added on the west side of the house, along with plantings around the foundation, the house, and on the north side of the lot.

In 1911, Overholser suffered from a stroke; it eventually led to his death in 1915. Henry Overholser, one of the founding fathers of Oklahoma, exemplified the pioneering spirit of the Eighty-Niners. Once the Overholser family moved on, the mansion served as the official residence of US senator Mike Monroney from 1956 to 1968. The mansion was acquired by the Oklahoma Historical Society in 1972 through funds raised primarily by the Oklahoma Chapter of the American Institute of Architects. Restoration and operation of the mansion has been aided through the efforts of the National Society of Colonial Dames of America; Historical Preservation, Inc.; the Women's Architectural League; and Friends of the Overholser. The mansion is operated by Preservation Oklahoma, a private nonprofit dedicated to preserving Oklahoma's historic places.

Study Director: Dr. Charles L. Leider, Landscape Architecture Program
Study Team Members: John Schroeder, team leader; Meredith Matthews; and Joseph Bettencourt

Sources:
www.overholsermansion.org
www.okhistory.org

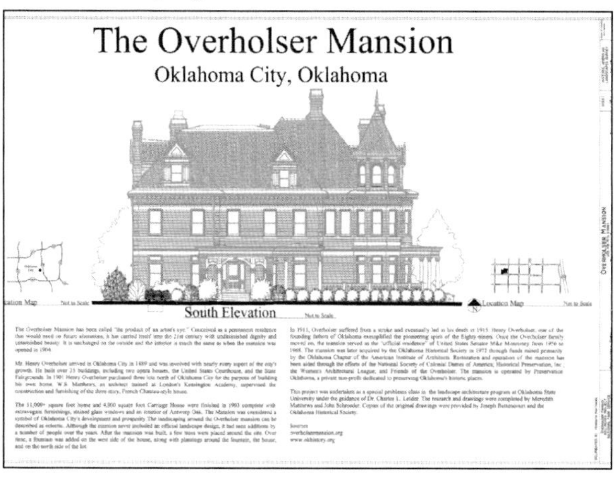

The poster gives the history of the Overholser Mansion and locates it within Oklahoma City and the Classen Highland Park neighborhood. The mansion is an early good example of the Queen Anne and Château architectural styles, as shown in this south elevation drawing from 2010. Built in 1903 for Henry Overholser, considered the father of Oklahoma City, it was designed by W.S. Matthews. The mansion is on the corner of Fifteenth and Hudson Streets.

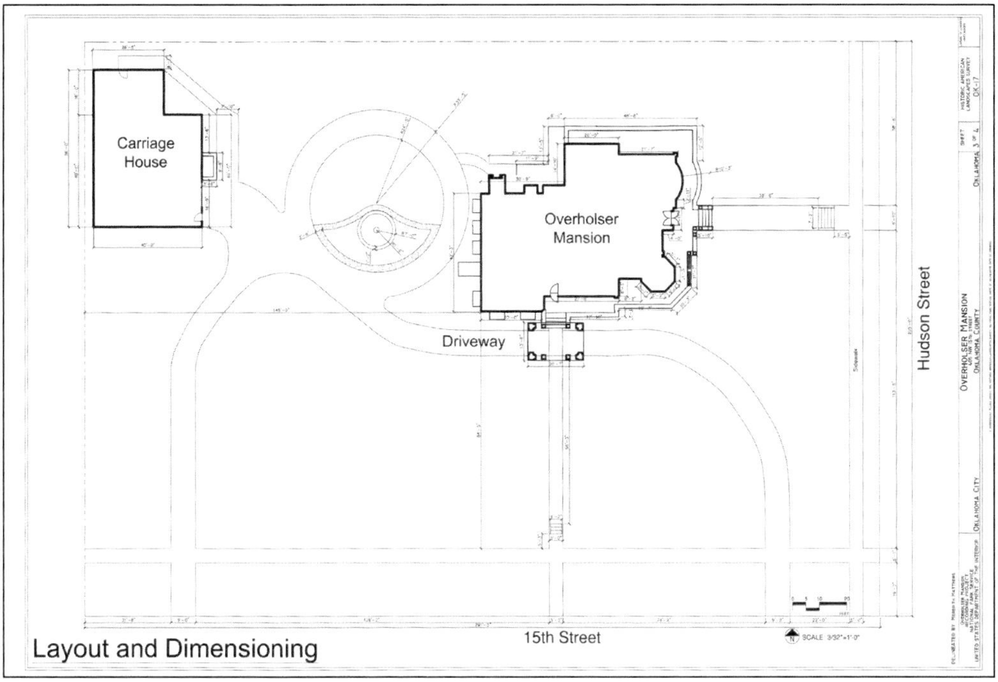

The as-built site plan drawing in 2010 shows one of the first major residences in Oklahoma City to integrate the use of the automobile into the site. A curvilinear U-shaped driveway off Fifteenth Street provides two-way access to the side door of the mansion, a circle drive provides for a turnaround, and space for a single car is provided in the carriage house in the rear yard. A sidewalk off Hudson Street provides access to the front door.

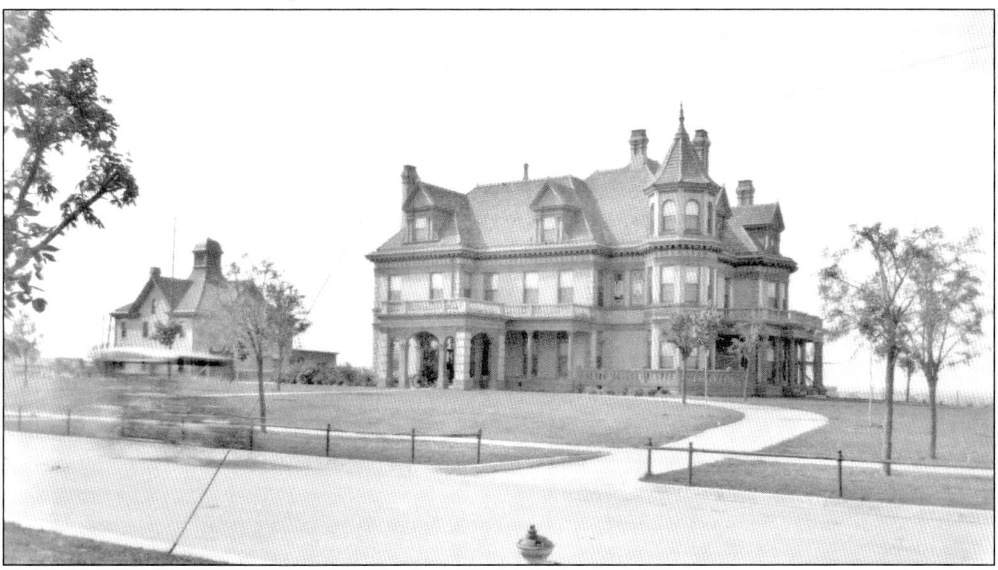

This view shows the 11,700-square-foot Overholser Mansion and 4,000-square-foot carriage house on the corner of Hudson and Fifteenth Streets in 1910. It shows a yard with an informal landscape design style with a large lawn, a few randomly planted shade trees, a foundation planting using shrubs by the mansion and carriage house, and a rail fence along the curb of the street to define the site. (Courtesy Oklahoma City Ronald J. Norwick Downtown Library.)

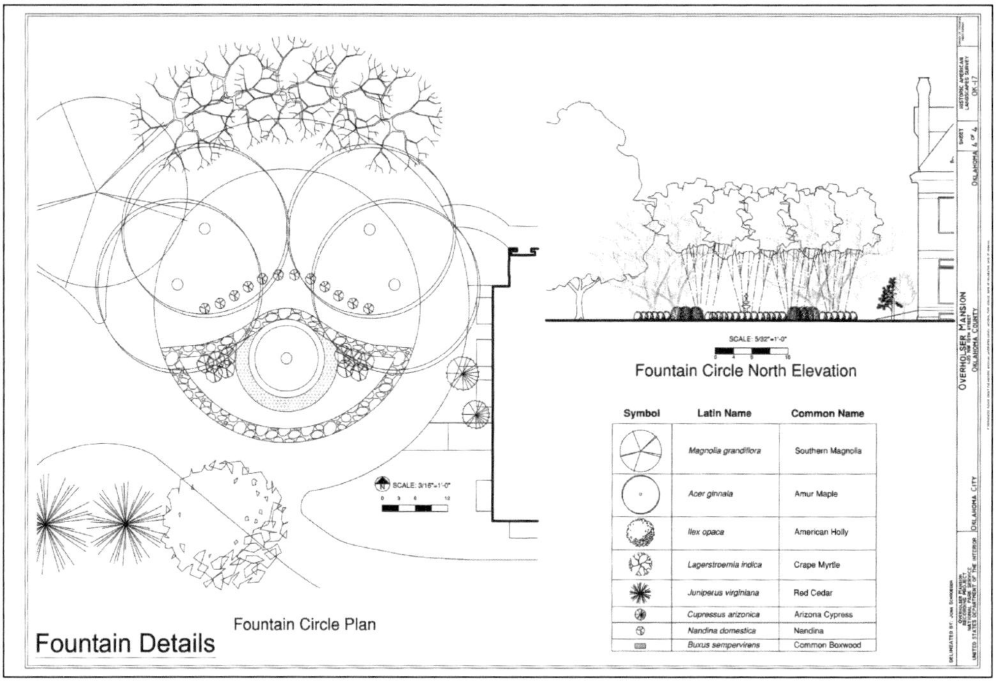

The as-built measured drawing in 2010 of the formal fountain circle area shows it set in an informal landscape design. The area has been enhanced with large shade trees and low-growing shrubs in between the circle drive to the mansion and carriage house. The fountain serves as the focal point for the design, as shown in the site plan, elevations, and plant list.

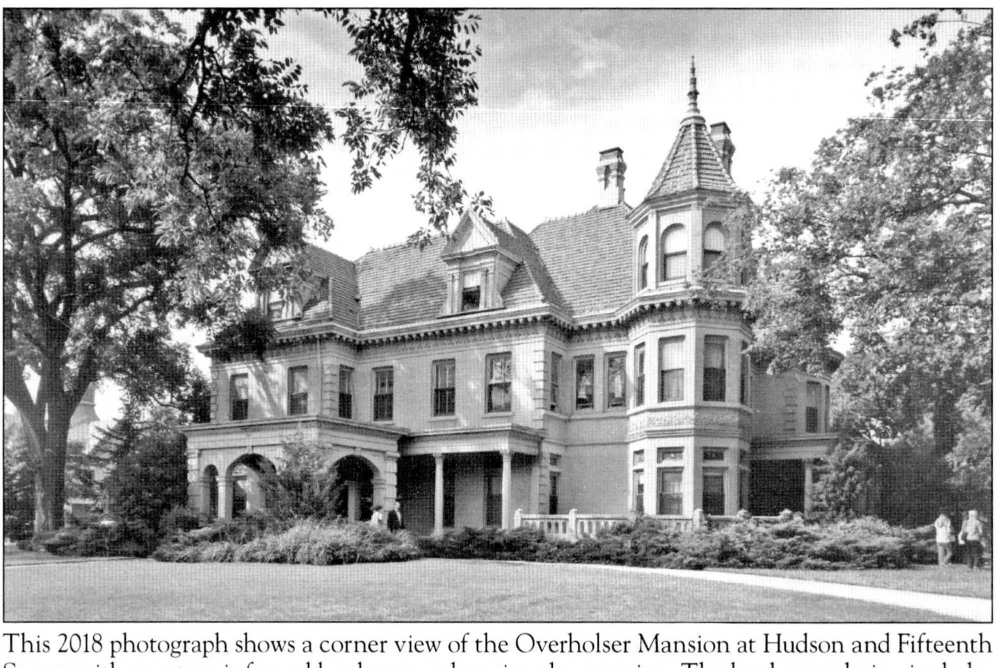

This 2018 photograph shows a corner view of the Overholser Mansion at Hudson and Fifteenth Streets with a mature informal landscape enhancing the mansion. The landscape design includes large trees that frame the mansion, while evergreen shrubs soften the foundation by making a smooth transition to the lawn. (Courtesy Oklahoma City Ronald J. Norwick Downtown Library.)

Two

CITY PLANNING AND INSTITUTIONAL GROUNDS

OKLAHOMA STATE UNIVERSITY, STILLWATER
Type of Project: Campus Master Plan
Designer: McCrary, Culley, and Carhart, Architects, Denver Date: 1928

The Oklahoma State University campus is the result of the 1930 twenty-five-year campus master plan. It is one of the few universities in the United States to be fully built out according to a master plan. Dr. Henry G. Bennett, upon his arrival as president of the Oklahoma A&M College in 1928, advocated the establishment of a 25-year plan for the campus. The idea came to fruition when the Denver firm McCrary, Culley, and Carhart— involved in preparing master plans for over 30 colleges in the West and Midwest—was retained to develop a conceptual campus master plan. After the plan was developed, President Bennett, with the assistance of Philip A. Wilbur, professor of architecture, and D.A. Hamilton, associate professor of architecture, revised the plan and established a Georgian Renaissance design theme using brick and limestone trim for the campus buildings. The English colonial capital of Williamsburg, Virginia, was the model for the plan and major buildings.

The plan called for the library to be the centerpiece of a cruciform design with north–south and east–west axes. The formal character of the campus was reinforced with buildings grouped in quadrangles adjacent to the axes. The site plan produced a formal landscape design to complement the strong, formal architectural elements of the plan. Major landscape features executed during the 25-year plan were the formal planting design and the intensive installation of indigenous and nonindigenous plant materials. The plan required ample circulation and service to each building, which has been maintained throughout the years. In addition, formal sight lines were created by malls and reinforced by the use of sidewalks, hedges, and tree-lined avenues. The red-orange brick, beige limestone trim, and Georgian architectural style of the buildings unified the campus, which was built out the according to the 1930 plan 15 years after World War II. The architectural theme and materials of the campus continued in the new building additions to the campus.

The campus owes its present existence to the leadership of President Bennett and Prof. Philip Wilbur. Building designs were by the architectural firm of Layton, Hicks, and Forsyth of Oklahoma City. In 1936, beautification of the Oklahoma A&M campus became a federal project. Funds were allocated to provide for an extensive tree and shrubbery planting program. Professor Wilbur, agronomy professor H.J. Harper, and Prof. Frank Cross, head of horticulture, worked together on both site plans and planting plans that assisted the WPA's installation program. Bryan Thompson, an OSU landscape design graduate, headed the campus beatification activities from 1938 to 1958. President Bennett lived to see the central elements of his 25-year plan executed before his accidental death in an airplane accident in Iran in 1953.

Study Director: Dr. Charles L. Leider, Landscape Architecture Program
Faculty Advisors: Dr. William Bryans, Department of History; Prof. Nigel Jones, School of Architecture
Study Team Members: William M. Cole, team leader; Kyle Clayton; Donna S. Decatur; Myra Ann Roberts; Gregory Fox; and Scott L. Kilgo

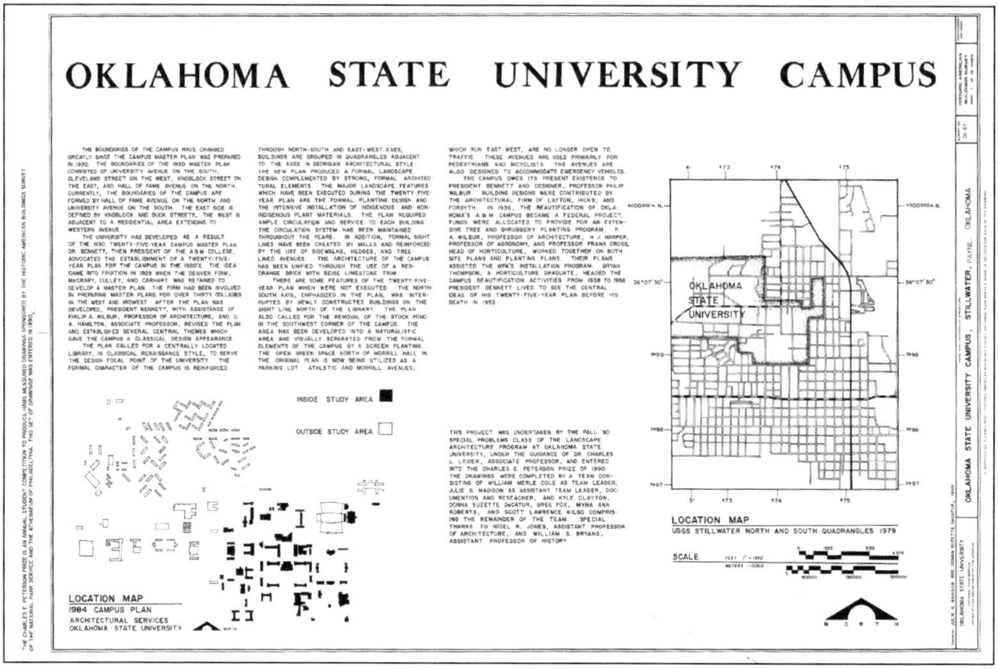

The poster gives the history of the Oklahoma State University campus. The campus map shows the built-up portion of the campus on its centennial in 1989, and maps show the relationship of the campus to Stillwater. The campus is in the northwest portion of the city's grid street system starting at the corner of Knoblock Street and University Avenue. The campus was laid out by landscape architect faculty member Frank Waugh with a curvilinear street, but with his departure, the street system reverted to a grid to match Stillwater's.

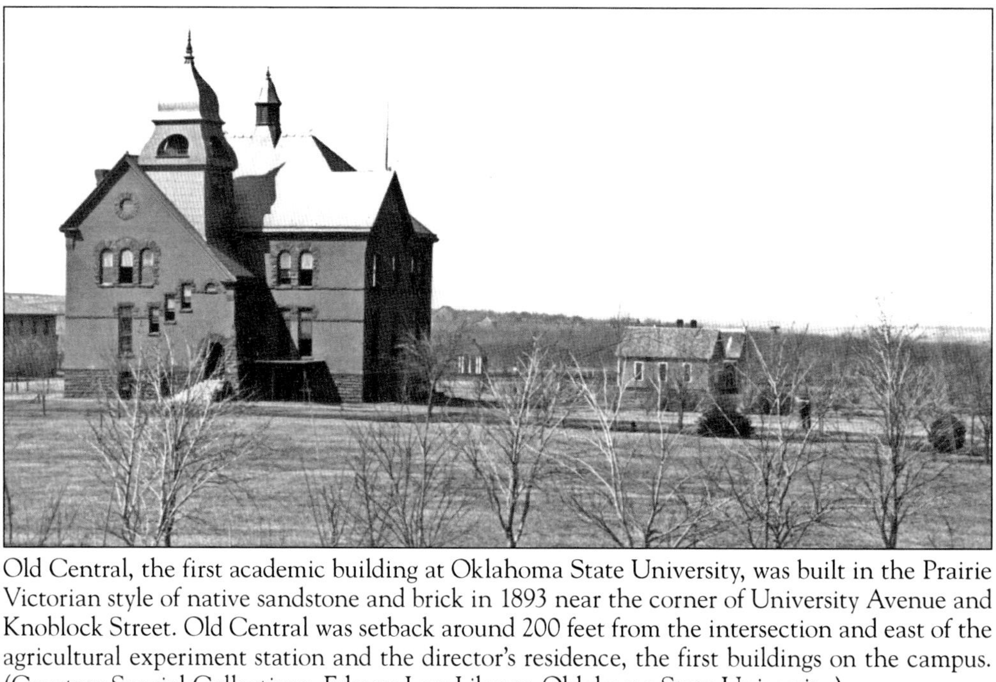

Old Central, the first academic building at Oklahoma State University, was built in the Prairie Victorian style of native sandstone and brick in 1893 near the corner of University Avenue and Knoblock Street. Old Central was setback around 200 feet from the intersection and east of the agricultural experiment station and the director's residence, the first buildings on the campus. (Courtesy Special Collections, Edmon Low Library, Oklahoma State University.)

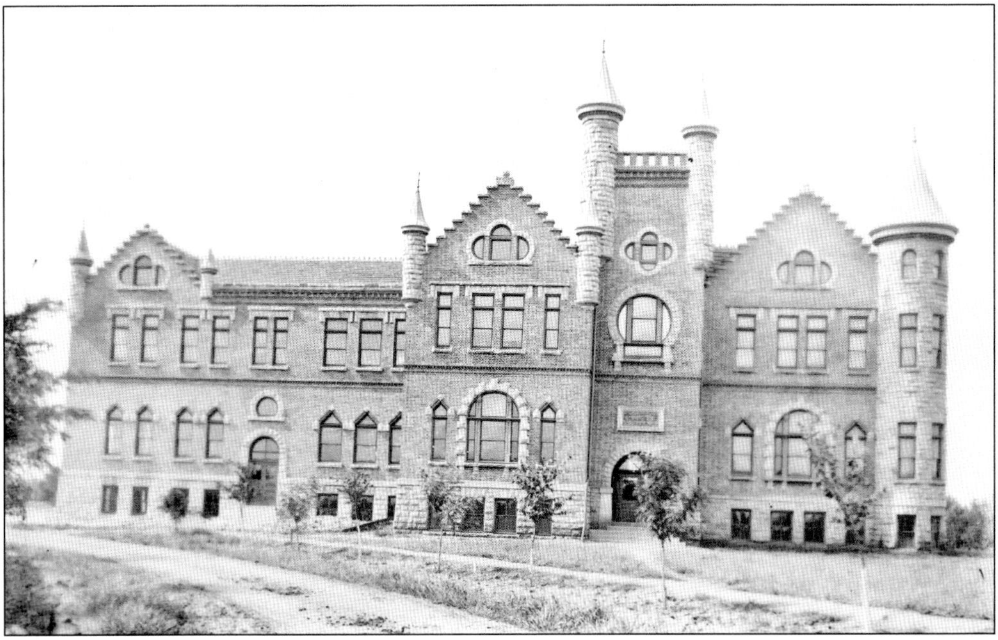

Williams Hall was constructed in 1900 as a multipurpose building in the Prairie Gothic Revival style by Joseph P. Foucart, a Belgian-born architect who gained professional experience on the design of the Paris Opera House. He arrived in Guthrie during the Land Run and set up a professional office. Williams Hall housed classrooms, laboratories, offices, a library, and an auditorium. The building of native sandstone was on the Knoblock Street side of Old Central. (Courtesy Special Collections, Edmon Low Library, Oklahoma State University.)

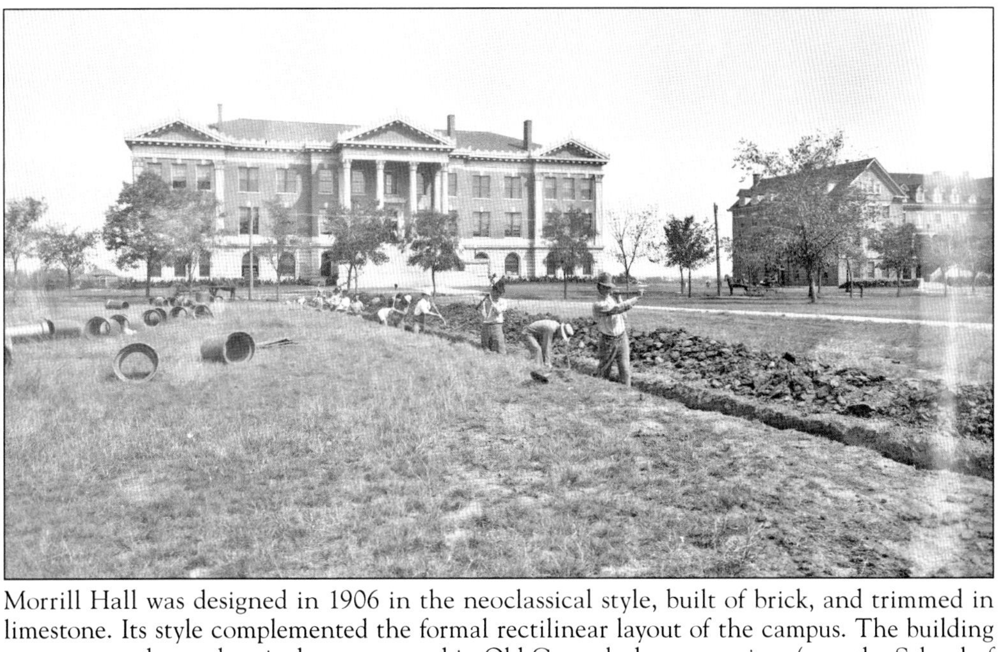

Morrill Hall was designed in 1906 in the neoclassical style, built of brick, and trimmed in limestone. Its style complemented the formal rectilinear layout of the campus. The building was on a north–south axis that connected it, Old Central, the gymnasium (now the School of Architecture), and the football stadium to the north. (Courtesy Special Collections, Edmon Low Library, Oklahoma State University.)

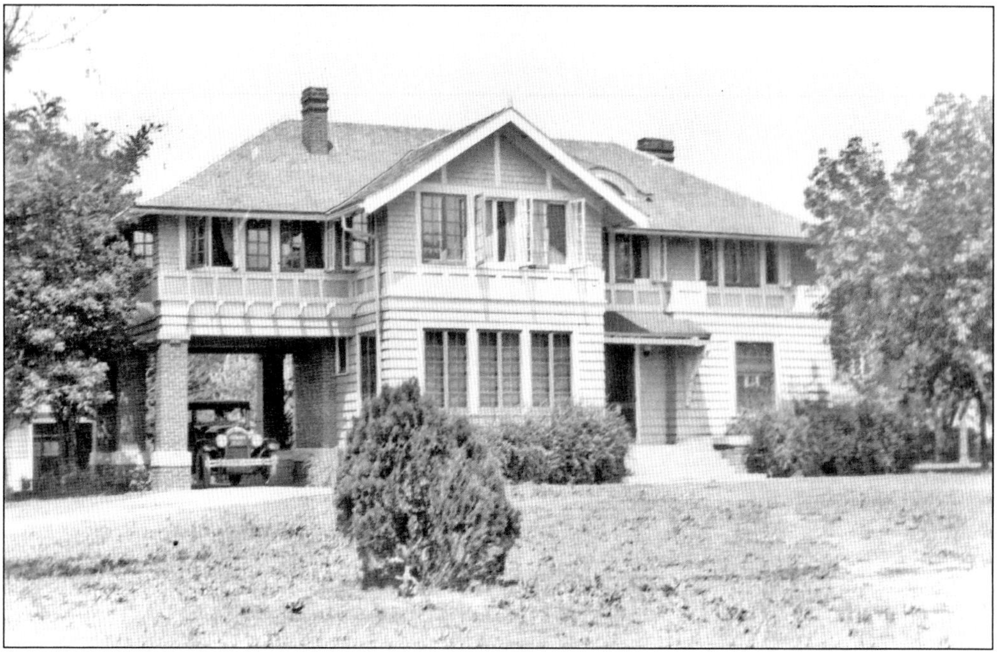

The president's house was built in 1917 at the corner of University Avenue and Hester Street and was demolished in 1952 to provide a site for Bennett Memorial Chapel. The president's new house was designed in Contemporary style and built in 1960. The house is off the campus on North Washington Street. (Courtesy Special Collections, Edmon Low Library, Oklahoma State University.)

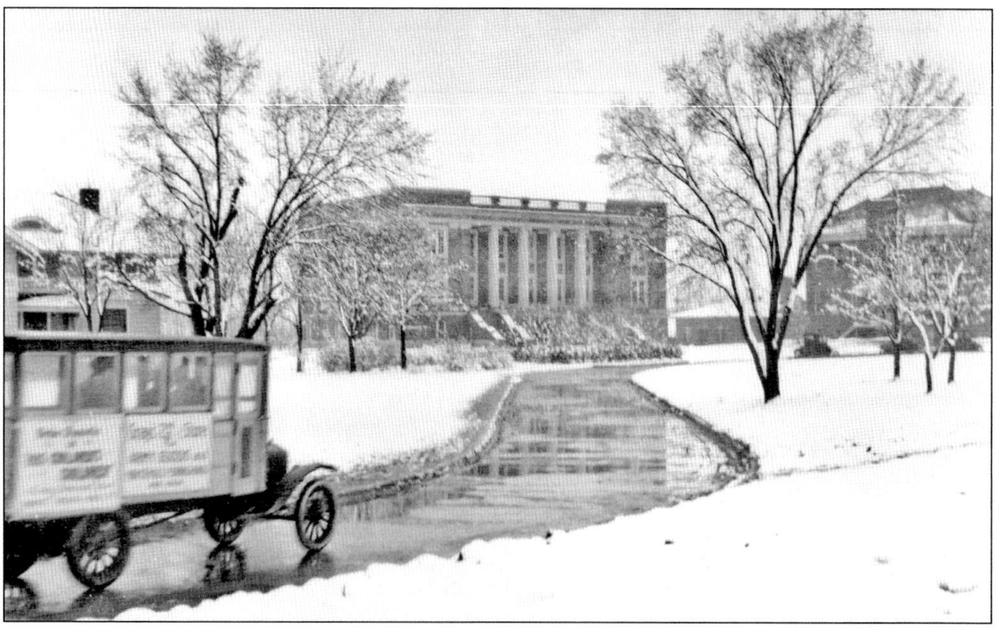

The rectangular street system was expanded to the north to serve more building sites, including an athletic area for a gymnasium, baseball field, and stadium. The design in 1920 of the New Science Hall, near Old Central, continued the neoclassical style to accommodate the expanding science programs. (Courtesy Special Collections, Edmon Low Library, Oklahoma State University.)

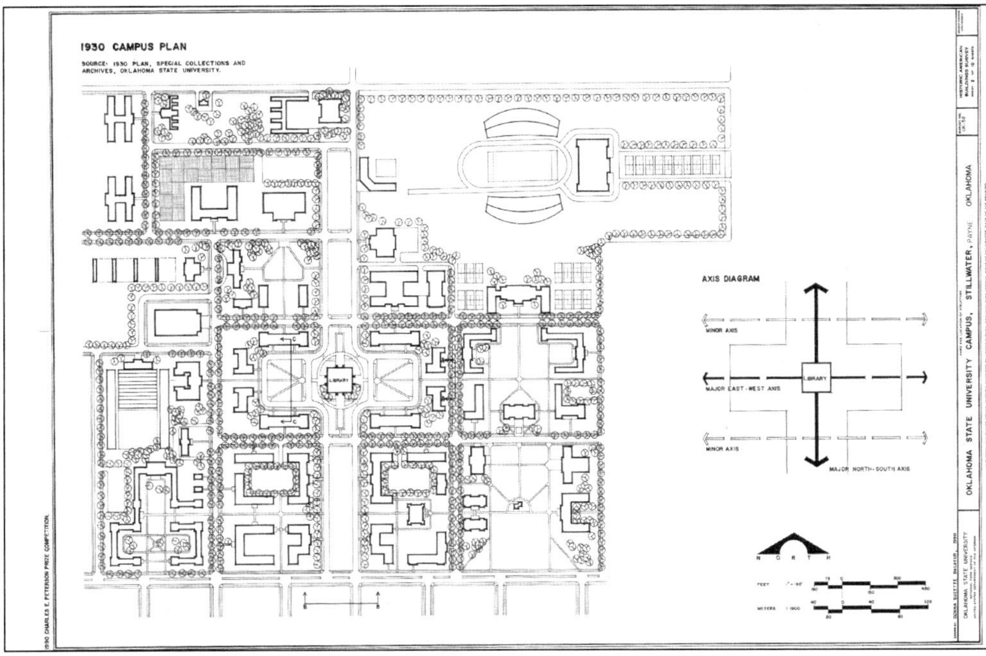

The as-built measured drawing of the 1929 Neo-Georgian-style master plan continued the extension of the rectilinear street system of the old campus. The new master plan established the library as the centerpiece of the cruciform plan. The library is positioned to be viewed from College/University Avenue on the south and Hall of Fame Avenue on the north. The plan shows other major buildings terminating at either end of the east–west axis and buildings grouped in quadrangles on either side of the north–south axis.

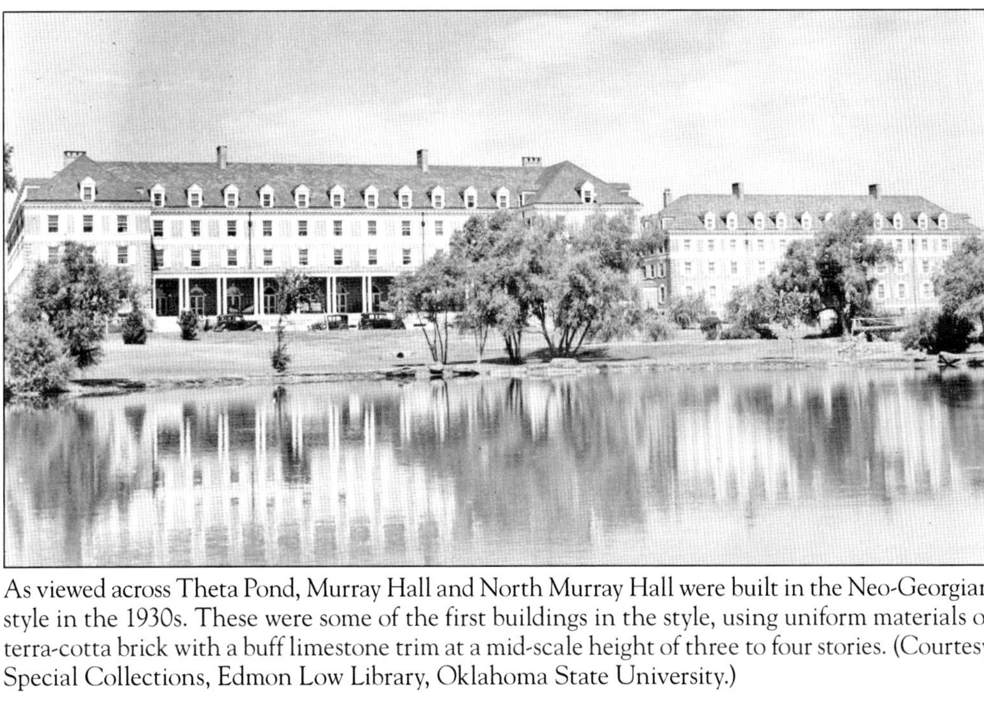

As viewed across Theta Pond, Murray Hall and North Murray Hall were built in the Neo-Georgian style in the 1930s. These were some of the first buildings in the style, using uniform materials of terra-cotta brick with a buff limestone trim at a mid-scale height of three to four stories. (Courtesy Special Collections, Edmon Low Library, Oklahoma State University.)

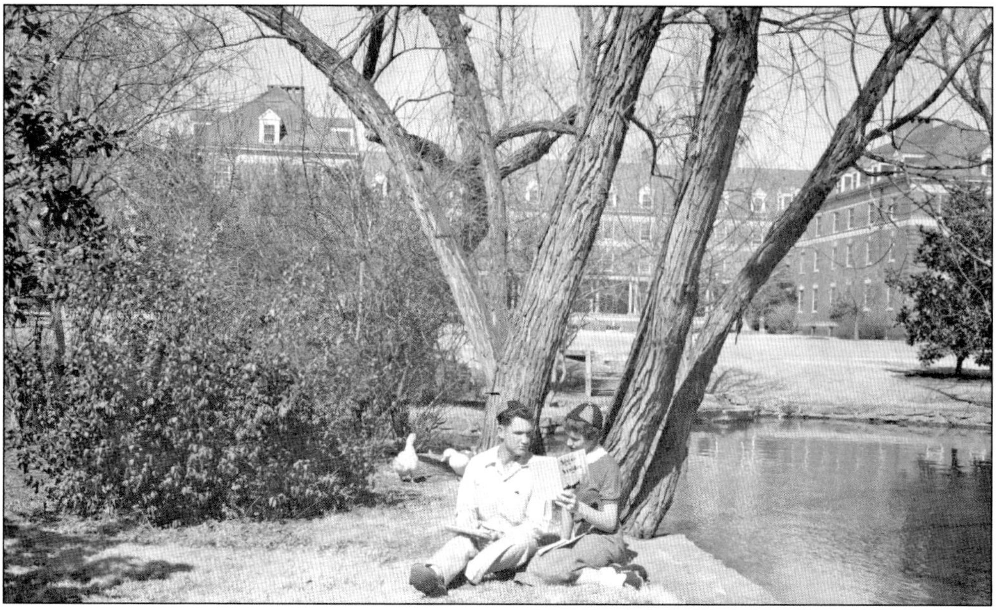

Theta Pond was converted from a stock-watering pond starting in the 1920s to become a park in the 1930s. It is located on the corner of University Avenue and Monroe Street on the campus. In the 1930 plan, the site was designated as a quadrangle for buildings. It evolved into a park in the naturalistic style, which runs counter to but complements the formal, rectangular Neo-Georgian style. (Courtesy Special Collections, Edmon Low Library, Oklahoma State University.)

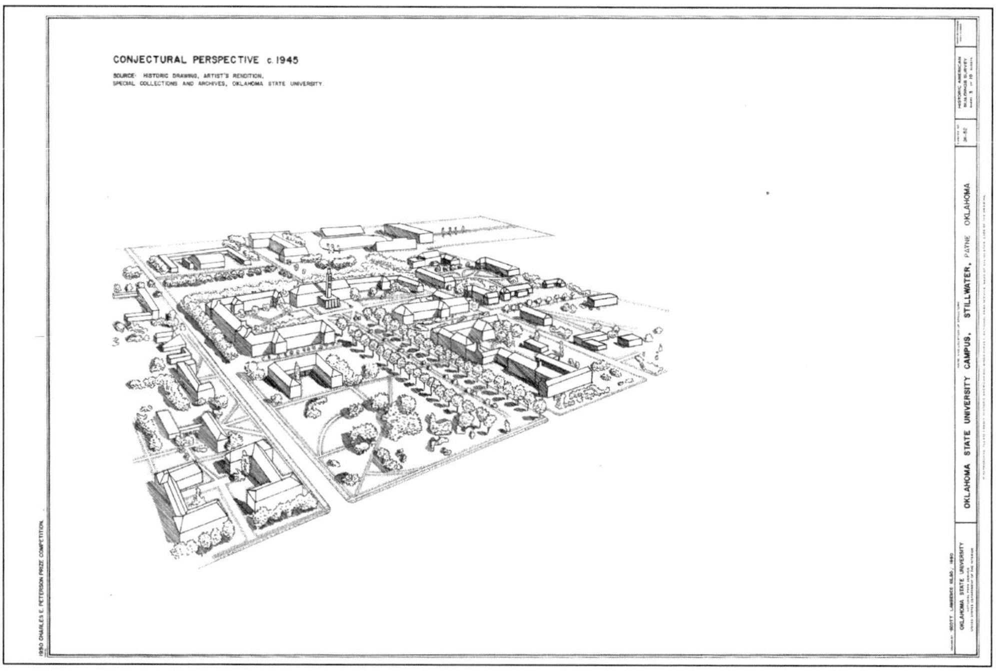

With a view looking north, an aerial sketch of the campus in 1945 from the southwest corner along University/College Avenue shows the campus 90 percent built out, based on the 1930 campus plan. The only area not built out is Theta Pond, in the foreground of the sketch along University Avenue.

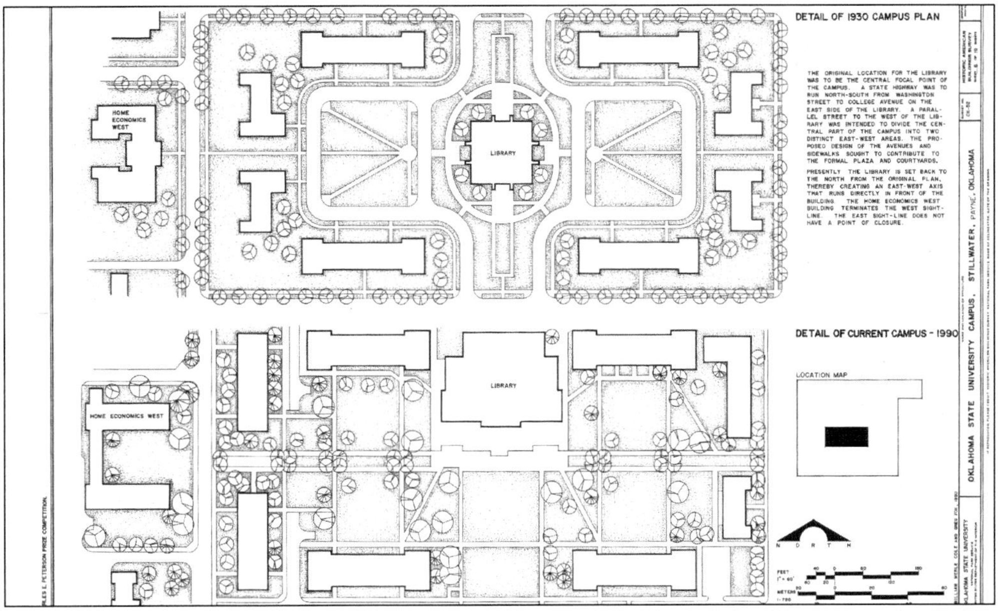

A comparison of the 1930 plan versus the as-built 1989 site plan of the library area for OSU's centennial shows that not all of the plan was fully implemented. The library was placed north of the cross axis instead on the cross axis, as proposed in the 1930 plan. The proposed one-way street system around the library from University Avenue to Hall of Fame Avenue was converted to a walkway to the library instead of a roadway, as proposed in the 1930 plan. The lawn north of the library to Hall of Fame Avenue was infilled with the power plant and the Noble Research Center.

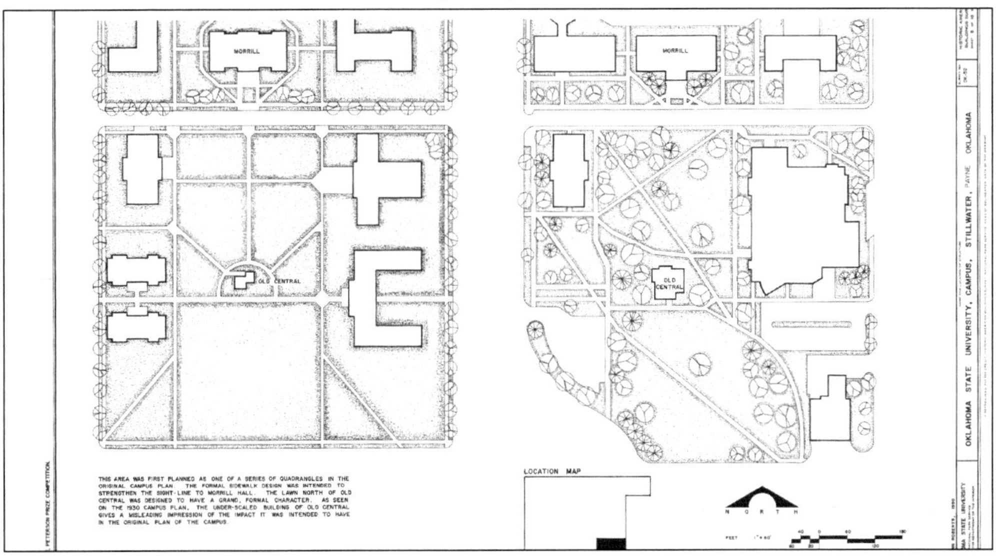

A comparison of the 1930 plan and the as-built site for the Old Central area in 1989 shows that only a few of the elements of the plan were implemented, such as the north–south axis visually connecting Old Central to Morrill Hall. The southwest corner of this area plan was changed when a parcel of land from the old campus was used as a site for the Bennett Chapel. The change resulted in a realignment of Hester Street at University Avenue. The pedestrian circulation system of the 1930 plan was essentially ignored, and sidewalks were built in response to desired walking directions instead of a grid system, as shown in the 1989 plan.

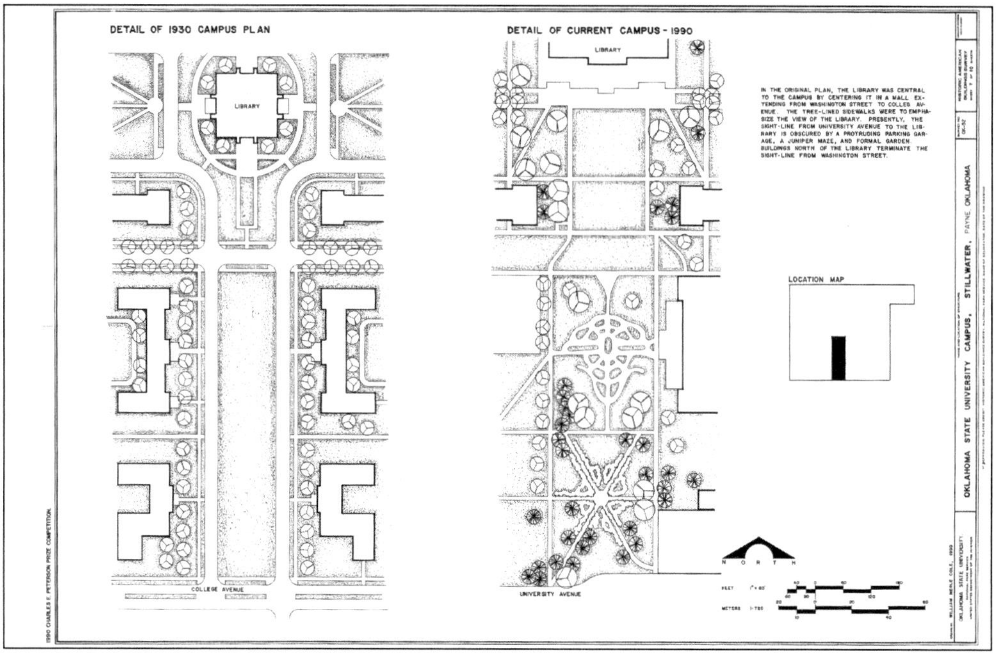

A comparison of the 1930 plan to the as-built 1989 site plan for the library mall area at OSU's centennial shows that some elements of the plan were modified and other fully implemented. The proposed north–south divided one-way roadway around the library from University Avenue to Hall of Fame Avenue was converted to a pedestrian walkway to the library on either side of the mall. The open green lawn of the mall was infilled with low-growing formal gardens. The layout of buildings on the east side of the mall was implemented by the building of the Student Union and a parking garage. Theta Pond was developed on the west side of the mall instead of buildings.

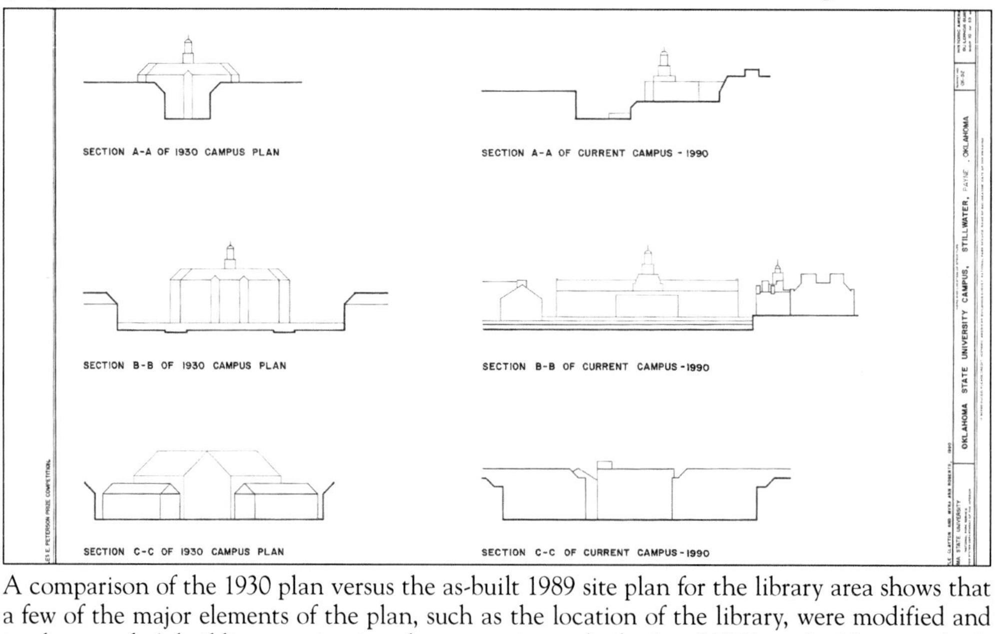

A comparison of the 1930 plan versus the as-built 1989 site plan for the library area shows that a few of the major elements of the plan, such as the location of the library, were modified and implemented. A building terminating the west axis was built. As of 1989, no building was built to terminate the axis on the east.

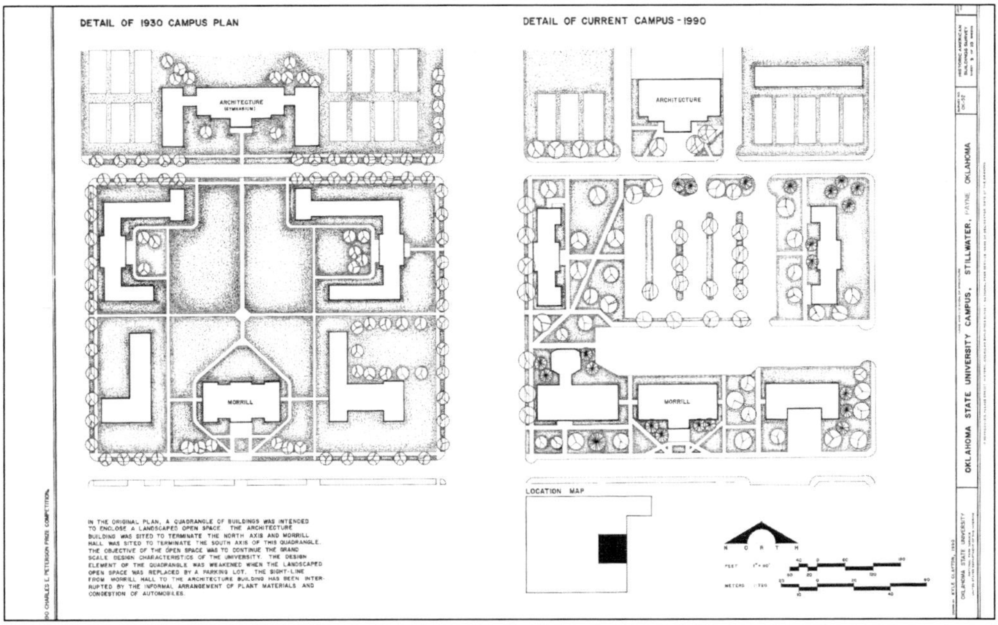

A comparison of the 1930 plan and the as-built 1989 site plan for the Morrill Hall plan area shows that most of the elements of the 1930 plan were implemented with the exception of the central green space between Morrill Hall and the gymnasium, which was converted into parking lots. The pedestrian circulation plan of 1930 was disrupted by the parking lots and not implemented.

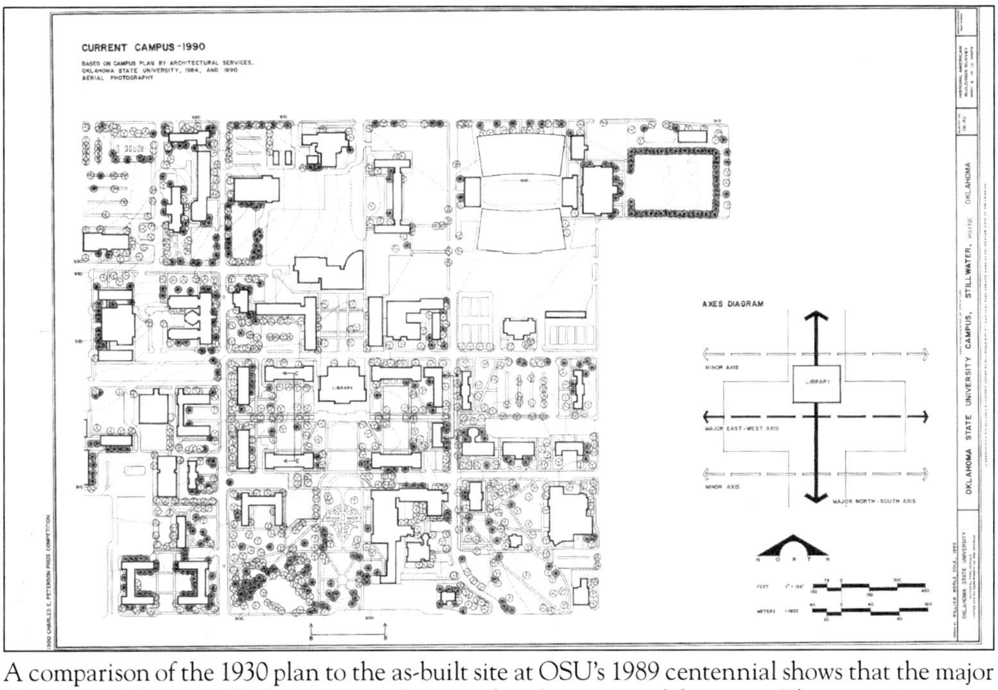

A comparison of the 1930 plan to the as-built site at OSU's 1989 centennial shows that the major elements of the overall plan were implemented with some modifications. The exceptions were not maintaining the great lawn north of the library to Hall of Fame Avenue by first placing the power plant on the north–south axis of the lawn and later placing the Noble Research Center between the library and the power plant on the north axis.

Oklahoma City Civic Center

Type of Project: Urban Design
Designer: Hare & Hare, Landscape Architect, Kansas City. Missouri; George Kessler, City Planner
Date: 1926–1936

The development of the Oklahoma City Civic Center grew out of the City Beautiful Movement, a trend that swept the nation at the beginning of the 20th century. The movement sought to improve the appearance of cities throughout the country by creating, transforming, and upgrading public spaces into beautiful, well-organized, and appealing destinations. Typical enhancements included majestic boulevards, grand park systems, and impressive railroad stations, along with recreational and playground facilities. One additional, immensely important aspect of the City Beautiful Movement, especially as it pertains to Oklahoma City, was the conceptualization and implementation of grand civic designs. The civic center scheme of grouping public buildings in close proximity to each other originated during the 1893 Chicago World's Fair and from the McMillan Plan for Washington, DC. The term "civic center," as it applies to a formal ensemble of public buildings, did not come into use until almost a decade later, when in 1902 it was introduced by John De Witt Warner, a leader of New York City's Municipal Art Society.

The City Beautiful Movement spread to Oklahoma as early as 1903, when a City Beautiful organization formed in Oklahoma City. In 1909, W.H. Dunn, superintendent of parks in Kansas City, Missouri, was hired to design a parks and boulevard plan for the city. This was not completely implemented due to insufficient funds. Nevertheless, in 1920, the city acquired the services of noted City Beautiful planner and consultant George E. Kessler of St. Louis, Missouri. He was to complete a comprehensive plan to ensure the city's planned development as it grew. Kessler died three years later in 1923, leaving his plan unfinished. Undeterred by these early obstacles, city commissioners charged forwards, and in 1928, they brought in the landscape architecture and city planning firm of Hare & Hare.

Hiring a landscape architect or landscape architecture firm to implement aspects of the City Beautiful planning ideology was not abnormal in cities across the United States. Actually, landscape architects played a larger role in the movement than architects, even though in 1909 the American Society of Landscape Architects only numbered 61 members.

The first site plan was prepared in 1936 by Hare & Hare based on the 1923 conceptual plan developed George Kessler, city planner from St. Louis, as part of a WPA project. The father-son landscape architecture firm Hare & Hare established itself as a successful city planner in the Southwest prior to its time in Oklahoma City and came highly recommended. The firm's primary task was to complete the unfinished Kessler plan.

Although the buildings within the civic center complex have received interior and exterior renovations over the years, the original structures remain. The landscape of the civic area in downtown Oklahoma City has experienced various modifications though, as plant materials were replaced or removed completely, monuments were built, and streets were widened to accommodate additional vehicular traffic around the site and to the business district. As recently as 2001, the landscape architecture firm Howard-Fairbairn redesigned the site. Included in this report are the original 1929 Hare & Hare plans, the implemented 1936 design, the result of Howard-Fairbairn's redesign, and the layout of the site as built by 2008.

Study Director: Dr. Charles L. Leider, Landscape Architecture Program
Faculty Advisor: Dr. William Bryans, Department of History
Study Team Members: Andrew Loverude, team leader; Randy Becker; Justin Kissman; Stephen Murphy; and Steven Eilers

Sources:
Hare & Hare archives, University of Missouri, Kansas City
Oklahoma City Park Department
Howard-Fairbairn, Landscape Architects, Oklahoma City

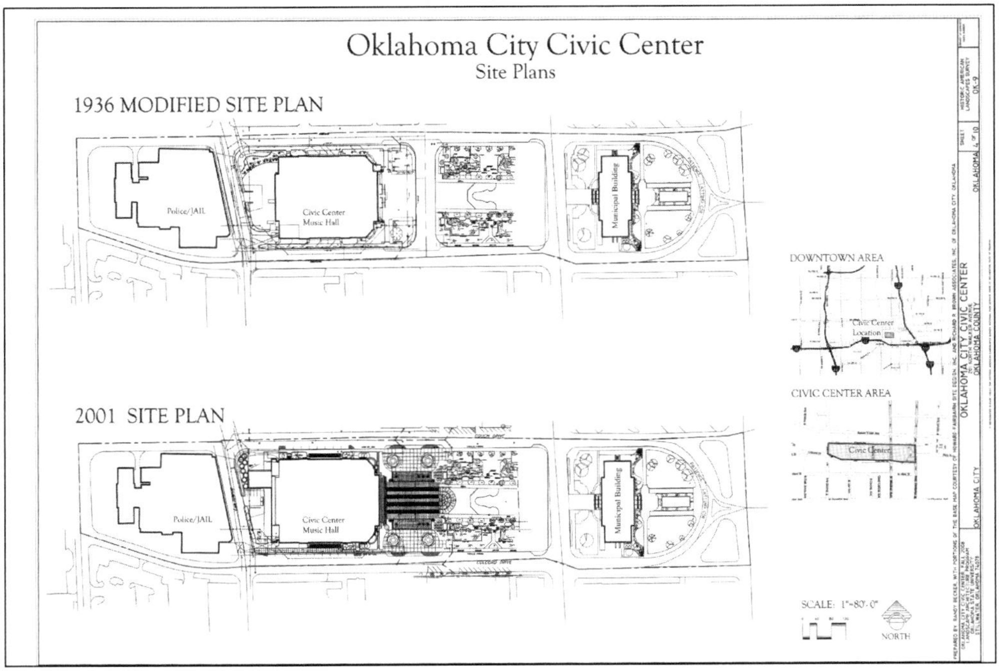

The locator diagrams in the drawing prepared in 2010 shows the location of the Oklahoma City Civic Center as well as the downtown area. The City Beautiful site shows its evolution in two plans. In the second plan, the site was renovated in 2001 when a larger plaza was created in front of the auditorium by eliminating one of the crossroads as shown in the site plan.

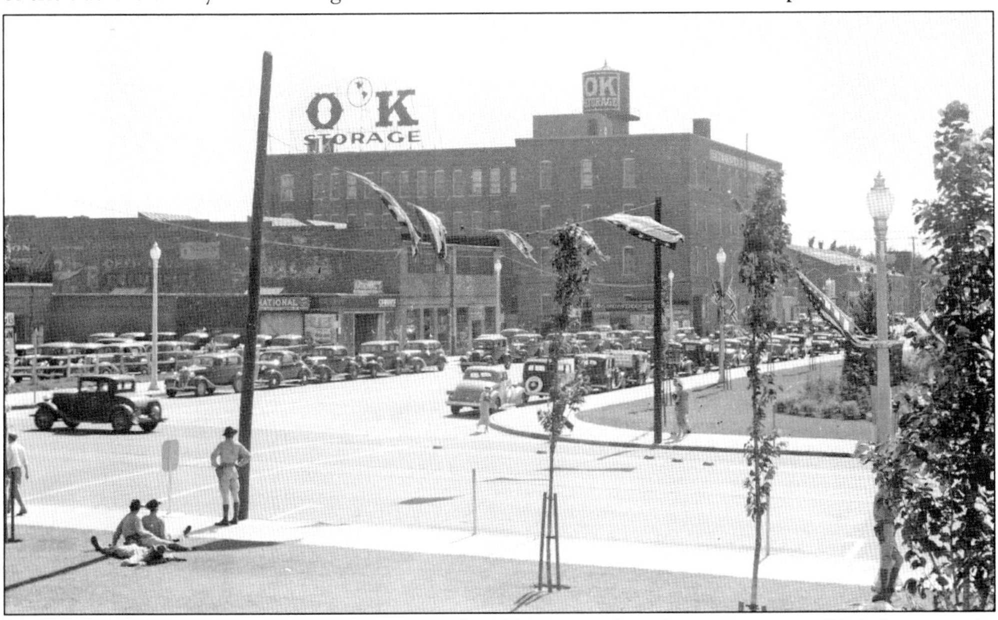

An image made the day of the dedication of the Oklahoma City Civic Center in 1936 shows newly planted and staked trees reflecting the integration of hardscape with landscape in urban design projects as part of the City Beautiful Movement to make cities greener. The dedication brought crowds, seen here on the streets with parked cars and newly planted trees. (Courtesy Oklahoma City Roland J. Norwick Downtown Library.)

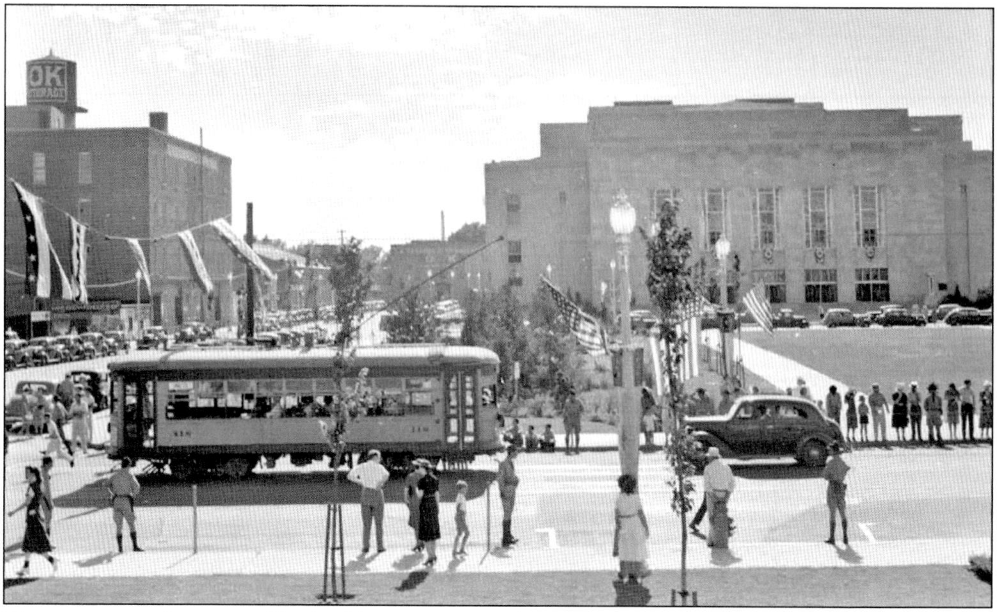

The grouping of major public buildings into an urban space was a planning concept of the City Beautiful Movement. This a view of the front of the Municipal Auditorium on the day of the dedication showing the flags, crowds, streetcars, parked cars, the green lawn, and the streets in the civic center in 1936. (Courtesy Oklahoma City Roland J. Norwick Downtown Library.)

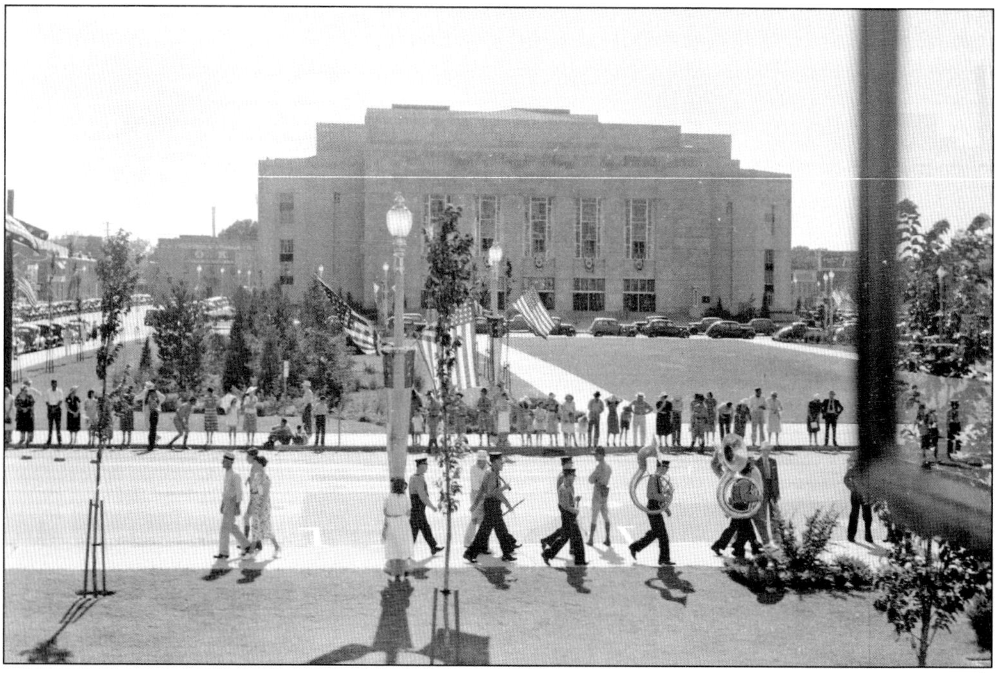

The front of the Municipal Auditorium is seen on the day of dedication in January 1936 when temperatures were at a record low of 23 degrees. This view shows the globe streetlights, with flagpole holders, for pedestrians. Rows of trees on either side of the plaza were planted to beautify the lawns on either side of the streets; they are seen newly planted and staked. (Courtesy Oklahoma City Roland J. Norwick Downtown Library.)

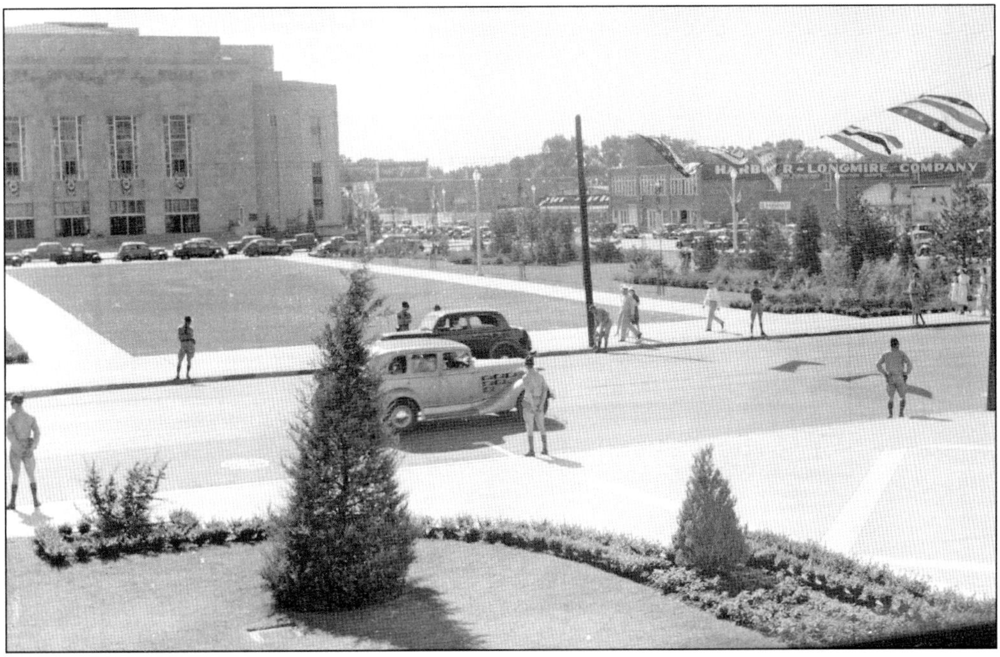

A partial view of the Municipal Auditorium and plaza in front of the Municipal Building on the day of dedication in 1936 shows the newly installed vegetation, consisting of annual flowers, evergreens, and trees and a lawn in front of the Municipal Building. Pedestrian-scale globe light fixtures were placed alongside the lawn. (Courtesy Oklahoma City Roland J. Norwick Downtown Library.)

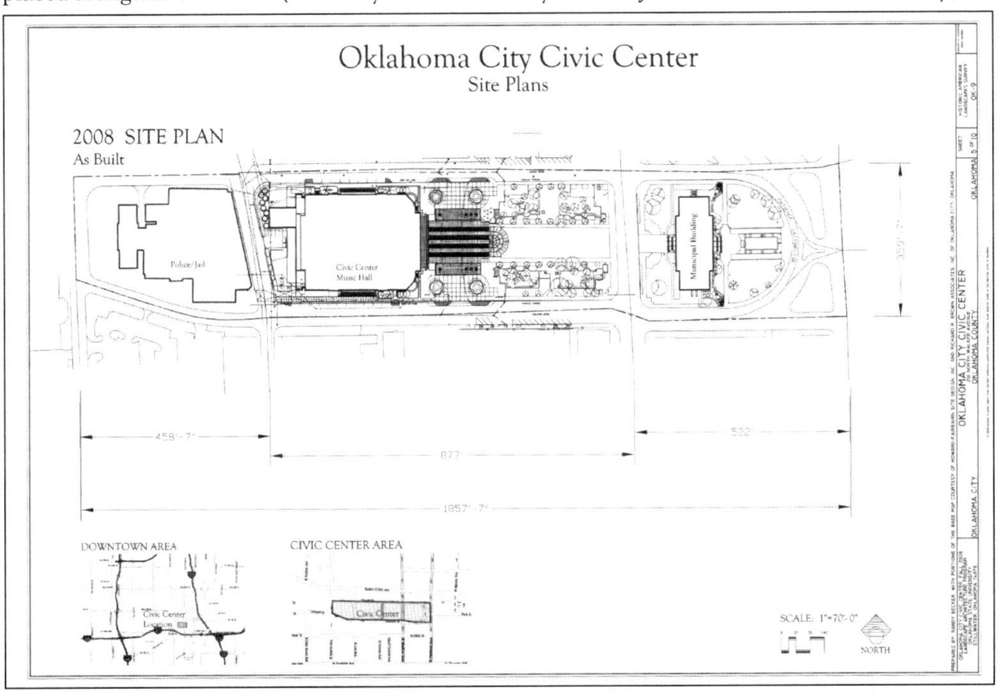

The 2001 site plan was renovated as shown in this 2008 as-built measured drawing. A decorative paving pattern was created for the plaza in front of the Municipal Auditorium, and the vegetation was upgraded, as shown in the plant list.

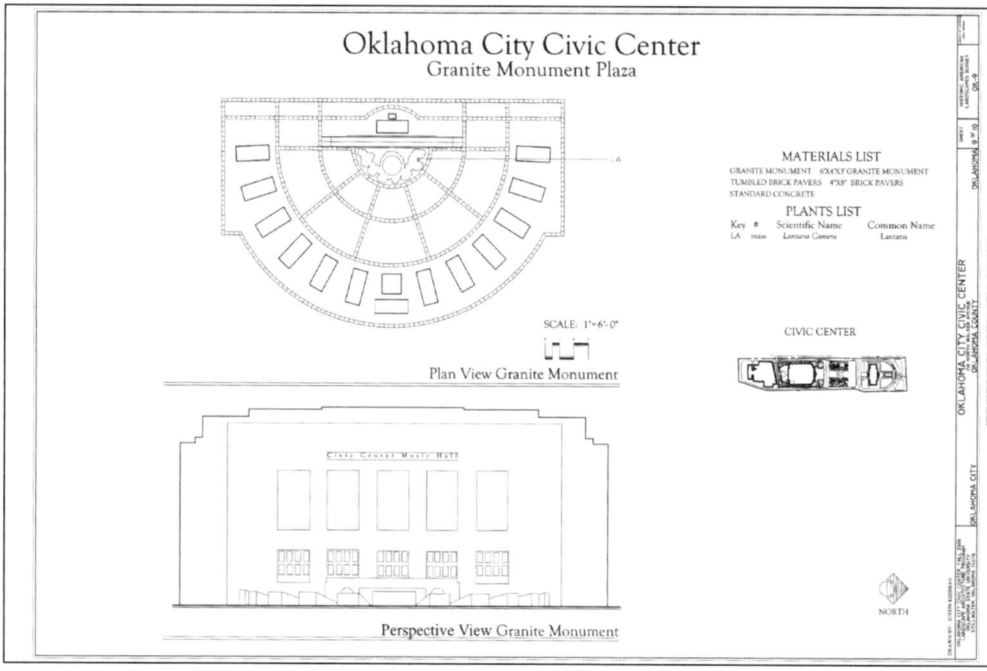

The 2008 as-built measured drawing shows the 2001 renovation site plan and background elevation of the facade of the Municipal Auditorium behind the granite monument plaza. The monument was built with granite, brick, and tumble brick pavers of various sizes. Lantana was used in the planting bed at the base of the monument.

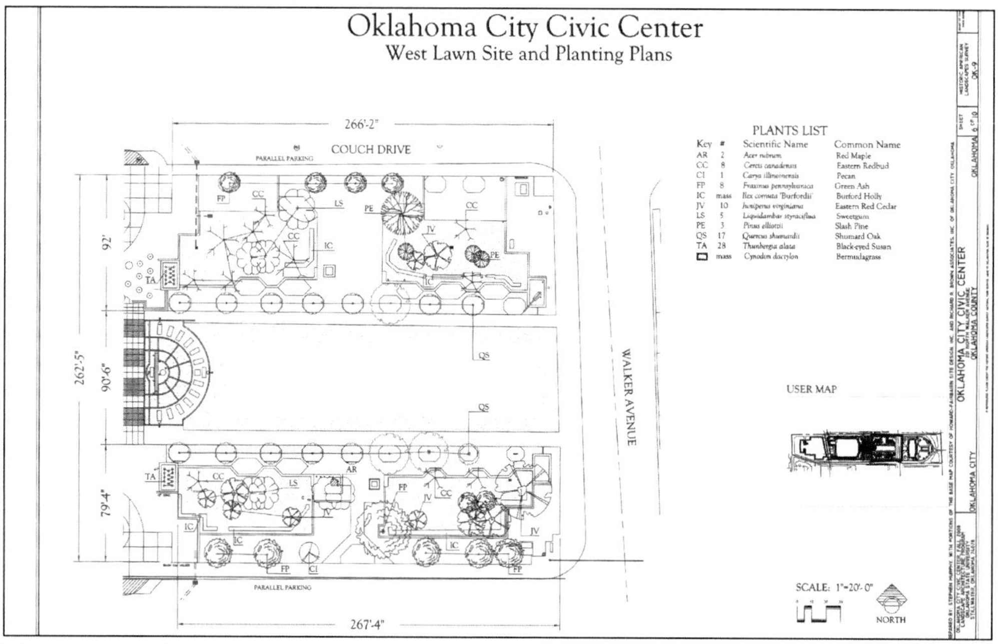

The 2001 site plan was renovated as shown in 2008 as-built measured drawing of the planting plan for the area between the Municipal Auditorium and Municipal Building west of Walker Avenue, known as the west lawn. The plant palette was expanded from the 2001 plan as shown in the plant list on the drawing.

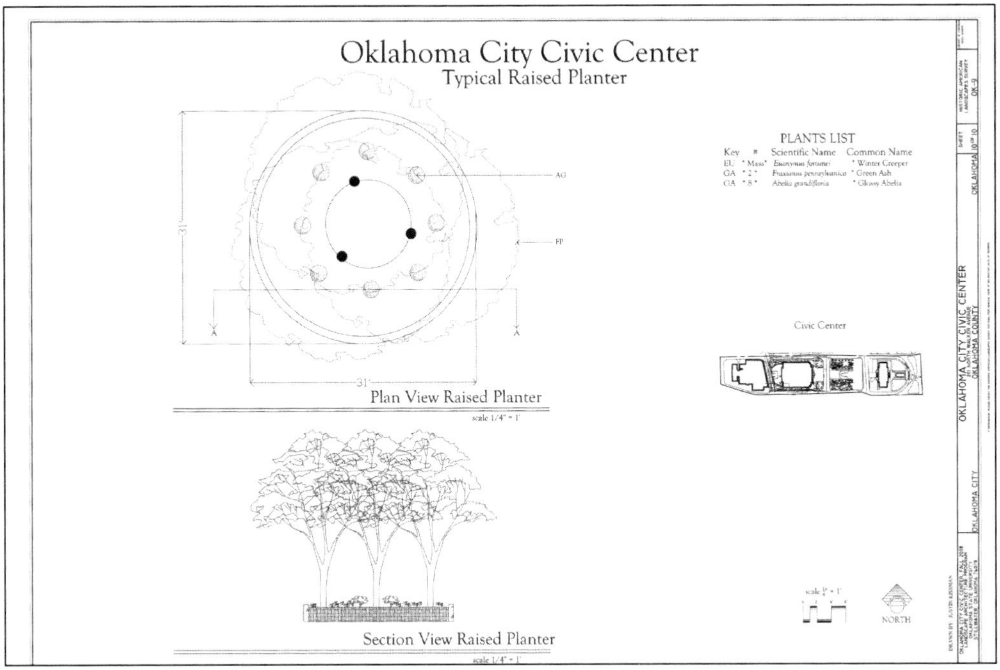

The 2001 site plan was renovated as shown in the 2008 as-built measured drawing of the typical raised planter in plan and section. The planter was designed to provide space for three medium-size trees with shrubs and ground cover. The plant list is provided on the drawing.

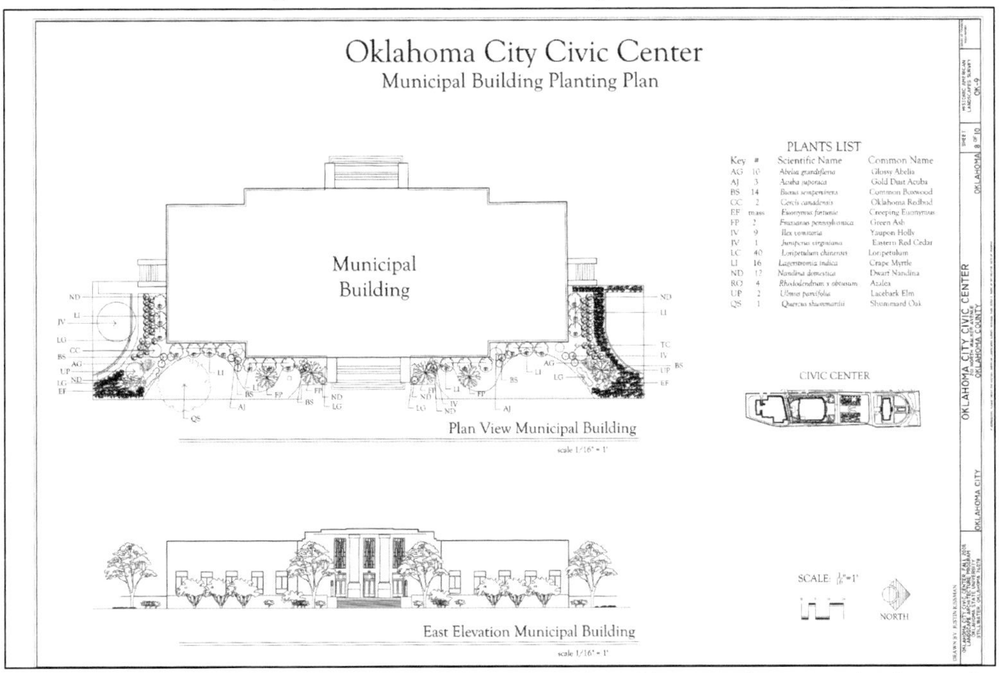

The 2008 as-built measured drawing of the Municipal Building on the west side, facing the Municipal Auditorium, shows the renovation of the 2001 site plan. The planting plan in the elevation shows small trees on either side of the doorway, with shrubs used to soften the building as shown in the plant list.

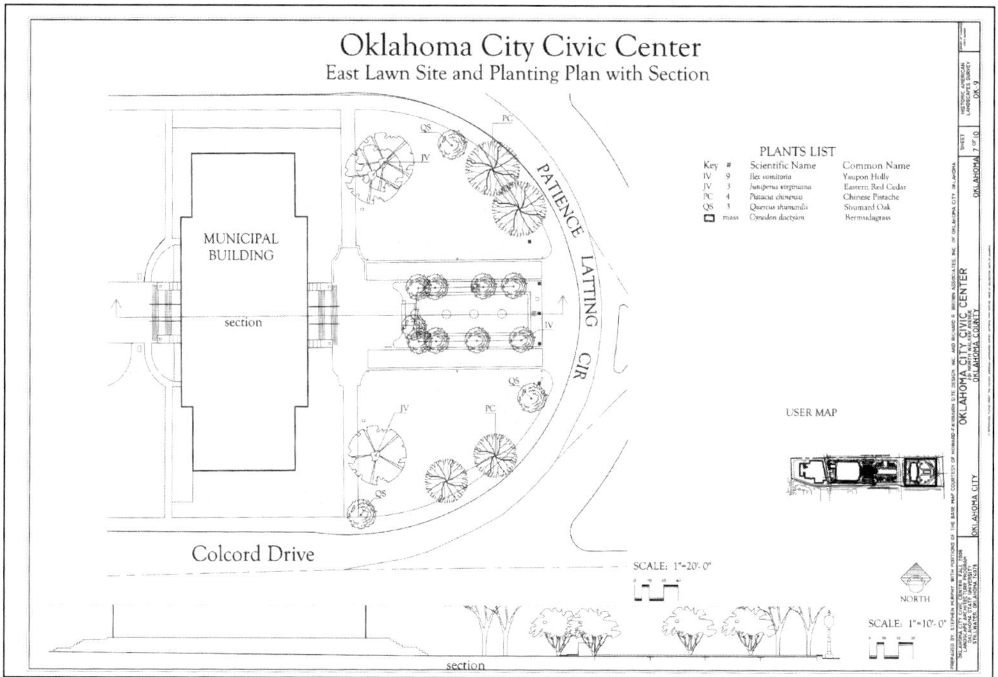

The 2001 site plan was renovated as shown in a 2008 as-built measured drawing of the planting plan for the area in front of Municipal Building on Walker Avenue, known as the east lawn. The plant palette was expanded from the 2001 plan as shown in the plant list on the drawing.

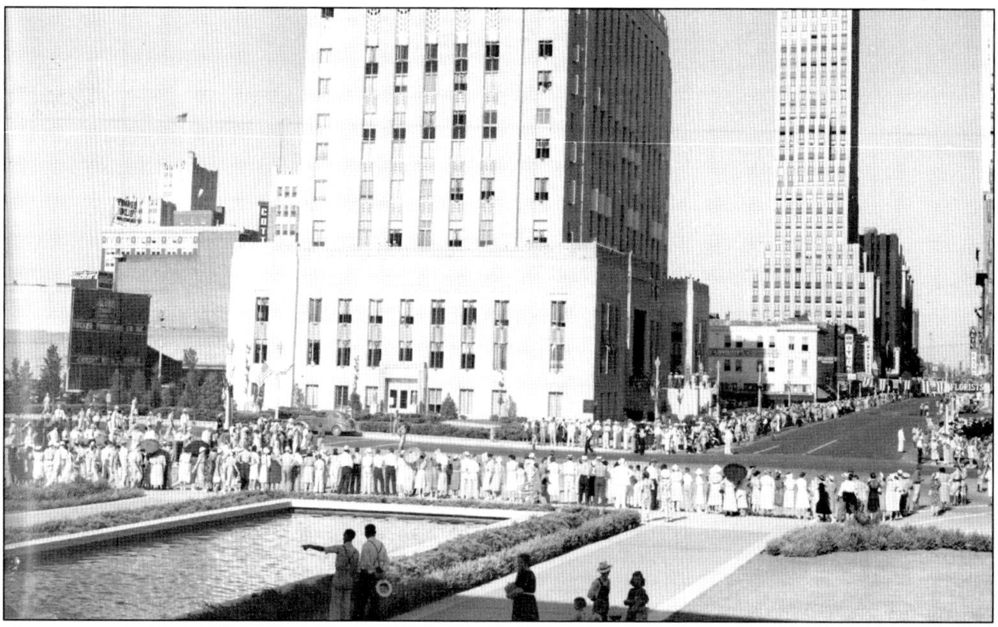

This view shows Walker Avenue in downtown Oklahoma City from the east entrance of the Municipal Building towards the county building across the street on the center's dedication day in 1936. No trees were used at the main entrance on the east side of the Municipal Building, only low shrubs under three feet around the pool in front and at the corners of the main entrance. (Courtesy Oklahoma City Roland J. Norwick Downtown Library.)

Three

Parks

Honor Heights Park, Muskogee
Type of Project: Park Design
Designer: George Palmer, Head Gardner Date: 1910

Honor Heights Park and the Union Agency sites adjoin each other in the city of Muskogee. The city created Honor Heights Park and acquired the Union Agency.

In 1910, landscape architect Charles Butterfield was hired as park superintendent, and English landscape gardener George Palmer was appointed head gardener and placed in charge of park development. Palmer became park superintendent in 1912, staying until his death in 1944. He created garden designs to promote passive recreation in a restful setting that were influenced by Chicago landscape architect Myron West. Honor Heights Park was fashioned after the naturalistic parks in England created during the Romantic period, with graceful curves, displays of beautiful plants, and an obvious attention to detail.

In 1921, Honor Heights Park was dedicated to honor the region's World War I veterans. It also was the winner of *Better Homes and Gardens*' "More Beautiful America" contest. Maintaining the high standards of beauty and function was a requirement for Palmer.

In 1948, Arthur Johnson became park superintendent. His tenure concentrated on increasing the park's economic productivity and providing more recreation facilities. Johnson envisioned a natural, informal landscape with mass color features made of blooming flowers. His vision began with 25 potted azaleas that were donated in 1951 after a funeral. The park's azalea gardens have since been recognized as one of the 10 top nationwide attractions by the North American Coach Association and as the second-best azalea garden in the Southwest. Currently, over 30,000 azalea plants of more than 625 varieties exist within the park. The Lynde Azalea Walk, with pecan and oak trees for shade, is an especially beautiful area of the park. The park's many other attractions include the J.E. Conrad Rose Garden, named for the rose grower who established the garden in 1954 with a donation of 1,000 plants. Today, the garden boasts 3,500 plants from the American Rose Society that are displayed in their annual sequence. The garden also holds the park's popular wedding gazebo. The Kirchner Memorial Recreation Area, just below the rose garden to the west, was established with funds raised by Muskogee oilman Phil Kirchner. The recreational area contains tennis courts and the Kirchner Memorial Fountain, a circular pool ringed by azaleas. The Kiwanis Day Camp, dedicated in 1979, is within Honor Heights Nature Preserve on the eastern face of Agency Hill. The Rainbow Memorial Amphitheater, built in 1982, sits north of the reservoir. It offers a panoramic view of the city and surrounding area.

Study Director: Dr. Charles L. Leider, Landscape Architecture Program
Faculty Advisors: Dr. William Bryans, Department of History; Prof. Nigel Jones, School of Architecture
Study Team Members: Donna Decatur, team leader; Greg Sutton; Brandon Gurley; and Sean Ackerson

Sources:
Honor Heights Park, Muskogee Park Department
Union Agency, National Register of Historic Places

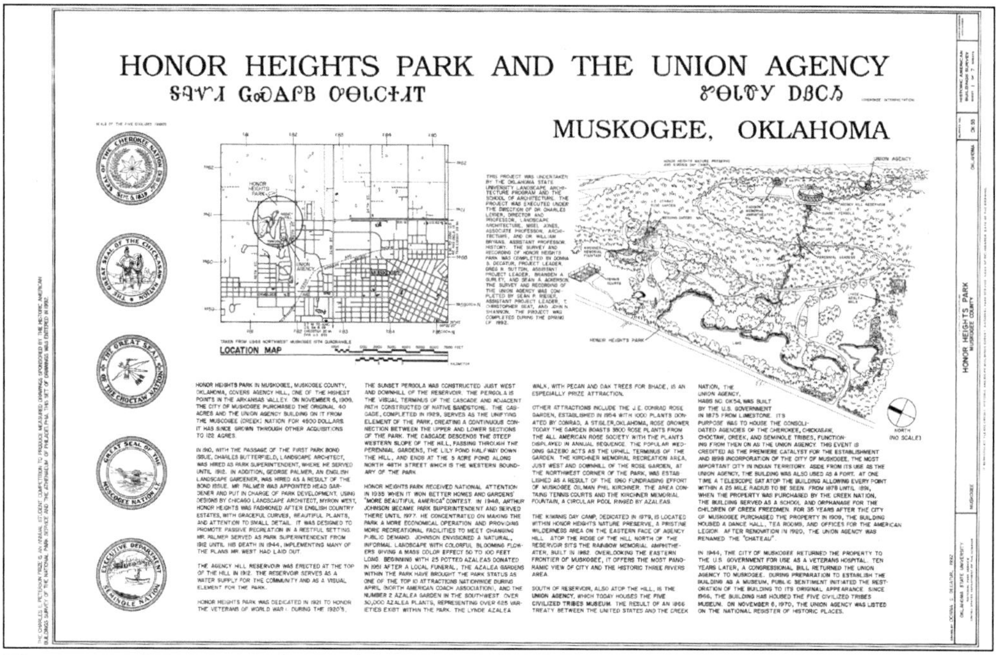

The poster of Honor Heights Park contains Cherokee language and emblems, the history of the park, maps showing the park in Muskogee and its neighborhood, and an aerial perspective sketch of the park as it appeared in 1997. The entrance of the park is at the intersection of North Fortieth Street and State Highway 16 and US Highway 62, adjoining Agency Hill and the veterans hospital.

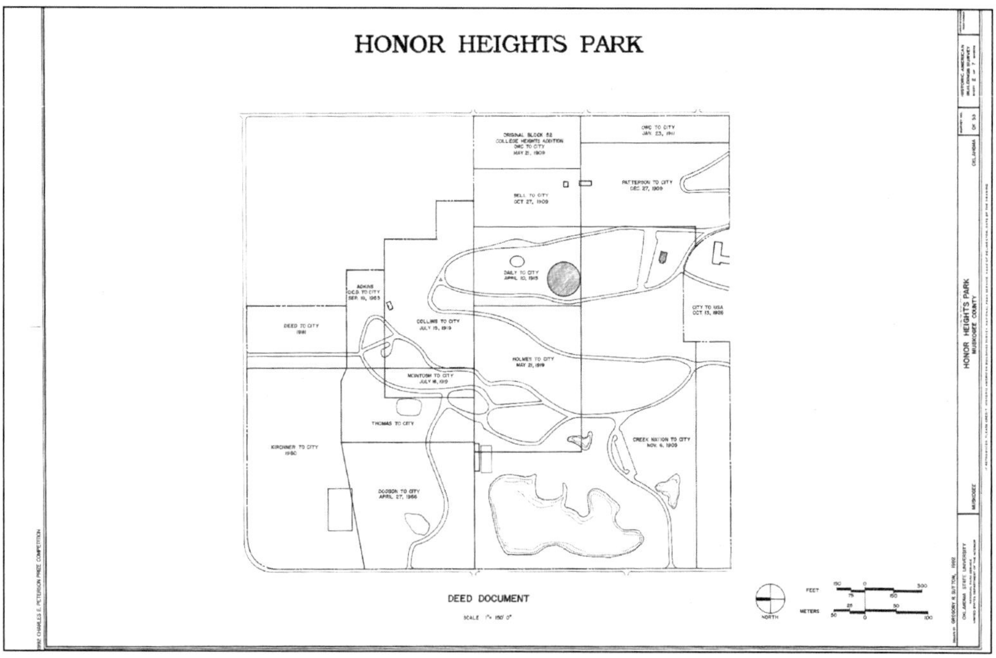

The Honor Heights Park parcel acquisition map shows the dates land was acquired from 1909 to 1981. The majority of the land parcels were acquired between 1909 and 1919. Over time, additional parcels were acquired as the park was expanded as a war memorial.

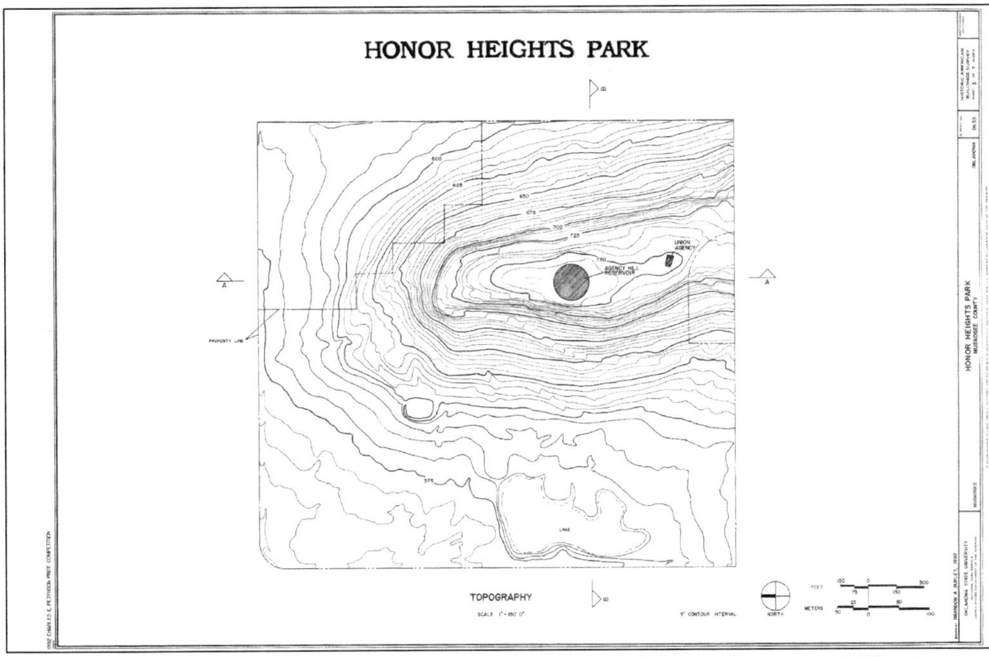

The topographic map of Honor Heights Park is drawn at a five-foot contour interval. The elevation ranges from 580 to 750 feet, with the highest elevation on Agency Hill Reservoir. The land below the reservoir at Agency Hill has a steep slope and has been retained in its natural state. The developable land for the park is found below Agency Hill at an elevation below 650 feet.

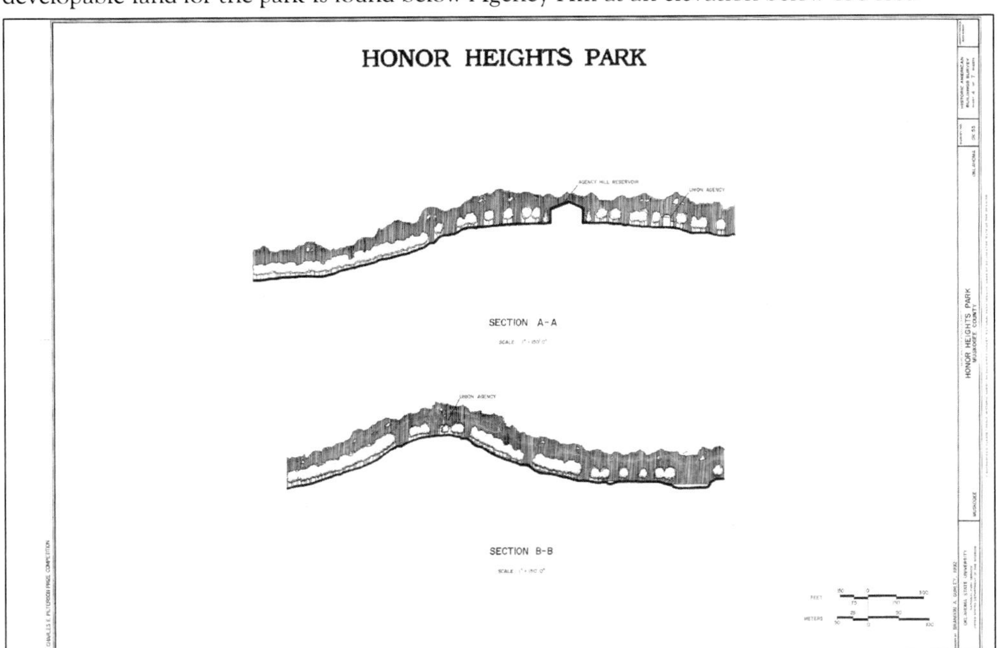

The drawing with two sections, one at the Union Agency, Section A-A, and the other at Agency Hill Reservoir, Section B-B, shows the elevation change at the Honor Heights Park site. The Union Agency and Agency Hill Reservoir, because of their locations at the highest points, are the most visible structures in the park.

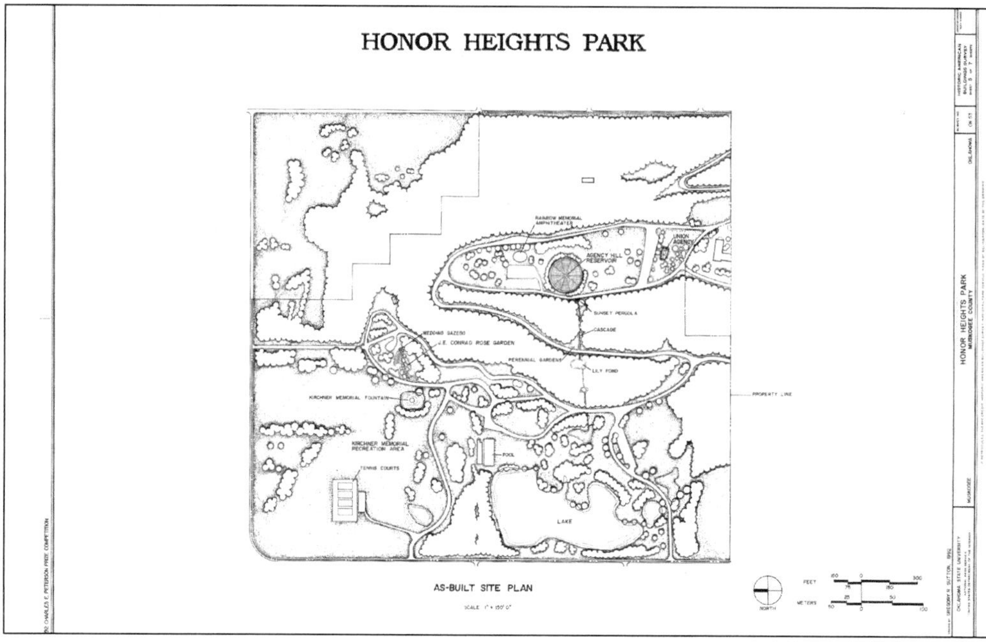

This as-built site plan drawing shows Honor Heights, designed in the English Romantic style by Myron West, Chicago landscape architect, and implemented by George Palmer, the park's English gardener from 1912 to 1944. The naturalistic style included curvilinear drives, a lake, meadows framed by trees, an amphitheater, a swimming pool, tennis courts, a fountain, a pergola, a lily pond, a waterfall, a rose garden, a perennial garden, and an azalea garden featuring one of the largest collections in Oklahoma and in the United States.

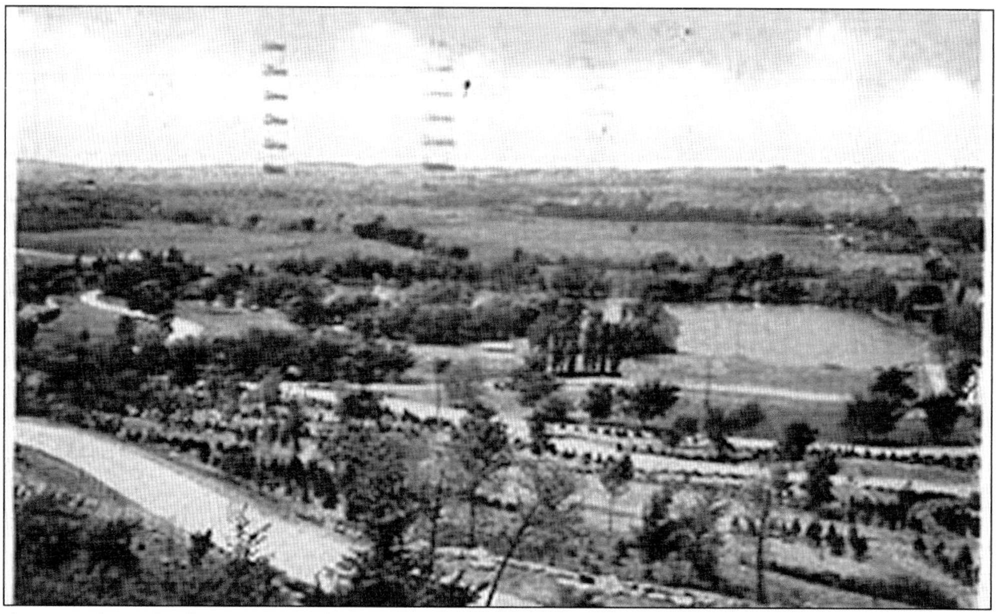

An aerial view of Honor Heights Park shows the developing implementation of the English Romantic style in the 1920s with a lake, open countryside, and curvilinear roadways. Both deciduous and evergreen trees have been planted to screen, define areas, and create an enclosed meadow. (Courtesy Muskogee Parks Department.)

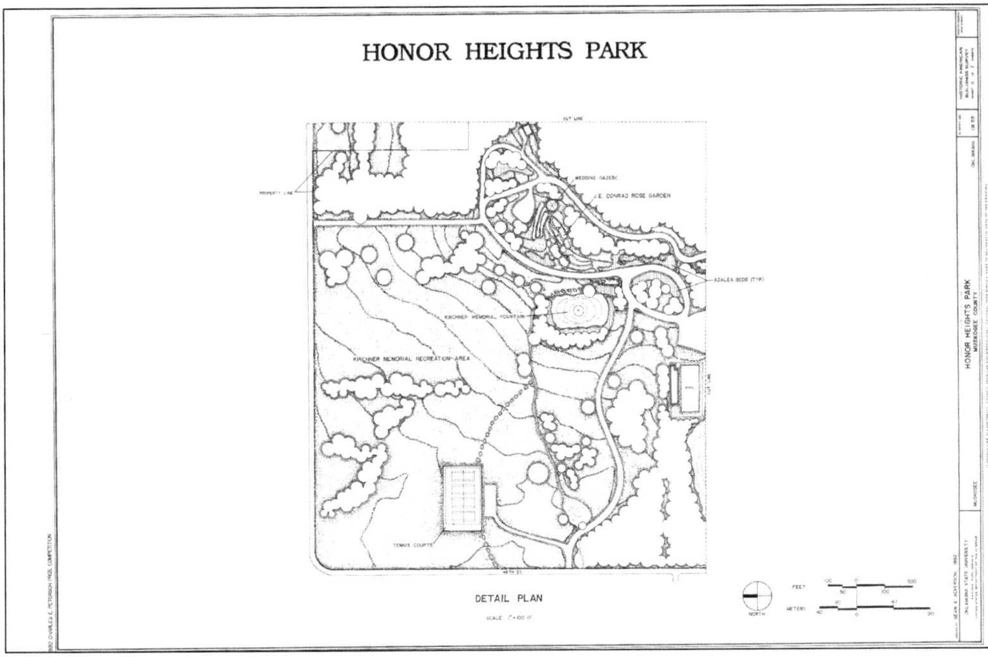

The 1997 as-built measured site plan shows the park's English Romantic style, with a curvilinear road system that provides an opportunity to view the partially enclosed meadows and open spaces. The driveways also provide views and access to the Kirchner Memorial Recreation Area, Kirchner Memorial Fountain, J.E. Conrad Rose Garden, tennis courts, swimming pool, wedding gazebo, and azalea gardens.

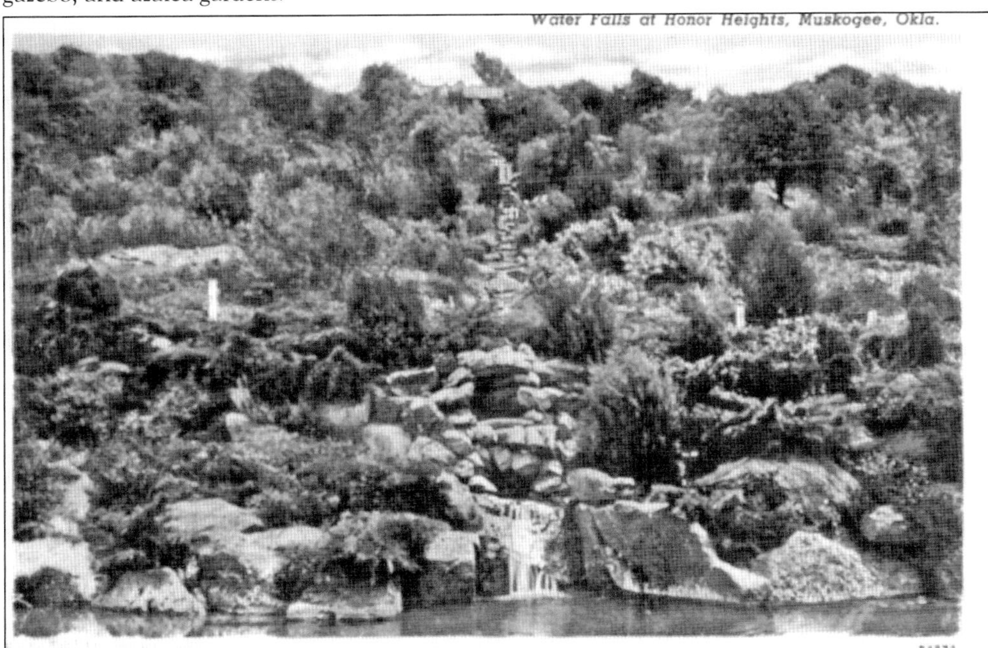

A 1930s view of Honor Heights Park shows the hillside covered with azaleas mixed with evergreen shrubs. A cascade passes through the azalea rock garden to a pool in the lower portion of the park. (Courtesy Muskogee Parks Department.)

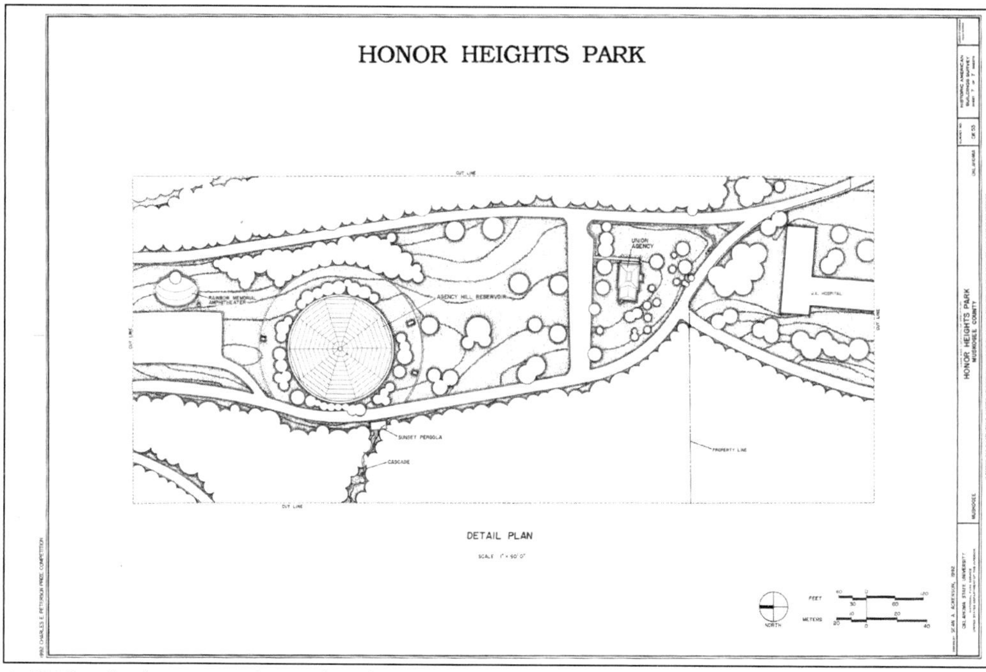

A 1997 as-built measured site plan shows the upper section of the Agency Hill Reservoir portion of Honor Heights Park, adjacent to the Union Agency and veterans hospital. The site is served by a curvilinear perimeter road with a cross street for better circulation. The site is designed in naturalistic style with the reservoir as the focal point.

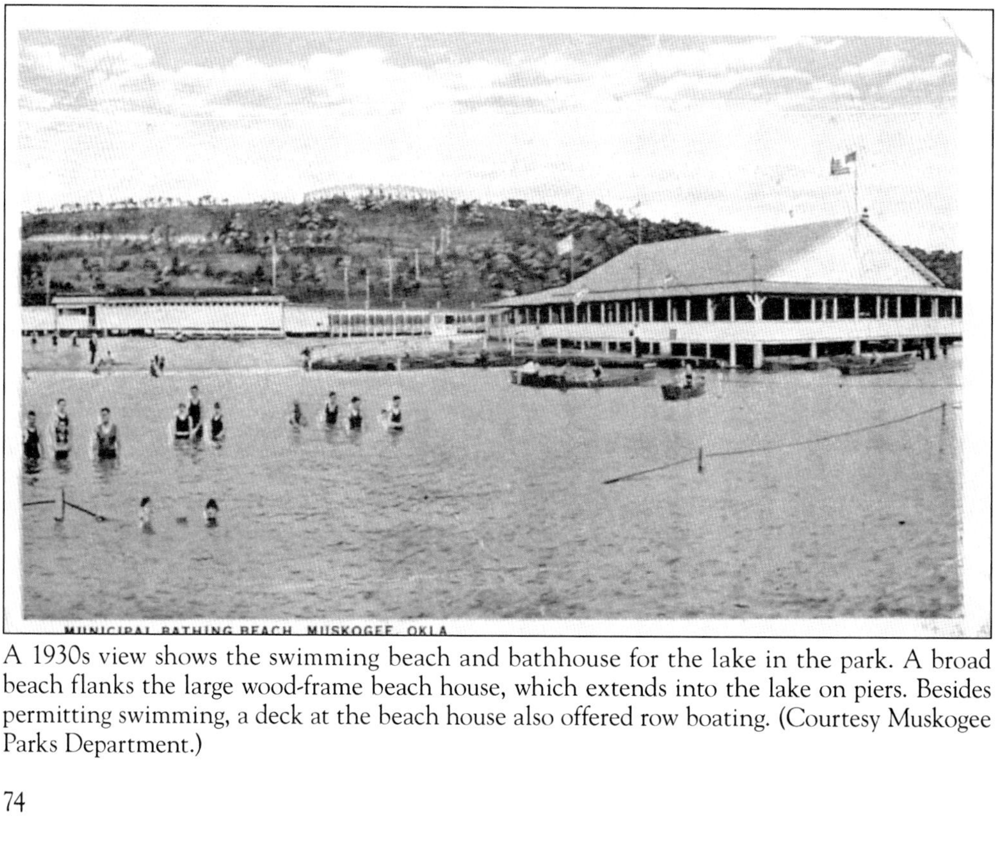

A 1930s view shows the swimming beach and bathhouse for the lake in the park. A broad beach flanks the large wood-frame beach house, which extends into the lake on piers. Besides permitting swimming, a deck at the beach house also offered row boating. (Courtesy Muskogee Parks Department.)

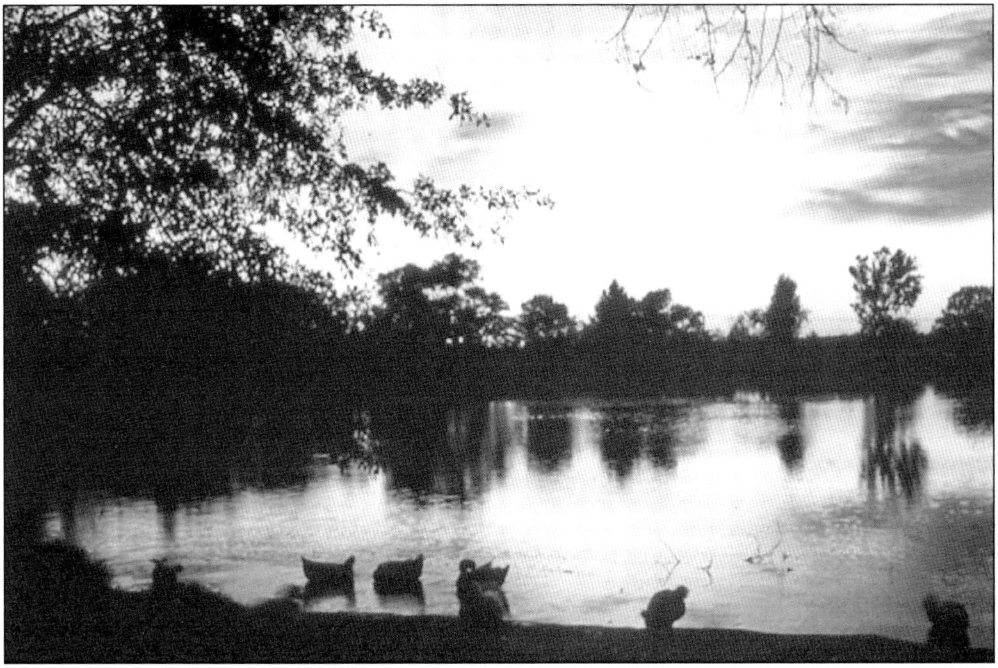

A view of the lake at sunset highlights the park's naturalistic landscape, with trees around the lake and ducks on the water. The calm water that creates a tranquil setting for visitors is a design feature of the English Romantic landscape design style. (Courtesy Three Rivers Museum.)

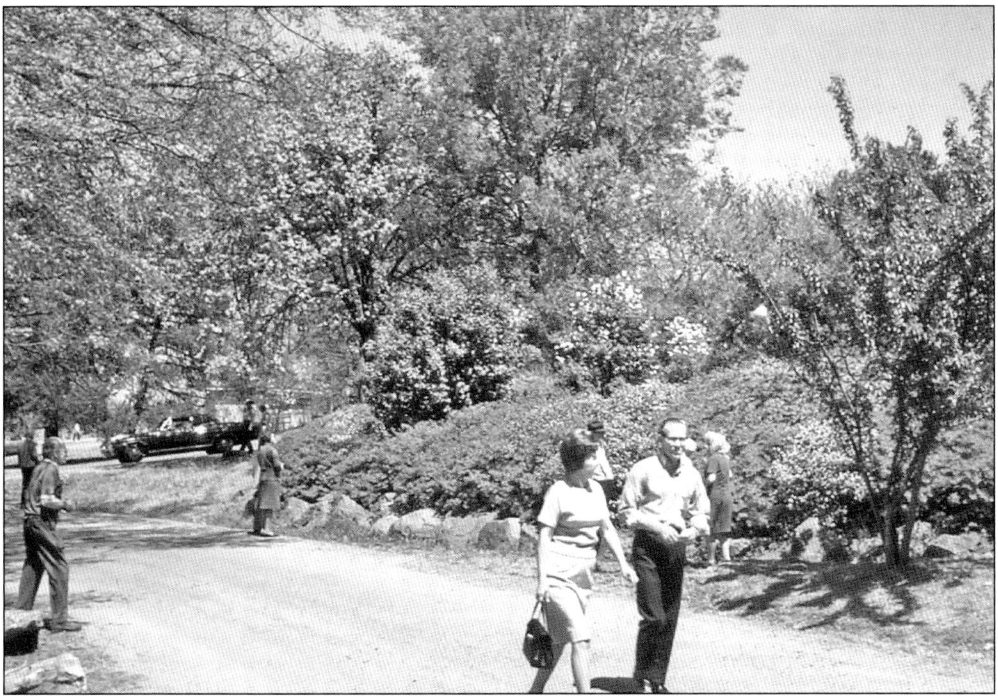

A springtime view shows the azalea gardens surrounded by flowering trees and shade trees in the background, with a rock edging along the walk in a naturalistic setting. The Romantic landscape design style invites visitors to stroll through the park. (Courtesy Three Rivers Museum.)

Agency Hill Park, Muskogee

Type of Project: Park Design
Designer: Park Department City of Muskogee

Agency Hill, one of the highest points in the Arkansas River valley, sits in Honor Heights Park in Muskogee. The City of Muskogee purchased the park's original 40 acres, which included the Union Agency building, from the Muscogee (Creek) Nation on November 6, 1909, for $4,500. The park has since grown through other acquisitions to 122 acres. The Union Agency, which stands atop the hill, was built by the US government in 1875 from limestone following an 1866 treaty between the United States and the Creek Nation to house the consolidated agencies of the Cherokee, Chickasaw, Choctaw, Creek, and Seminole tribes. This agency became the center of the local community and led to the incorporation of the city. The building has served many purposes. It was used as a fort, with a telescope that sat atop the building having an unobstructed view for 25 miles. After it was purchased by the Creek Nation, it was a school and orphanage for the children of Creek freedmen from 1878 until 1891. For 35 years after the city purchased the property in 1909, the building housed a dance hall, tearooms, and offices for the American Legion. The Union Agency was renovated in 1920 and renamed the Chateau. In 1944, the City of Muskogee returned the property to the federal government for use as a veterans hospital. Ten years later, a congressional bill returned ownership of the Union Agency to Muskogee. The building was restored to its original appearance by the Da-Co-Tah Club, a local group of women of Native American decent, and since 1966, the building has housed the Five Civilized Tribes Museum. On November 6, 1970, the Union Agency was listed in the National Register of Historic Places.

In 1912, the Agency Hill Reservoir was erected at the summit of Agency Hill. The reservoir serves the community and is a prominent visual element for the park. During the 1920s, the sunset pergola was constructed just west of the Agency Hill Reservoir. The pergola, which provides a visual terminus for the cascade, and its native sandstone path were completed in 1929. The cascade unifies the park by connecting the upper and lower sections. It trickles down the steep western slope of Agency Hill, passes through the perennial gardens and the lily pool below, and ends in the park's five-acre pond.

Study Director: Dr. Charles L. Leider, Landscape Architecture Program
Faculty Advisors: Dr. William Bryans, Department of History; Prof. Nigel Jones, School of Architecture
Study Team Members: Donna Decatur, team leader; Greg Sutton; Brandon Gurley; and Sean Ackerson

Sources:
Honor Heights Park, Muskogee Park Department
Union Agency, National Register of Historic Places

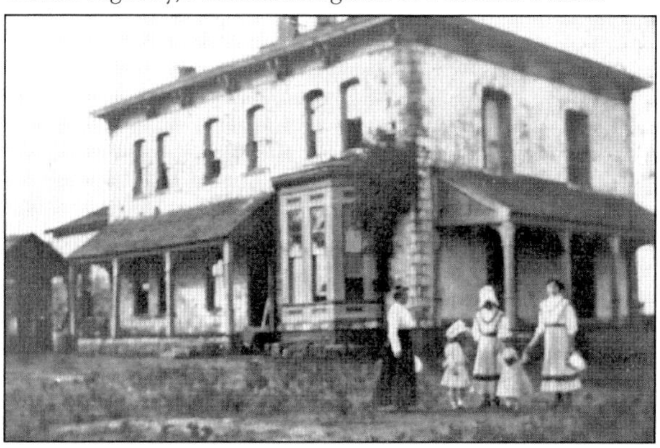

The Union Agency office was built of limestone by the US government in 1875 to serve as an administrative center for the Cherokee, Chickasaw, Choctaw, Creek, and Seminole tribes. A vernacular landscape design evolved in an attempt to beautify the site by randomly planting shade trees throughout and permitting pathways to develop by desired walking directions. (Courtesy Five Civilized Tribes Museum.)

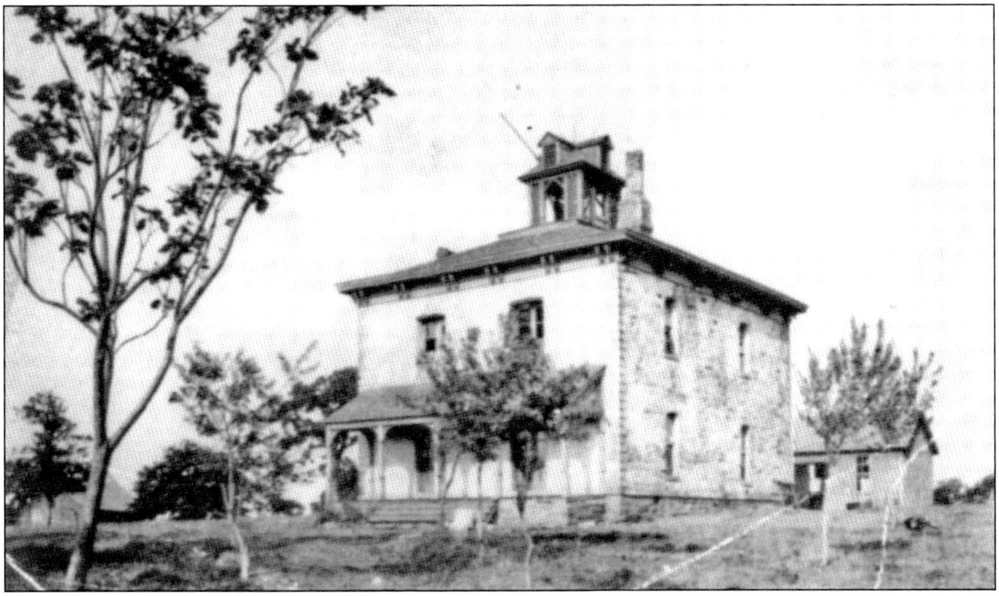

A front view of the agency building in 1890s shows a widow's watch cupola on the roof. From 1878 to 1891, a telescope atop the building allowed officials to view an area within a 25-mile radius of the building to assist in managing the tribal area beyond Muskogee. (Courtesy Five Civilized Tribes Museum.)

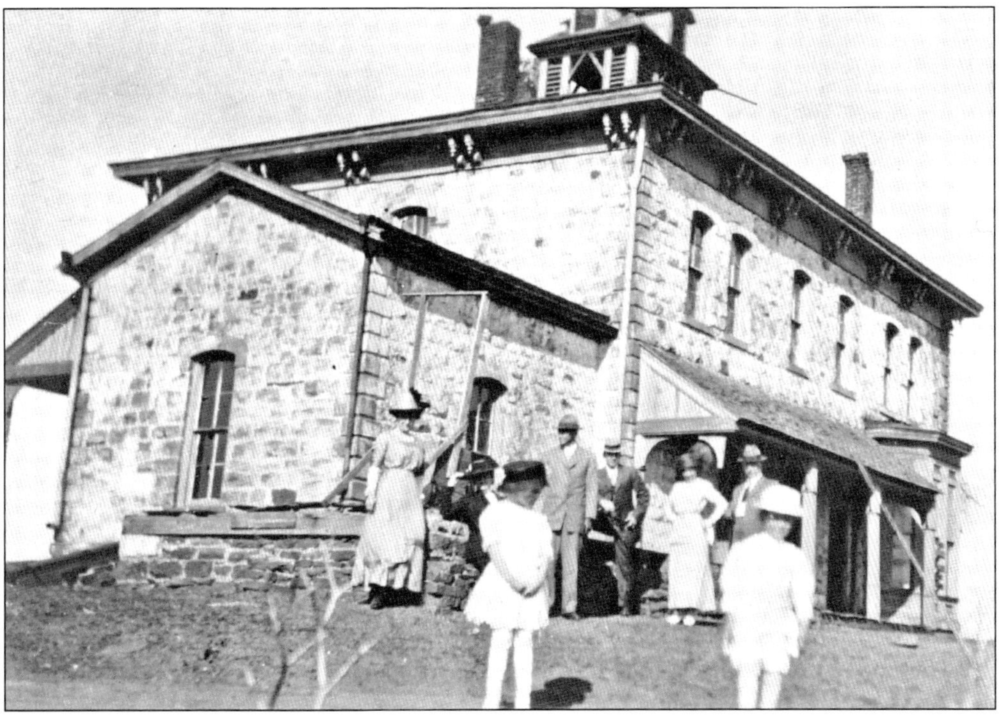

This view shows the Union Agency building in 1890s. The building was purchased by the Creek Nation and served as a school and orphanage. There was a minimal effort to beautify the site by establishing a vegetable garden and permitting a vine to grown on the corner of the building. (Courtesy Five Civilized Tribes Museum.)

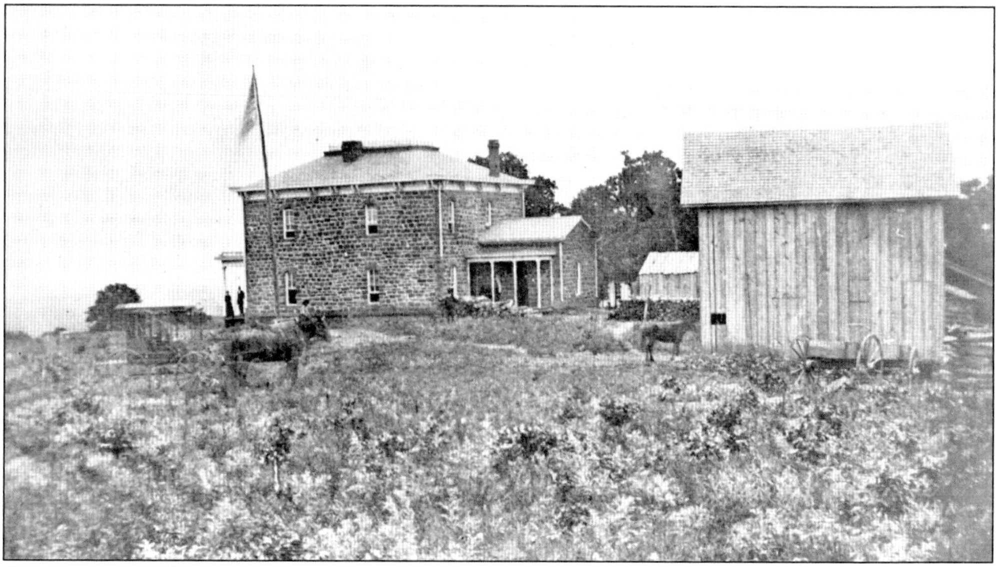

A rear view of the agency's main building shows its attached storage addition and the yard in the 1900s, when the building was used by the Creek Nation as a school and orphanage. The vernacular landscape shows a bare yard with no designated walkways and shade trees around the building. (Courtesy Five Civilized Tribes Museum.)

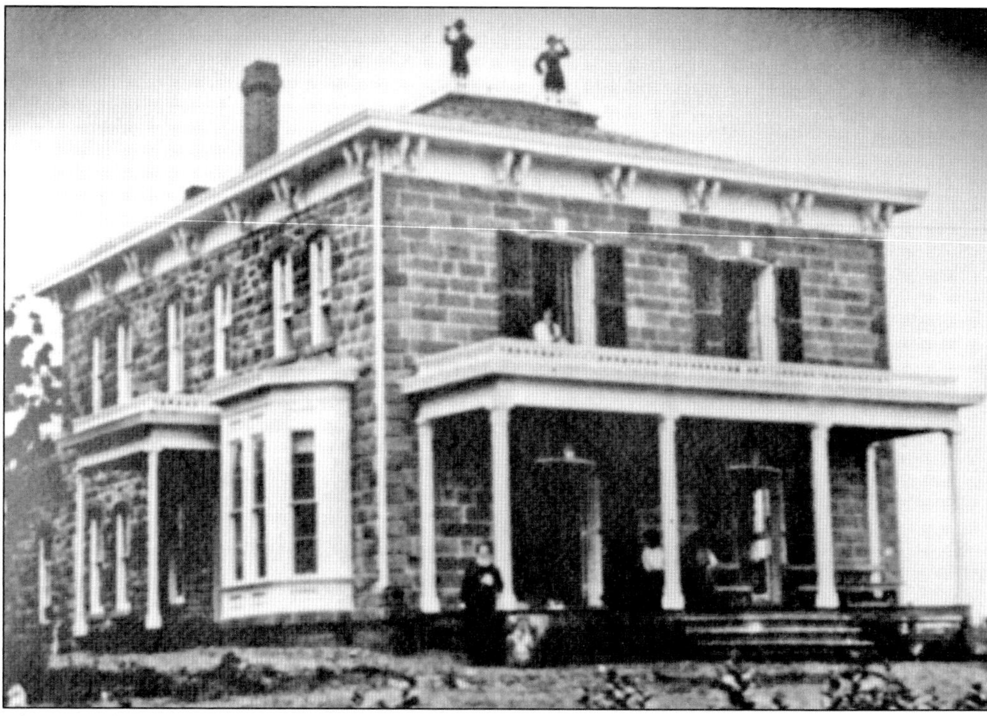

This view shows the agency building in 1909, when the City of Muskogee purchased and refurbished it for used as a dance hall, tearooms, and offices for the American Legion. The cupola on the roof was removed. Decorative columns and balustrades have been added to the front and side porticos. Planting beds were established in the yard around the building. (Courtesy Five Civilized Tribes Museum.)

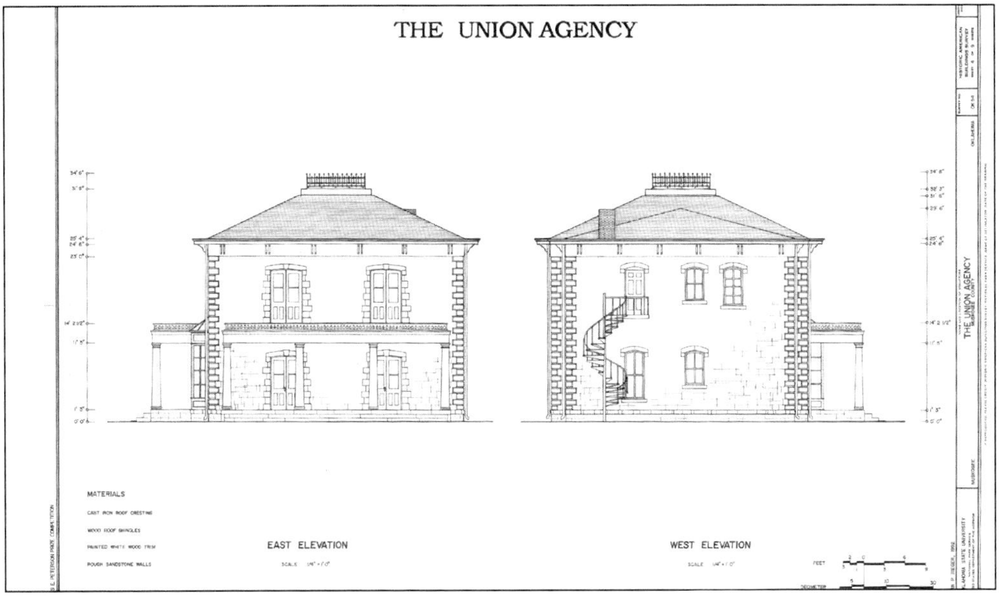

In 1954, the US government returned the agency building, which had been acquired as part of the veterans hospital in 1944, to the city to be used as a museum. In the 1960s, the process to restore the building and site to its original appearance started. The 1989 as-built measured drawing shows the east and west elevations of the building. The elevations show the decorative corners. The covered portico entrances, with decorative railings on the roof and columns with capitals, are located on both sides of the building arrival area with two steps leading into the building. The original cupola on the roof was not restored, but a decorative balustrade was installed in place of it. An outside spiral staircase for fire protection was added to the west wall.

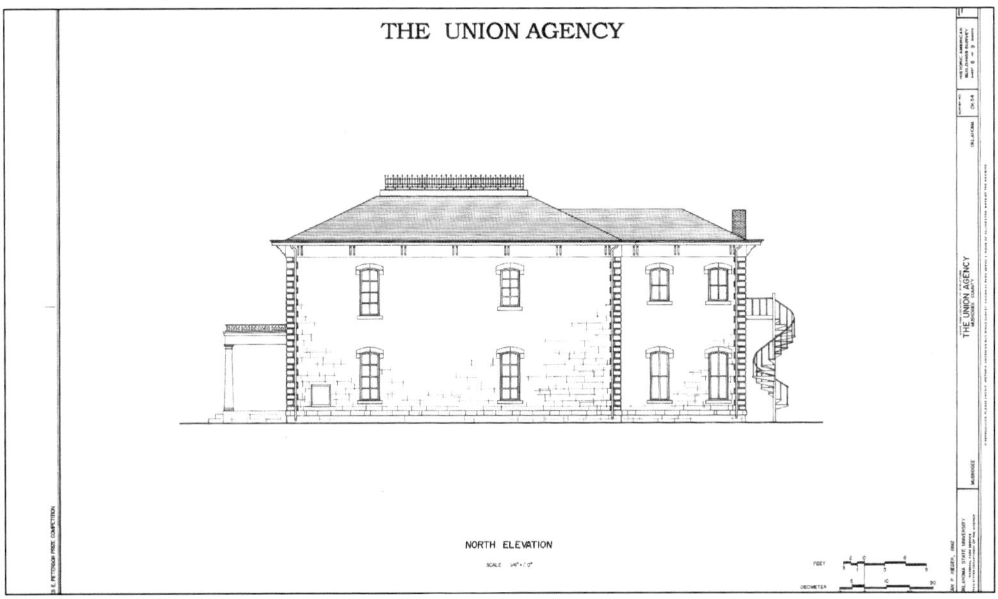

The 1997 as-built measured drawing shows the north elevation with decorative corners, a railing on the roof where the cupola once stood, and an outside spiral staircase for fire protection. The portico with two steps is on the front of the building and features a decorative railing on the roof and columns with capitals.

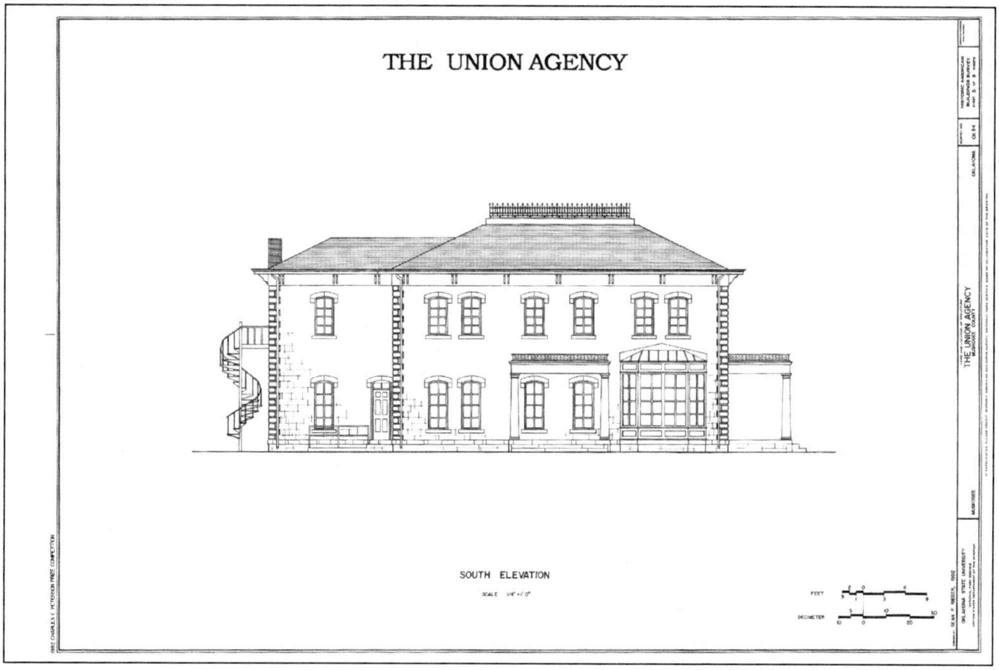

The 1997 as-built measured drawing shows the south elevation. Porticos featuring columns with capitals are on both sides of the building, with two steps leading into the house, decorative corners, a railing on the roof where the cupola once stood, and an outside spiral staircase for fire protection.

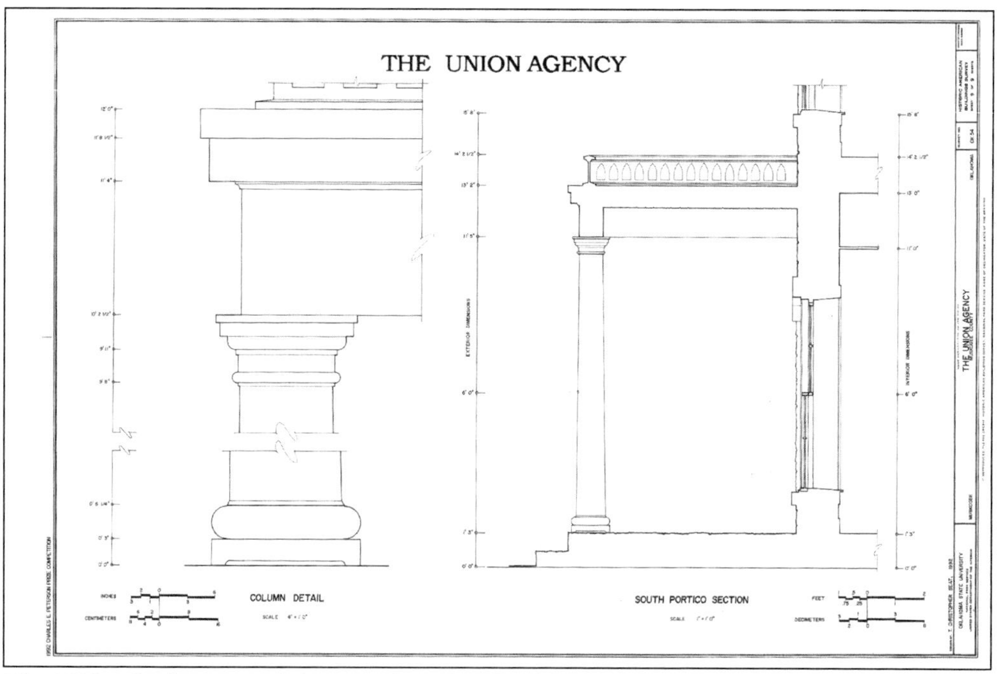

The 1997 as-built measured drawing show details of the portico with two steps and columns on the front (south) side of the building.

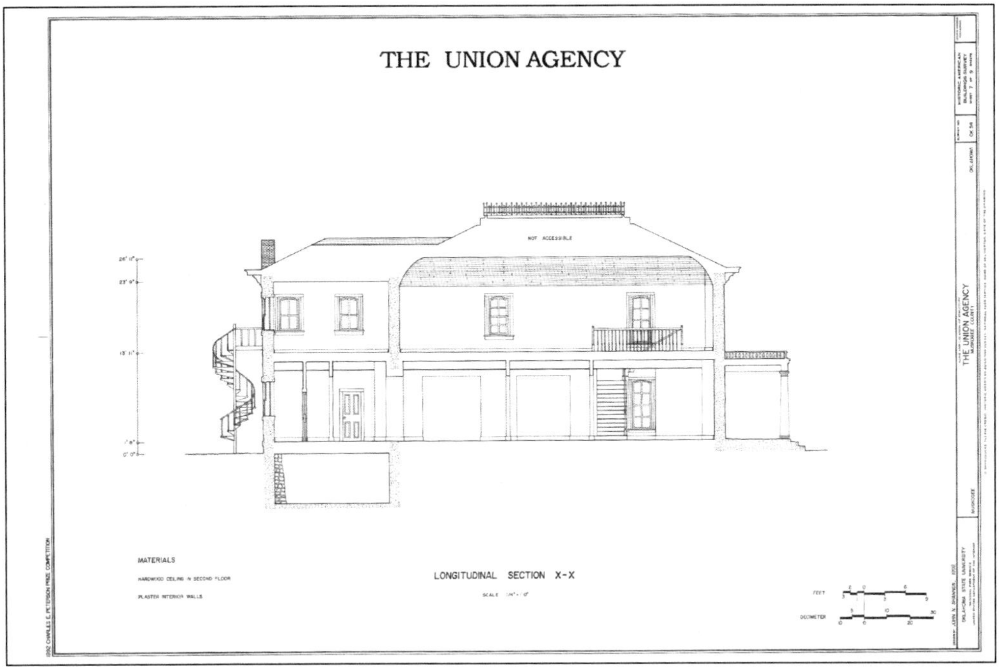

This longitudinal section is featured in a 1997 as-built measured drawing to show the relationship of the rooms from the attic to the basement. Circulation inside the building is handled by a stairway between the first and second floors. The original stairway to the third-floor cupola and attic has been removed and was not restored. To address fire protection on the second floor, a spiral stairway was added to the rear outside wall.

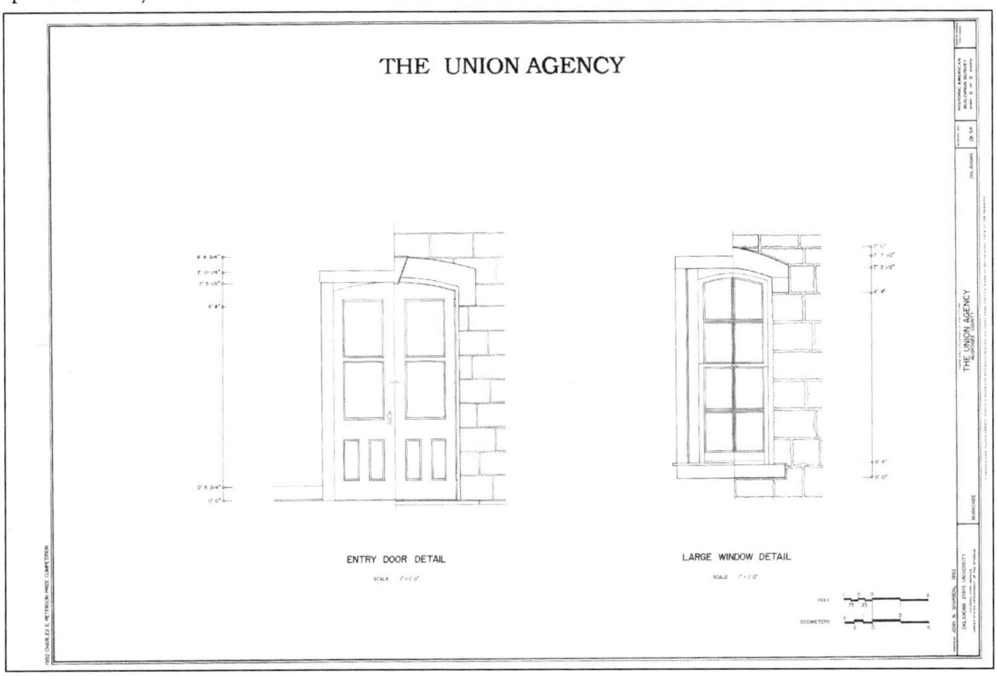

The 1997 as-built measured drawing shows the double wood entry doors and wood window details. There are 32 windows and two double entry doors in the building.

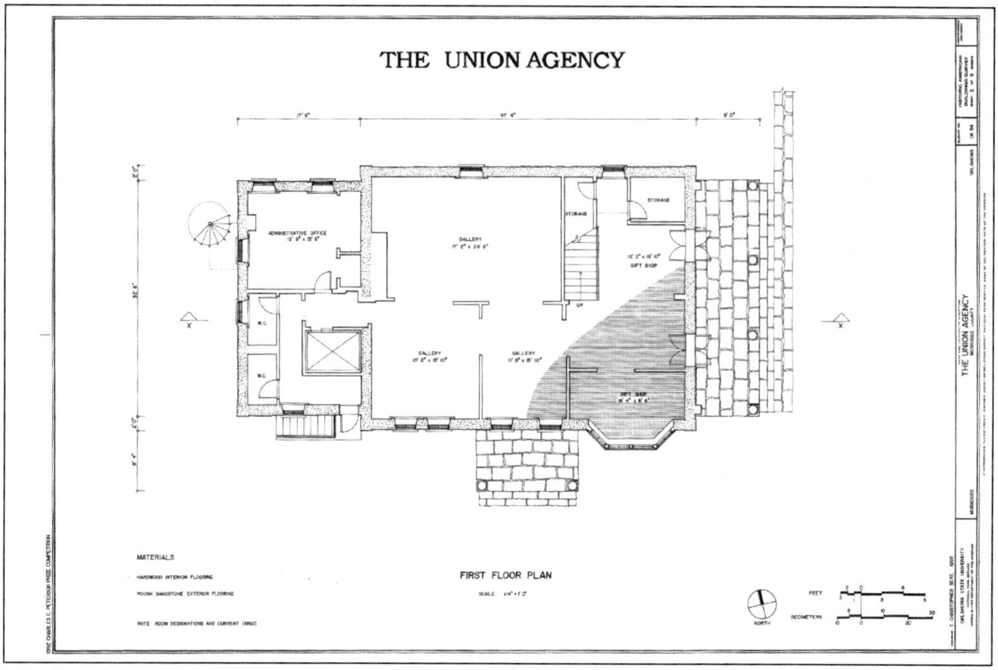

The first-floor plan is shown in this 1997 as-built measured drawing with gift shop, gallery, library, administrative office, men's and women's restrooms, storage room, and stairways to the basement and the second floor. The gallery is divided into three rooms of different sizes. The gift shop is located at the entrance and is divided into two spaces with a storage room.

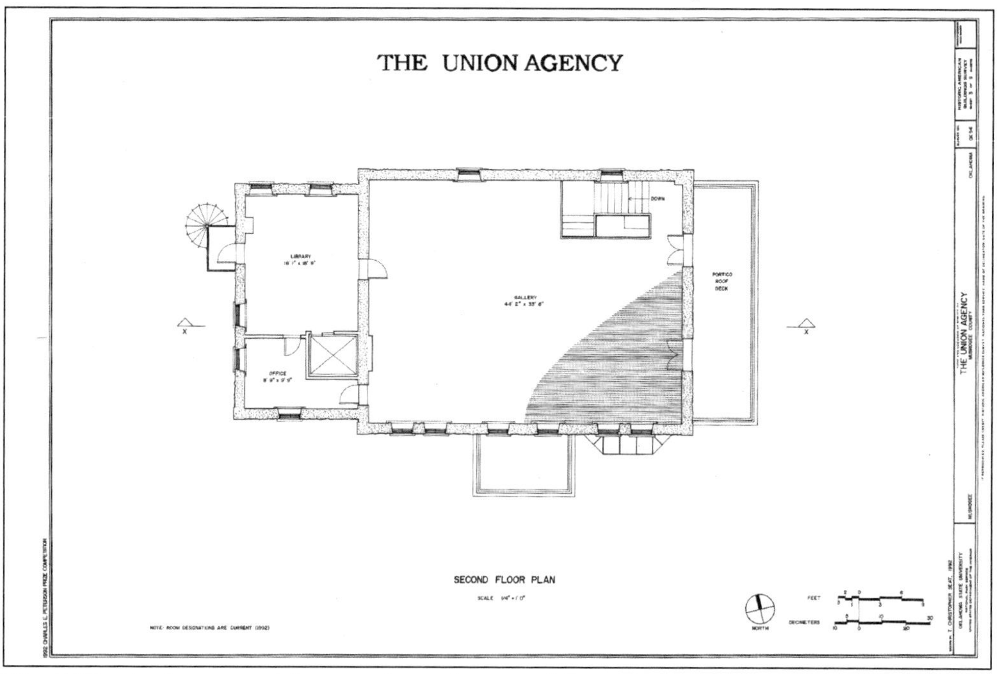

The 1997 as-built measured drawing shows the second-floor plan with rooms for a gallery, library, closet, and stairway to the first floor. The gallery is designed for large display and exhibit space; it uses over 80 percent of the second floor.

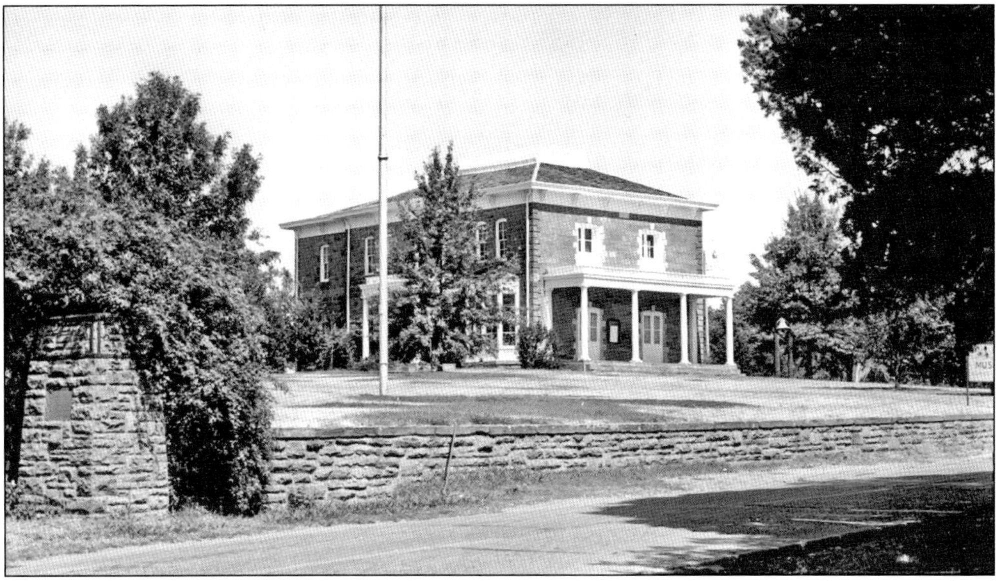

This view shows the former Union Agency building after it was converted into the Five Civilized Tribes Museum in 1970. The building and site are listed in the National Register of Historic Places, and it is one of the few such properties listed recognizing Native American history. (Courtesy Five Civilized Tribes Museum.)

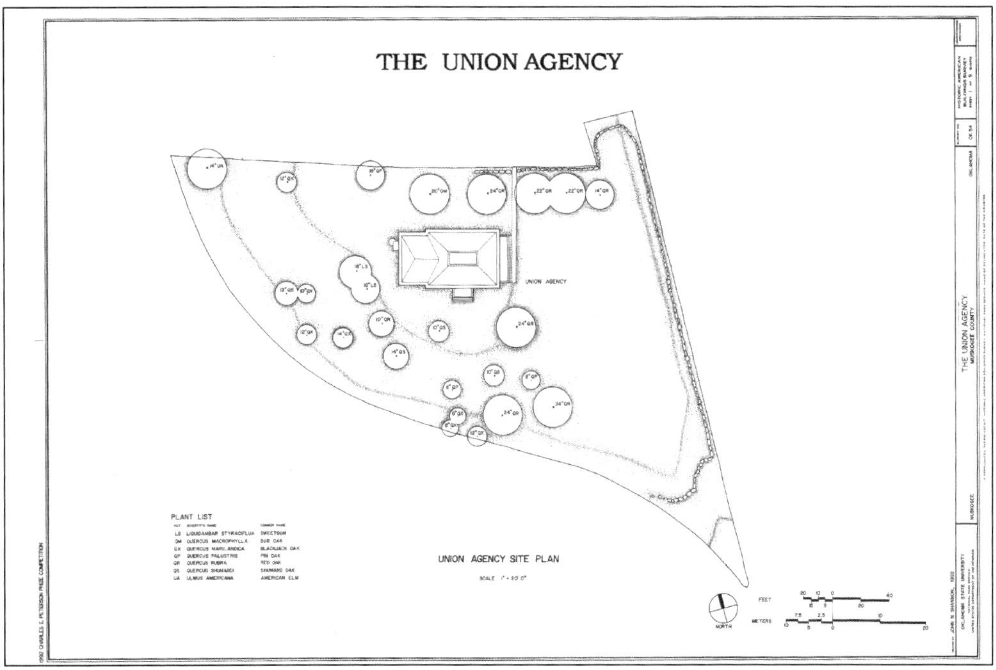

The 1997 as-built measured site plan shows the restored agency building above the surrounding landscape with a three-foot retaining wall in the foreground. The site is near the park entrance at the intersection of North Fortieth Street and State Highway 16 and US Highway 62, adjoining Honor Heights Park and the veterans hospital. The plan focuses on an informal landscape design by creating views of the agency building and flagpole across an open lawn framed by background trees and accented by shrubs.

Tulsa Municipal Rose Garden

Type of Project: Formal Garden
Designer: C. Burton Fox, Landscape Architect Date: 1935

The Tulsa Municipal Rose Garden is located at Twenty-First Street and Peoria Avenue, between Woodward Park and the Tulsa Garden Center. The four-and-a-half-acre garden consists of six terraces beginning at street level on Peoria Avenue that rise up a gentle slope for a distance of 850 feet. The garden was designed by landscape architect C. Burton Fox in the Italian Renaissance style; the plan was completed by 1935, making it ready for its first rose plantings that year.

The planned cost of the garden was $750,000, but the project quickly ran over budget. However, Fox donated six months of his time to ensure that the garden was finished. The rose garden has won national awards from *Better Homes and Gardens* and the National Council of Garden Clubs.

Study Director: Dr. Charles L. Leider, Landscape Architecture Program
Faculty Advisors: Dr. William Bryans, Department of History; Prof. Nigel Jones, School of Architecture
Study Team Members: Jeffrey Pugh, team leader; Sarah Crawford; and Cory Rust

Source:
Tulsa Park Department

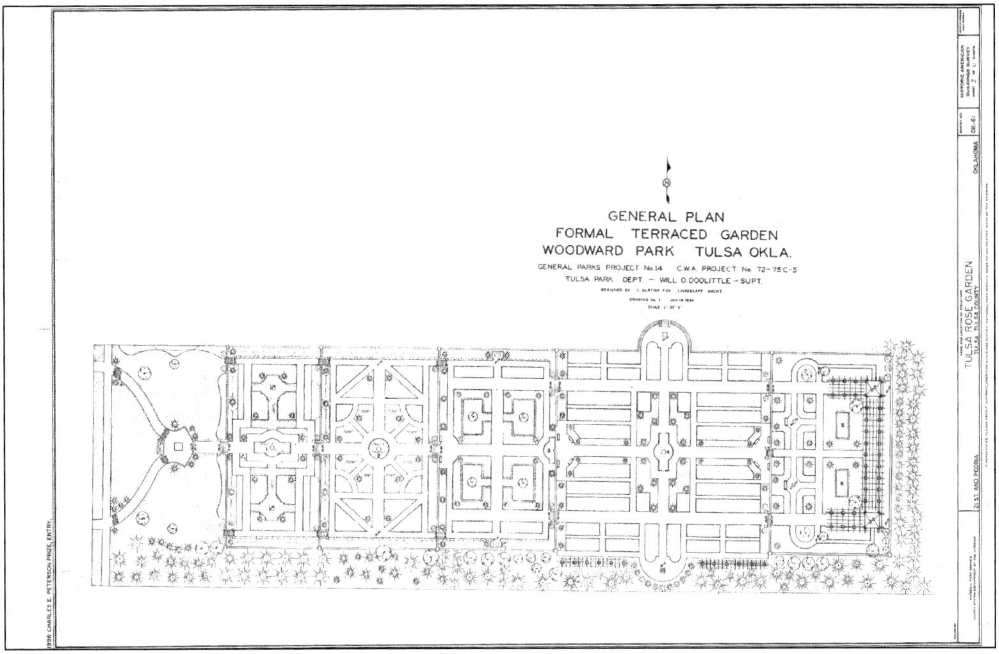

The original symmetrical site plan was designed by Tulsa landscape architect C. Bertram Fox in 1934; the garden was built as a WPA project in 1936. It consists of six terraces with connections to the adjoining Woodward Park and Tulsa Garden Center. The park fronts on South Peoria Street.

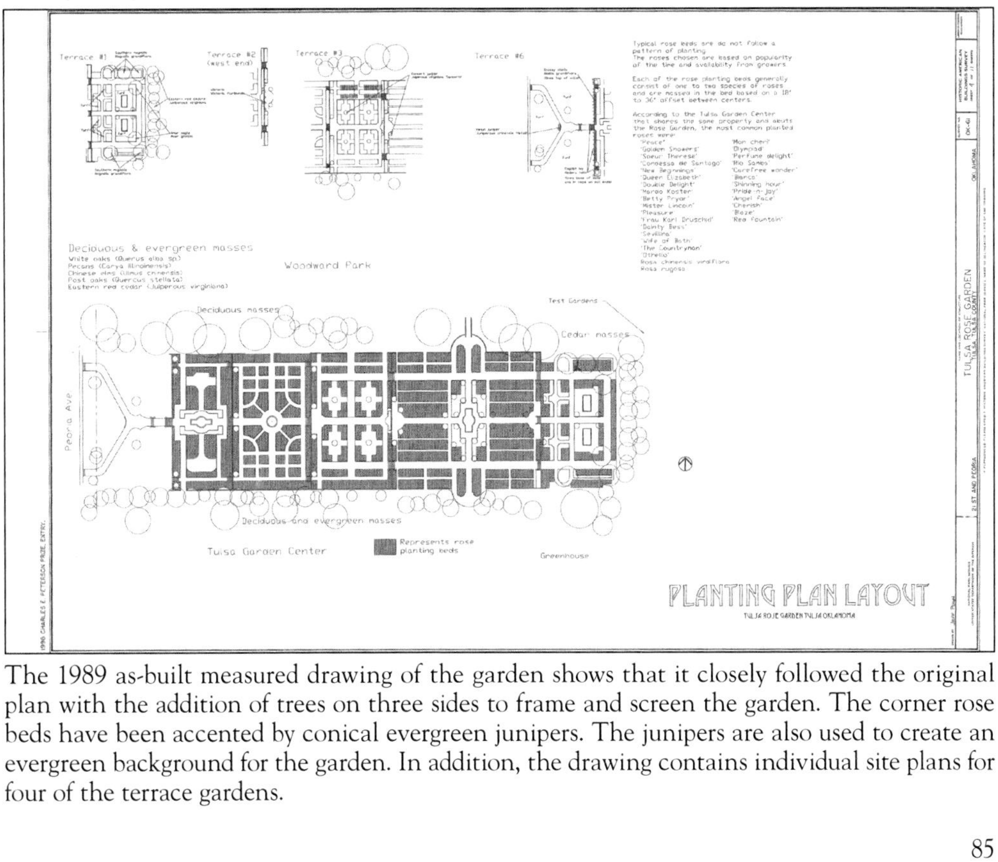

The 1989 as-built measured drawing of the garden shows that it closely followed the original plan with the addition of trees on three sides to frame and screen the garden. The corner rose beds have been accented by conical evergreen junipers. The junipers are also used to create an evergreen background for the garden. In addition, the drawing contains individual site plans for four of the terrace gardens.

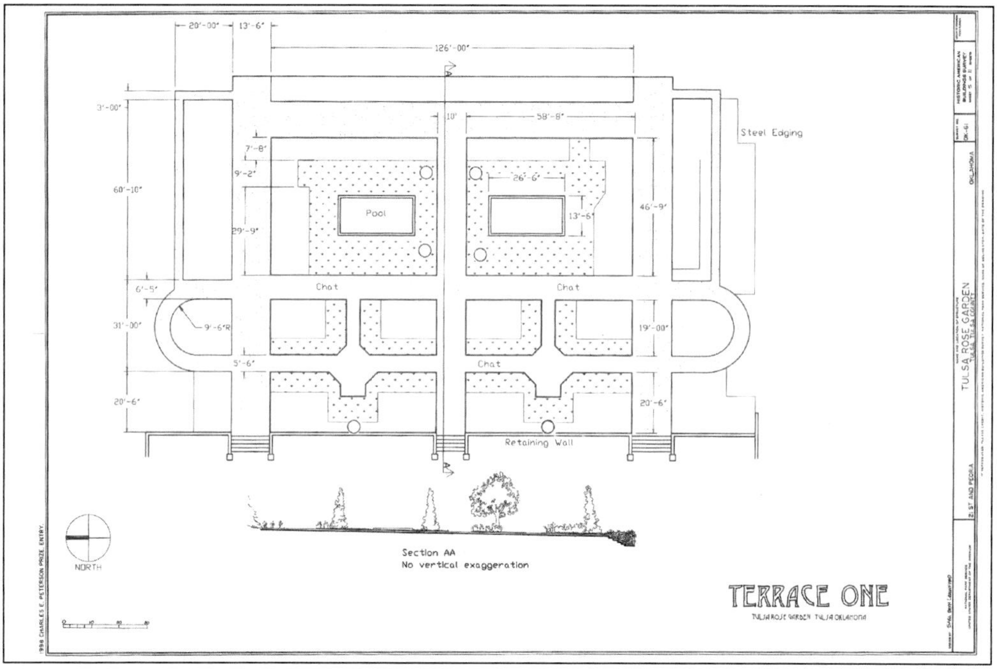

The as-built site plan and section for Terrace One shows a central walkway with parallel walks on either side. The section shows a slightly sloping site to a retaining wall separating Terrace One from Terrace Two below with three entrances and steps to Terrace Two.

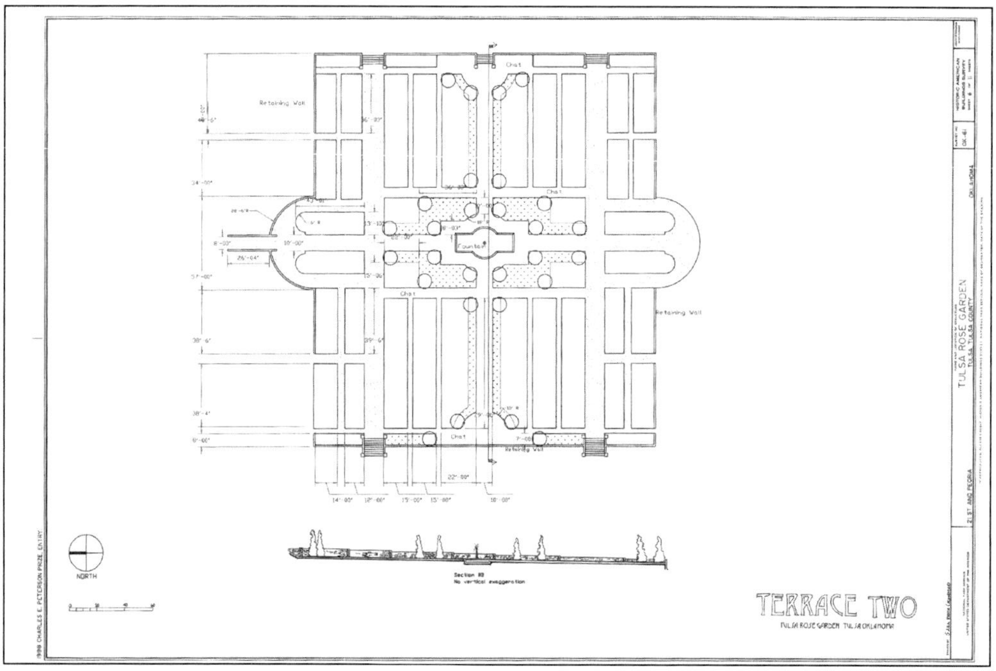

The as-built site plan and section for Terrace Two shows a central walkway with parallel walks on either side and a cross axis, with a pool and fountain as the focal point for the entire garden. The section shows a slightly sloping site to a retaining wall separating Terrace Two from Terrace Three below with three entrances and steps to Terrace Three.

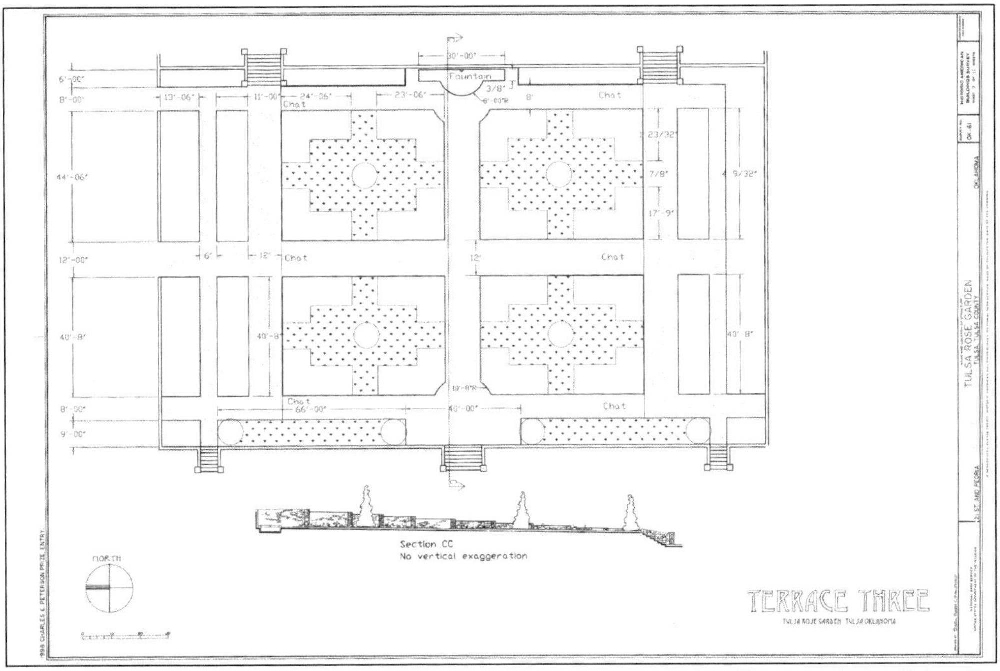

The as-built site plan and section for Terrace Three shows a central walkway with parallel walks on either side. The section shows a slightly sloping site to a retaining wall separating Terrace Two from Terrace Three below with three entrances and steps to Terrace Four. Terrace Three is accented by conical junipers.

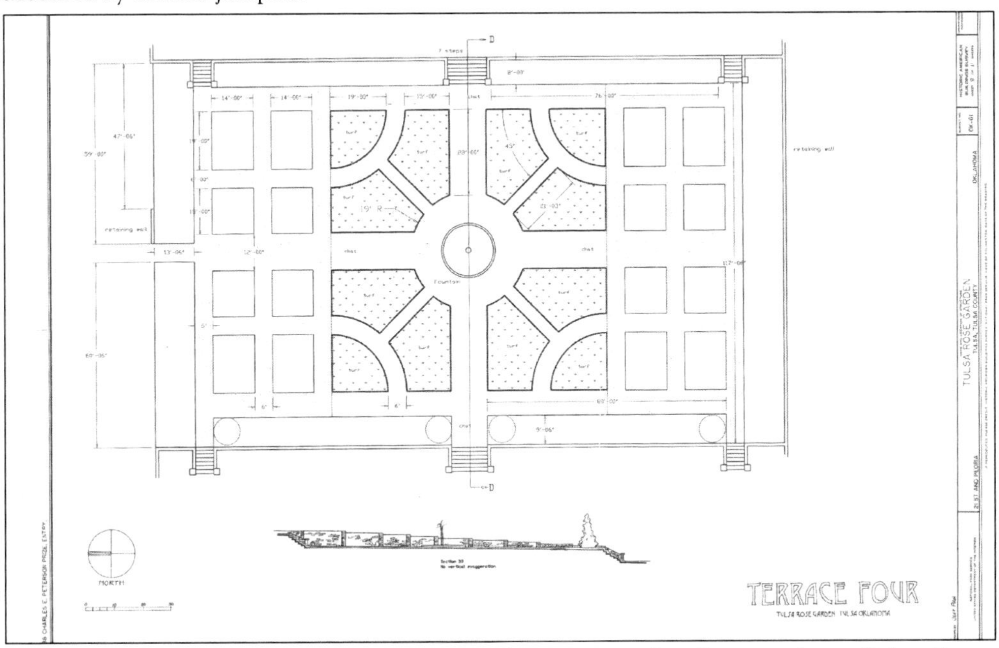

The as-built site plan section for Terrace Four shows a central walkway with parallel walks on either side. The section shows a slightly sloping site to a retaining wall separating Terrace Four from Terrace Five below with three entrances and steps to Terrace Five. Terrace Four features four separate square beds with a focal point in its design.

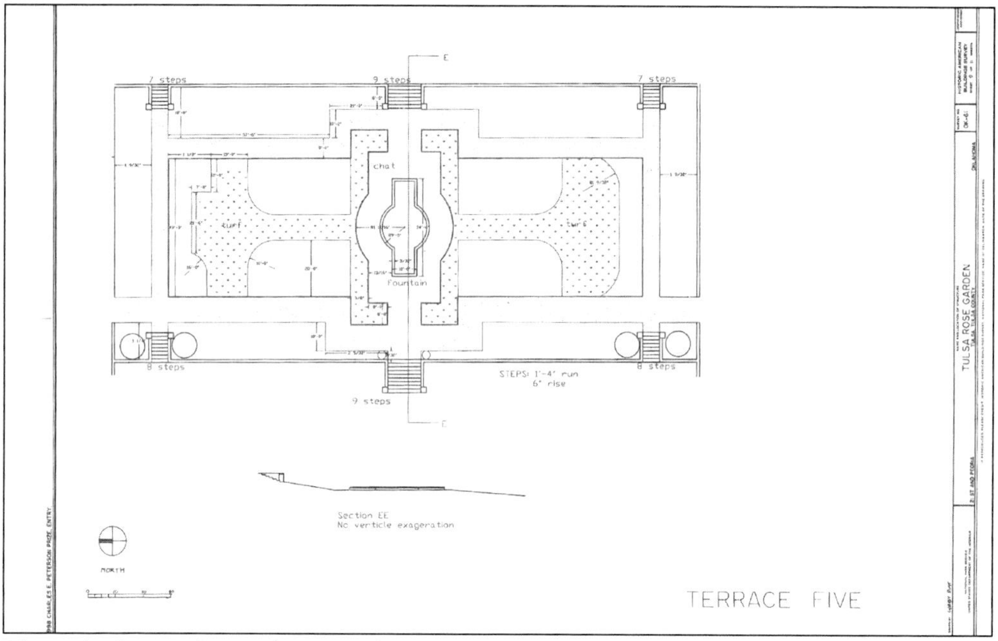

The as-built site plan and section for Terrace Five maintains a central sight line with walks through and around the central bed. The section shows a slightly sloping site to a retaining wall separating Terrace Five from Terrace Six below with one central entrance and steps to Terrace Six. Terrace Five is symmetrical with a pool as its center focal point in a rose bed larger than the other terraces.

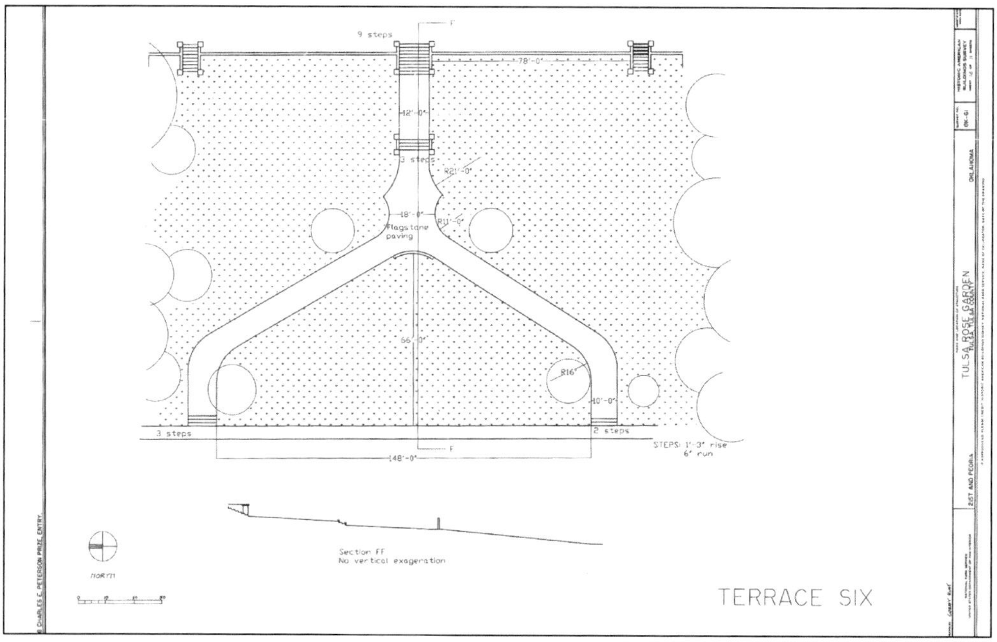

Terrace Six, in this as-built site plan and section, serves as the main entrance to the overall rose garden with a lawn framed by trees and a sloping Y-shaped walkway with three sets of steps from South Peoria Avenue to Terrace Five. The section shows a moderate upward-sloping site from South Peoria Avenue to Terrace Five.

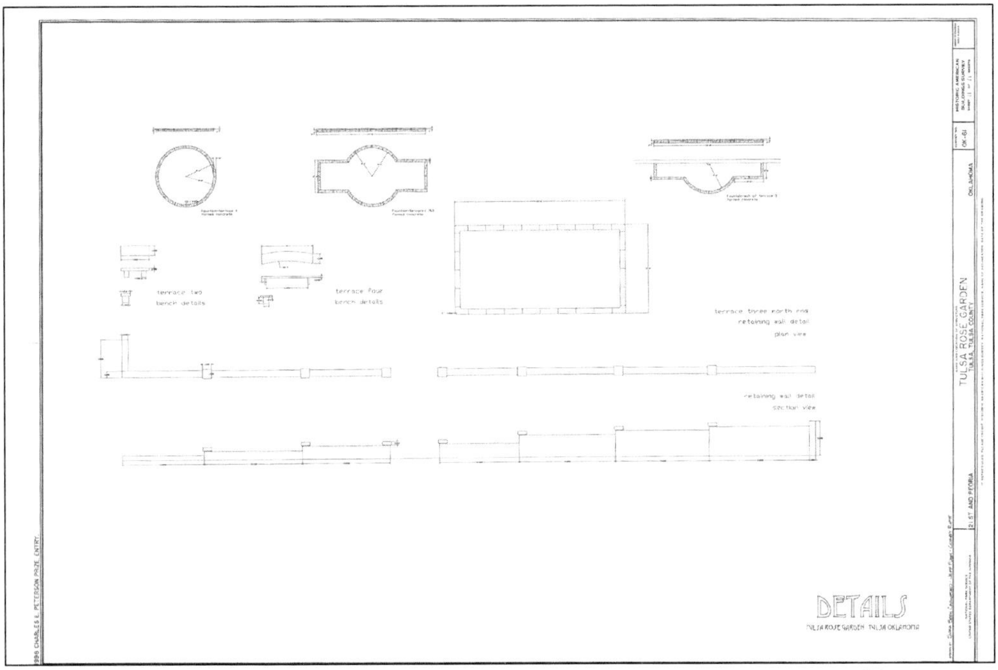

The as-built drawings show the plans and sections of the design features prepared by Bertram Fox and used to construct the garden. These features include pools, fountains, retaining walls, and benches throughout the park.

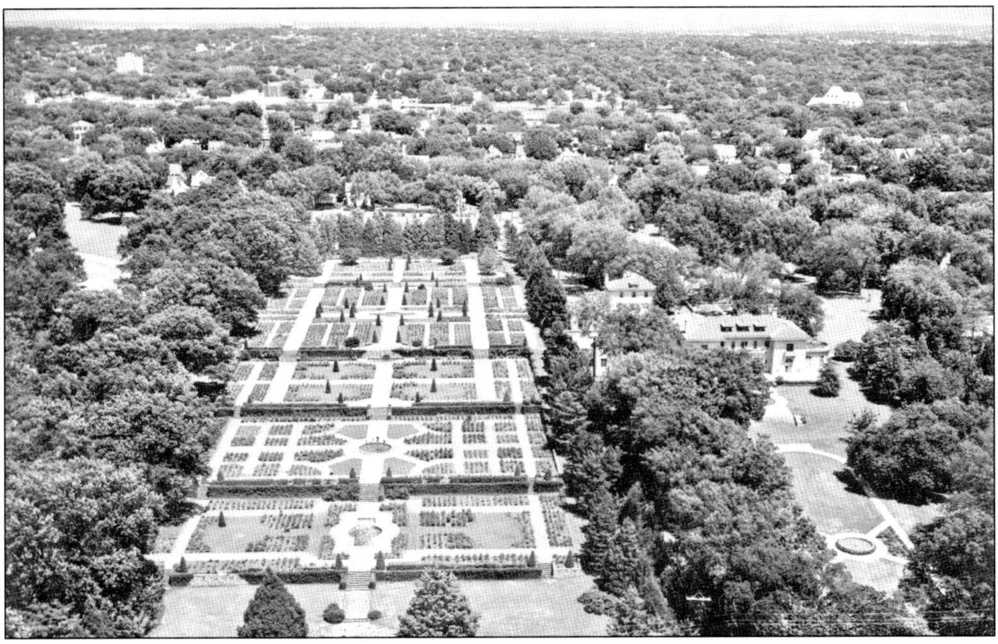

A 1960s aerial view of the rose garden shows a highly delineated formal landscape design through the use of light-colored walkways and conical accent evergreen trees through the site. The site is enclosed and screened by trees on three sides from Woodward Park and the Tulsa Garden Center. The park's main entrance faces South Peoria Avenue. (Courtesy the Beryl Ford Collection/Rotary Club of Tulsa, Tulsa City-County Library and Tulsa Historical Society.)

Capitol Hill Park: Scottish Rite Temple, Guthrie

Type of Project: Public Grounds
Designer: Hare & Hare, Landscape Architects, Kansas City, Missouri Date: c. 1924

Capitol Hill Park consists of four city blocks for a site of 10.62 acres. The site on Oklahoma Avenue is the highest point in Guthrie and was originally laid out to accommodate the state capitol and other state office buildings. Initially the site contained one large building on the east side that was used as the convention and legislative hall until the state capital moved to Oklahoma City in 1910. After the capital was moved, the site had two different owners. In 1911, it was acquired for use as a Methodist university, but it was returned to the city over a contract dispute in May 1919. The Guthrie Scottish Rite acquired the property in June 1919 and retained the firm of Hawk and Parr to renovate the convention hall and prepare plans for a temple. The cornerstone for the temple was laid on January 20, 1924.

The landscape architecture firm of Hare & Hare from Kansas City was retained in 1924 to prepare a site and planting plan. The plan called for 171 trees, 5,200 evergreens, and 388 perennials, all of which had to be at least three to four years old. The original plan called for a water fountain and tennis court, but budget restrictions prevented these features from being built. A full-time landscape maintenance staff was retained for the first 50 years, but with declining membership, the use of a part-time staff caused the landscape to fall into disrepair.

Study Director: Dr. Charles L. Leider, Landscape Architecture Program
Study Team Members: Derek McCall, team leader; Kristin Hattey Farrell; and Dean Wilson

Sources:
Hare & Hare archives, University of Missouri, Kansas City

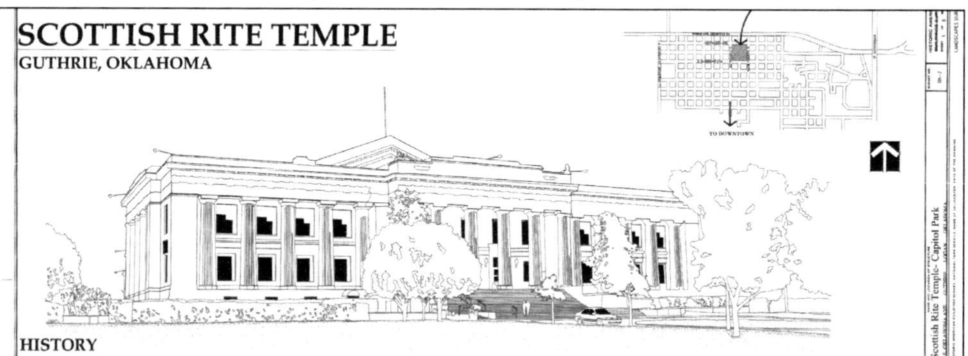

This 1998 poster describes the history of Capitol Hill and the Guthrie Scottish Rite Temple, shows the location of the park, and provides a sketch of the building. Guthrie was the territorial capital of Oklahoma. Its street system was laid out to provide a high point for the location of the future state capitol at a terminus for Oklahoma Avenue, Guthrie's main business street. After Oklahoma City was chosen as the state capital, the site was sold to the City of Guthrie in 1911; the city leased the property to a Methodist university until 1919, when the city sold the property to the Scottish Rite Masons for a temple. The Scottish Rite Masons retained the architecture firm Hawk and Parr in 1921 to design the temple, as shown in the sketch.

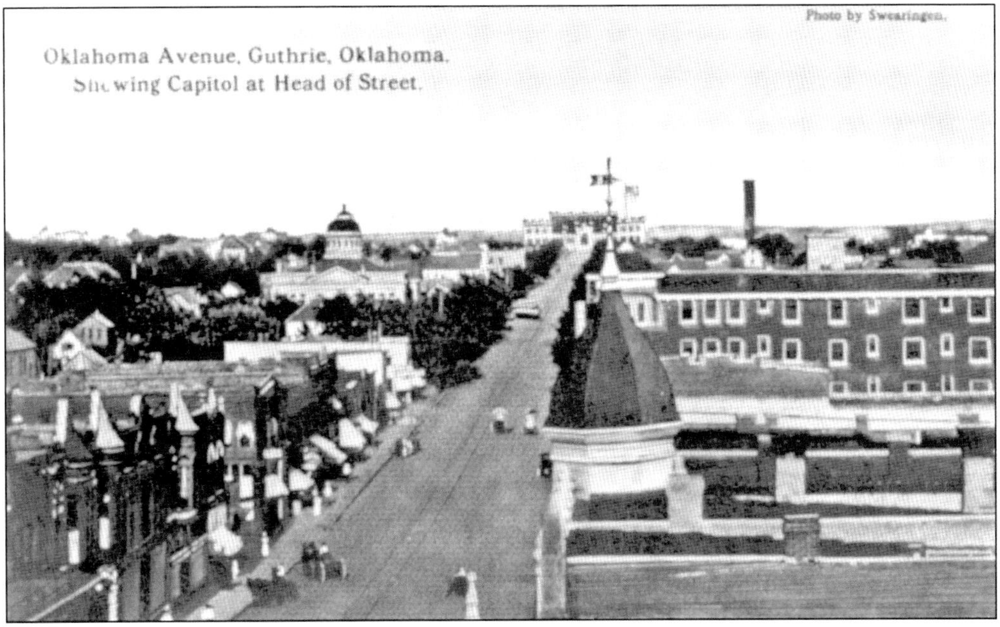

This 1910s aerial view shows the downtown business district of Guthrie along Oklahoma Avenue, which terminates at a proposed neoclassical design for a college building. The majority of the buildings along Oklahoma Avenue are two stories, except for the library with a tall dome where the constitutional convention was held and the state of Oklahoma was created. (Courtesy Special Collections Department, Metropolitan Library System of Oklahoma County.)

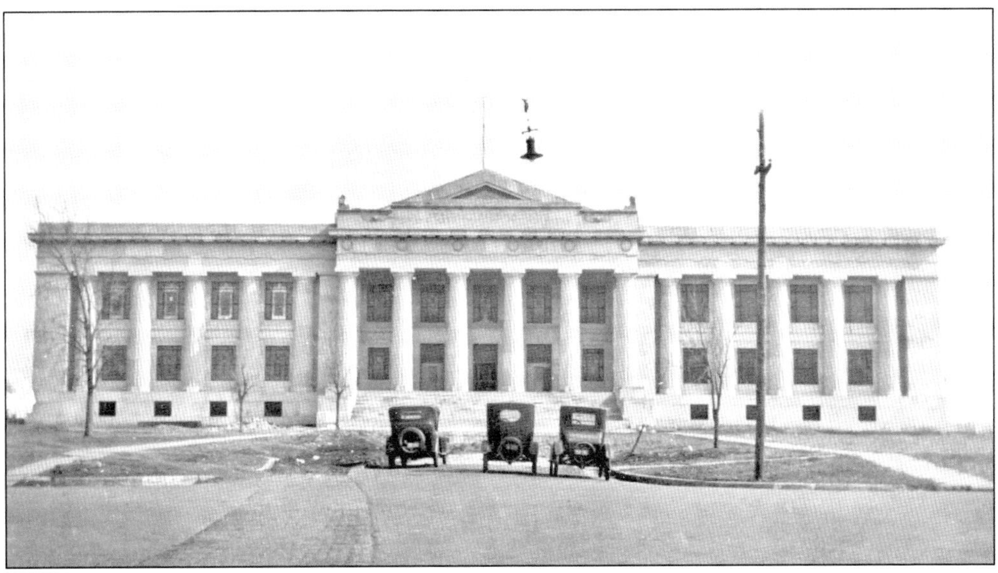

The Guthrie Scottish Rite Temple is seen after it was completed in 1924 with a symmetrical neoclassical facade. The rear portion of the temple incorporated the incomplete anticipated state capitol building. The imposing size of the temple on Oklahoma Avenue met the community's expectations for a building resembling a state capitol. The unlandscaped site reflects the need to relate the site and building into the tree-lined neighborhood. (Courtesy Special Collections Department, Metropolitan Library System of Oklahoma County.)

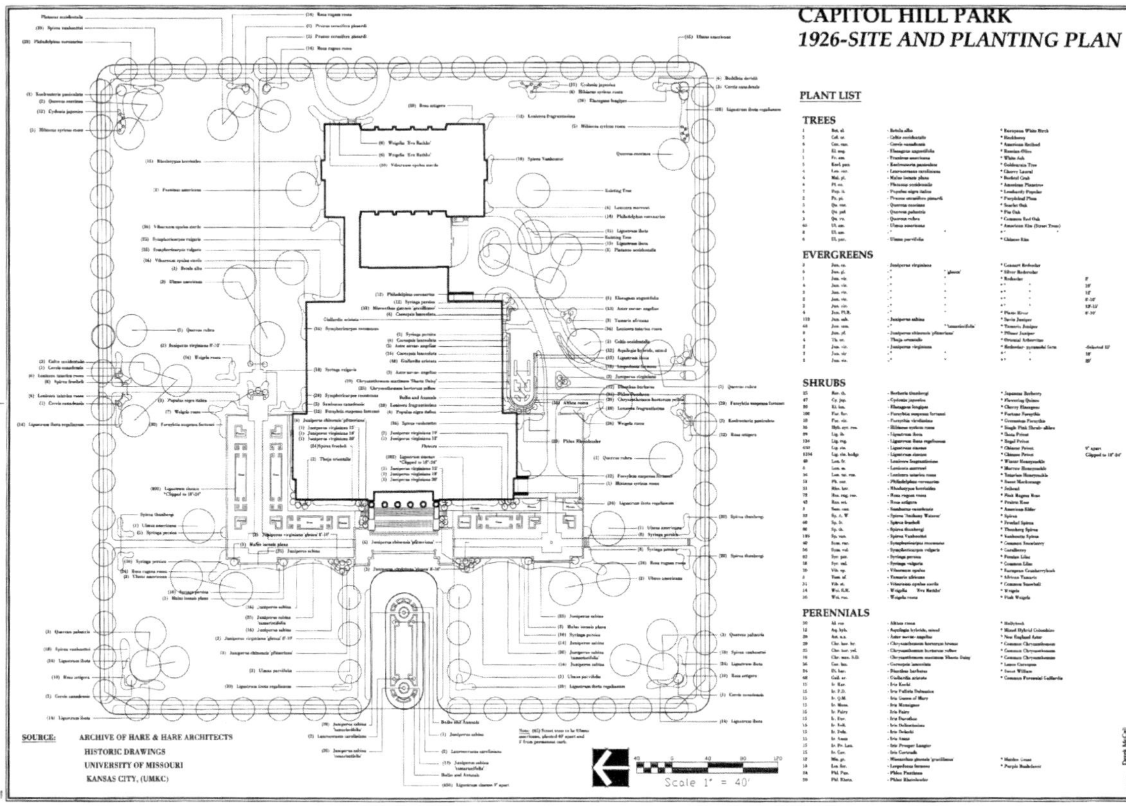

The 1998 as-built drawing shows the 1926 design of Hare & Hare, who prepared an informal site and landscape plan to complement the imposing neoclassical temple. Hare & Hare proposed a formal U-shaped entrance drive off Oklahoma Avenue on both the front and rear sides of the temple and a service driveway on the east side to both ends of the building. A rectangular sidewalk system alongside the temple and the streets surrounding the site was built. The plant material list identifies the plants by name that exist on the site plan in 1989.

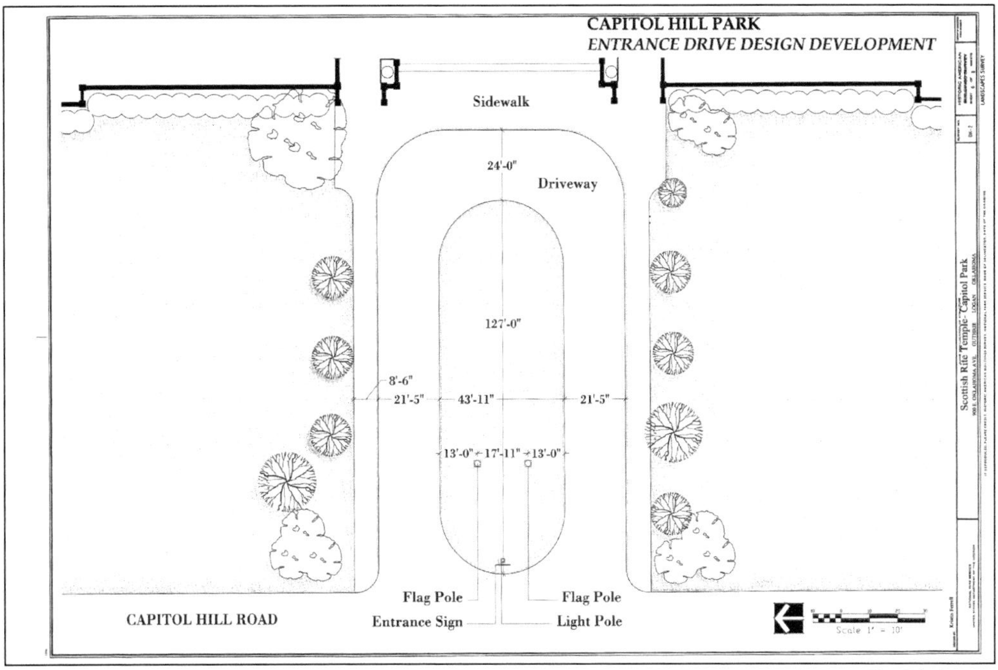

The 1998 as-built measured drawing show the formal U-shaped entrance drive off Oklahoma Avenue, focusing on the temple entrance. Rows of small trees on either side of the driveway enhance the arrival experience to the temple.

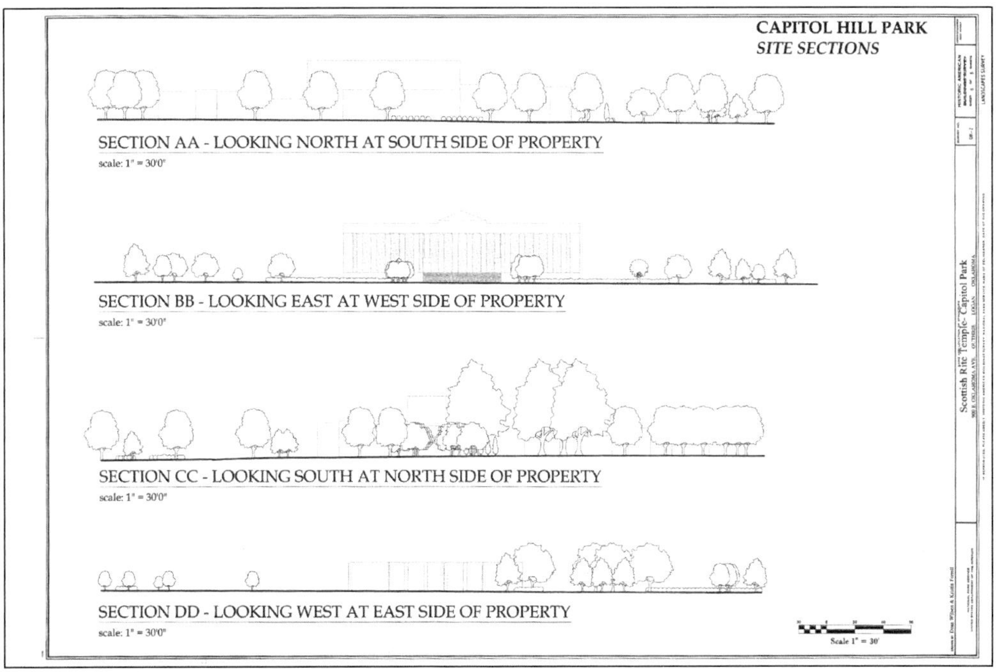

The 1998 as-built measured drawings as shown through four sections on each side of the park reveal a very level building site for the park and temple. The sections also show a relatively open site with small trees that are out of scale with the temple.

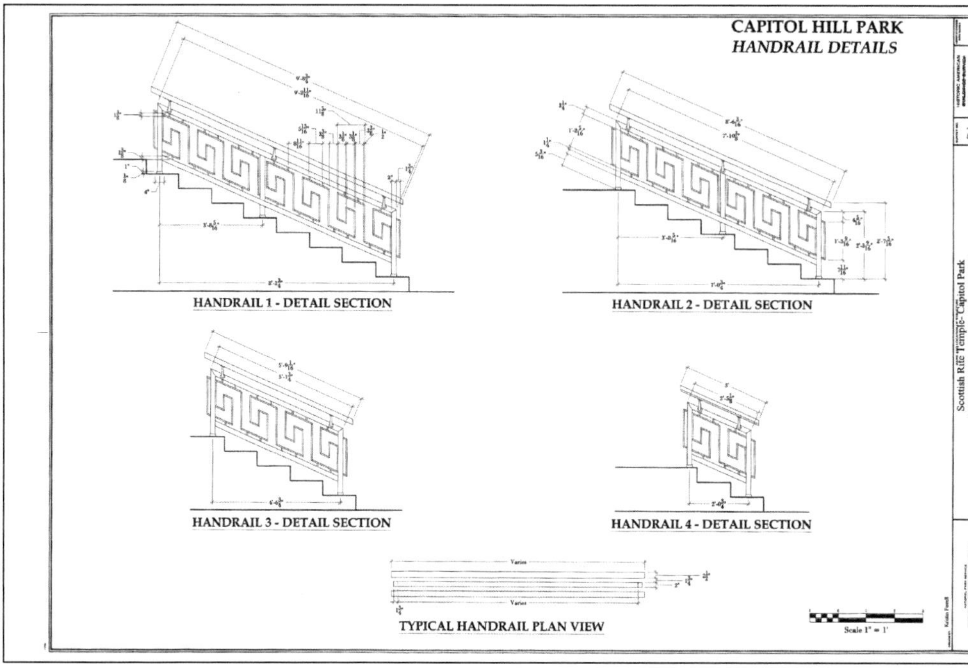

The 1998 as-built measured drawings show a variety of detailed handrails attached to the steps on four different-sized outdoor stairways. The stairways range from three to nine steps at the main entrance to the temple.

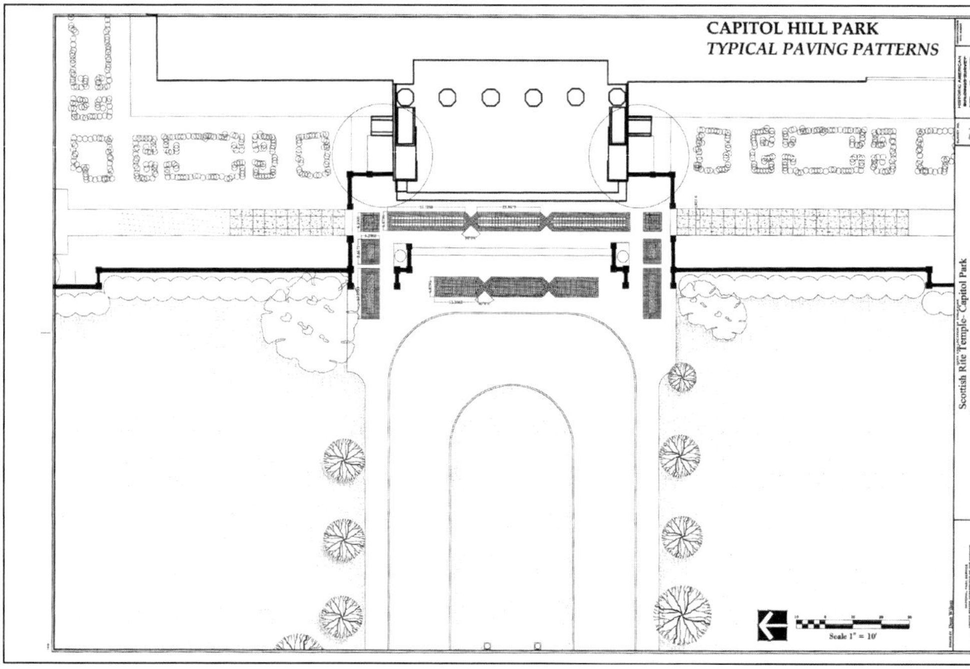

The 1998 as-built measured drawings show a variety of small panels of decorative geometric paving patterns for the arrival plaza and the front-door terrace. Three interlocking decorative paving pattern panels enhance the visitor's experience at the end of the U-shaped driveway and on the terrace at the entrance.

Woodward Park, Tulsa

Type of Project: Public Grounds
Designers: C. Burton Fox and Arthur S. Phillips — Date: 1930s
Renovation Designer: Howell & VanCuren, Landscape Architects — Renovated: 2006

From a cattle pasture used by prominent citizens of the Creek Nation in the late 1800s to its current use as an urban respite, the story of Woodward Park chronicles significant local, state, and national history within its own history. The park contains examples of the immense wealth that was quickly made and lost during Oklahoma's heyday in the oil boom during the first quarter of the 20th century. It also has structures built by Tulsans as part of the Works Progress Administration during the Great Depression. Over the years, the park has grown into a recognizable landmark within Tulsa.

Woodward Park has a rich cultural heritage that is evident in its history. Parts of the park offer snapshots of certain eras that were significant to the city of Tulsa, the state of Oklahoma, and the United States. Its early history is rooted in lands given to Native American tribes who moved to Oklahoma after being forced from their lands in the Southeastern United States as the country marched westward. The land where the park is located today was allotted to a Native American girl whose father sold it to the city. This transaction resulted in four years of litigation that was finally settled in Tulsa's favor in 1929 by the Oklahoma Supreme Court. The same year, the country spiraled into an economic crisis. As part of Pres. Franklin Roosevelt's New Deal policies, the WPA provided the construction of Woodward Park's rock gardens and rose garden, two of the most recognizable features of the park. The two mansions within the park complex, which now house the Tulsa Garden Center and the Tulsa Historical Society, were products of the era when Tulsa was the "Oil Capital of the World." The mansions have been preserved in their transition from private homes to public museums. Over the years, the park has offered a place to relax and enjoy nature while also offering educational services to the city's residents. As the second park in Tulsa's history, it has grown with the city from an undeveloped pastureland to one of Tulsa's premier parks.

Study Director: Dr. Charles L. Leider, Landscape Architecture Program
Faculty Advisor: Dr. William Bryans, Department of History
Study Team Members: Steve Eilers, team leader; Corbin Francis; Jonathan Miller; Chery Lyn Reeves; Shelly Wolf; and Peter Anderson

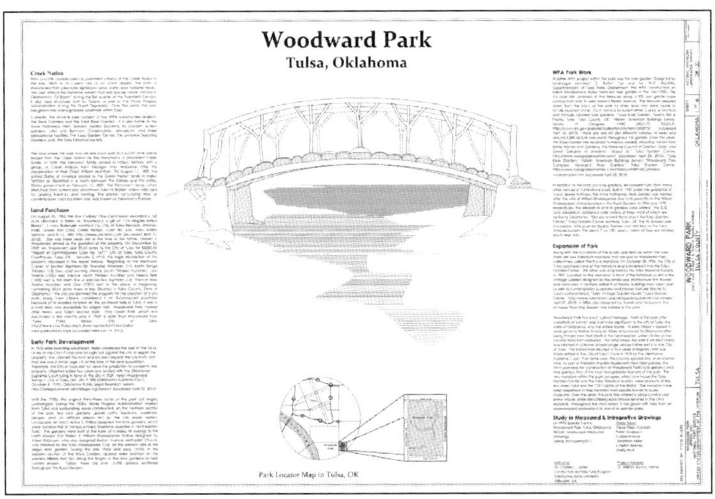

The poster describes the long history of Woodward Park; the maps show the location of the park on East Twenty-First Street and South Peoria and South Rockford Avenues; and included is a sketch of its principal landmark, the arched bridge. The landmark is the main entrance to the park at the intersection of East Twenty-First Street and Rockford Avenue.

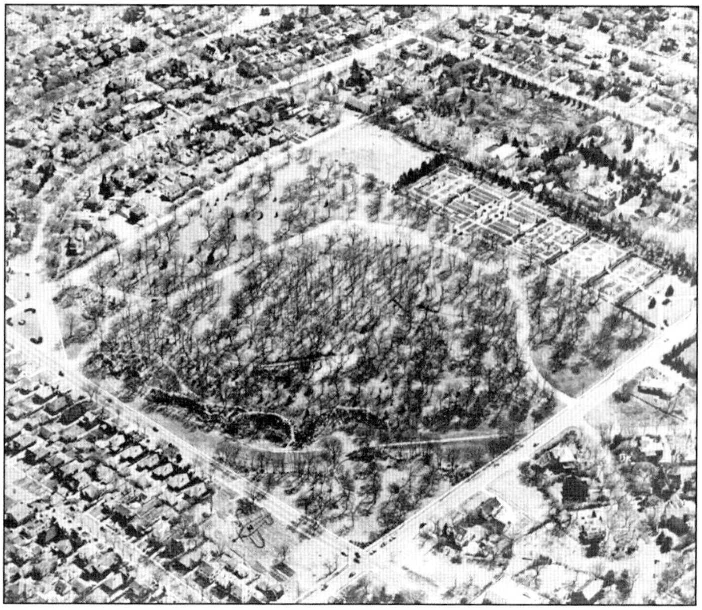

The aerial view of Woodward Park and the Tulsa Rose Garden was taken looking southeast towards the northwest corner of Woodward Park at East Twenty-First Street and South Peoria Avenue. The park and Tulsa Garden Center constitute approximately 90 percent of the area, while the rose garden occupies only 10 percent of the site. (Courtesy the Beryl Ford Collection/Rotary Club of Tulsa, Tulsa City-County Library and Tulsa Historical Society.)

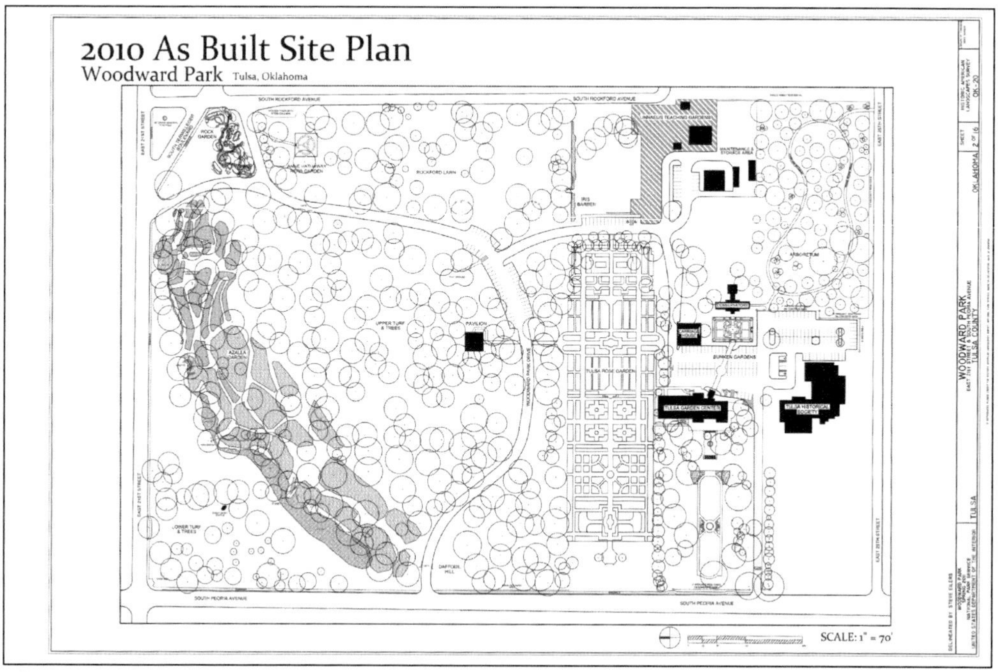

The 2010 as-built measured drawing of the site shows of the park's naturalistic design and its relationship to the adjoining rose garden and Tulsa Garden Center. There are two entrances to the park: the main entrance is at the intersection of East Twenty-First Street and Rockford Avenue, and the other entrance is off Peoria Avenue near the rose garden. One major curvilinear drive with the park connects the two entrances and provides service road access to the rear of the rose garden. (Courtesy Tulsa Historical Society.)

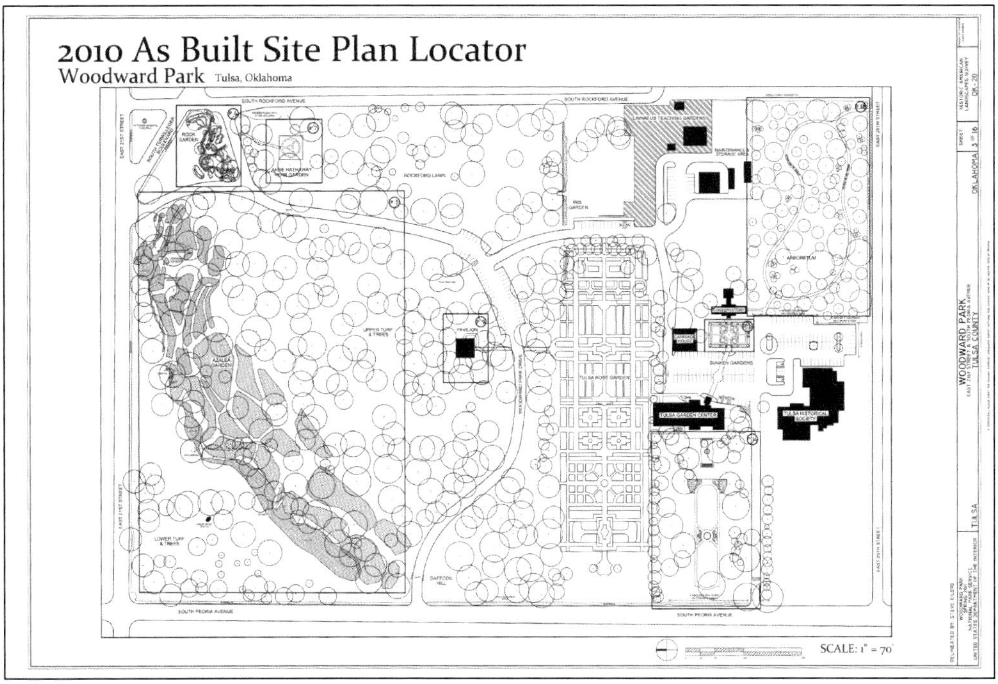

The as-built measured drawing of the site shows the boundaries and the location numbers of the individual area site plans in the park. The individual plans include the rock garden, Anne Hathaway Herb Garden, azalea garden, pavilion, sunken garden, arboretum, and garden center lawn.

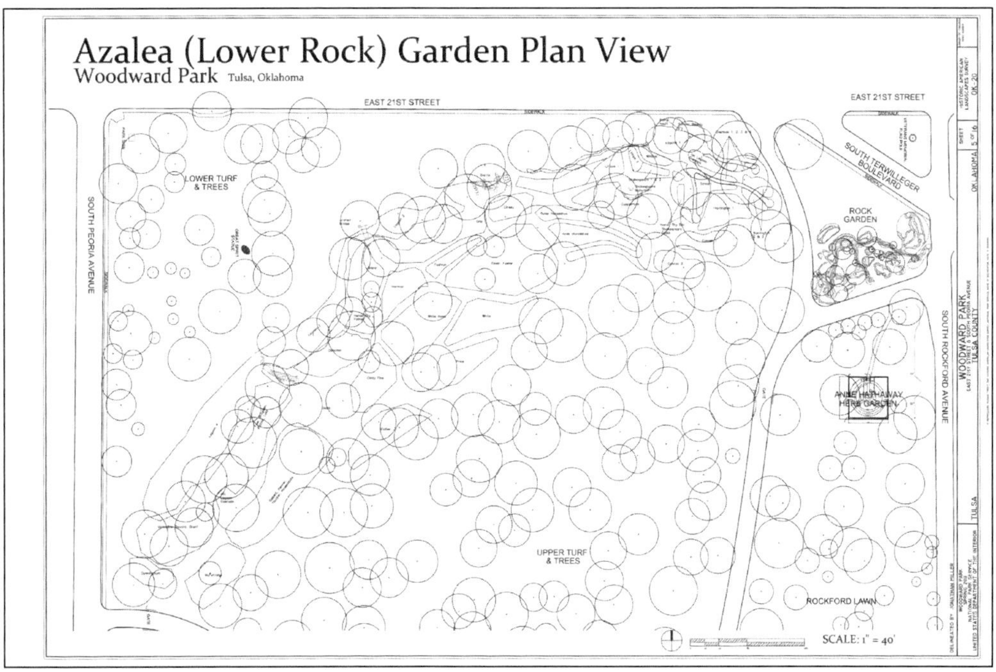

The as-built measured site plan shows the azalea (lower rock) garden, located at the entrance to the park on the west of the entrance drive off Twenty-First Street. The rock garden is on the east side of the azalea garden off Woodward Park Drive, the entrance road.

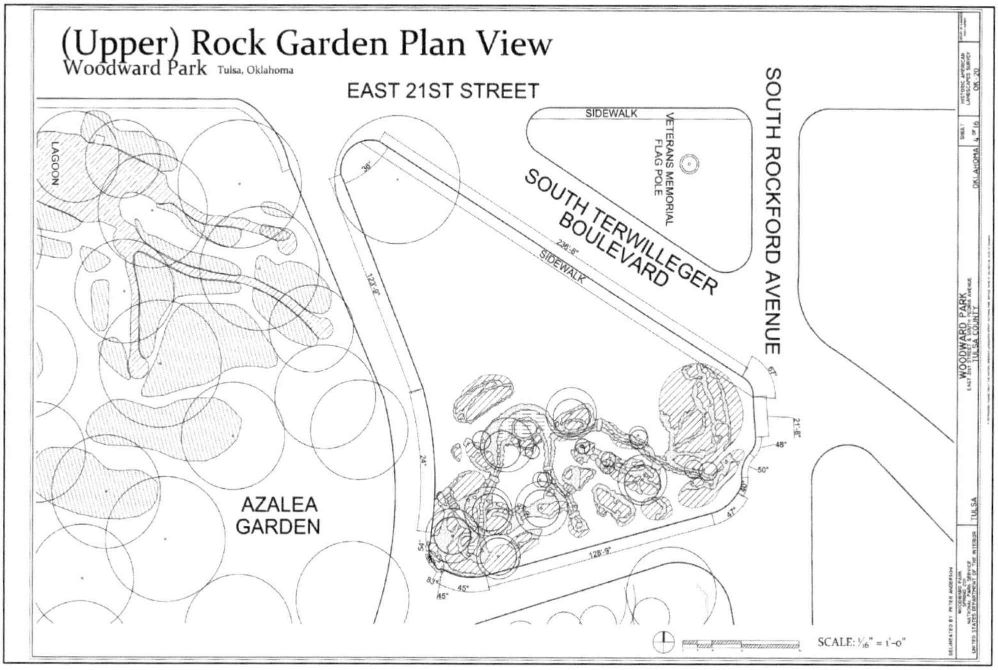

The as-built measured site plan shows the upper rock garden. It is at the entrance to the park in a triangular piece of land at the intersection of Twenty-First Street and Terwilleger Boulevard adjacent to the azalea garden on the west side. The site plan shows a lawn in the foreground and the rock garden in the background at the entrance to the park.

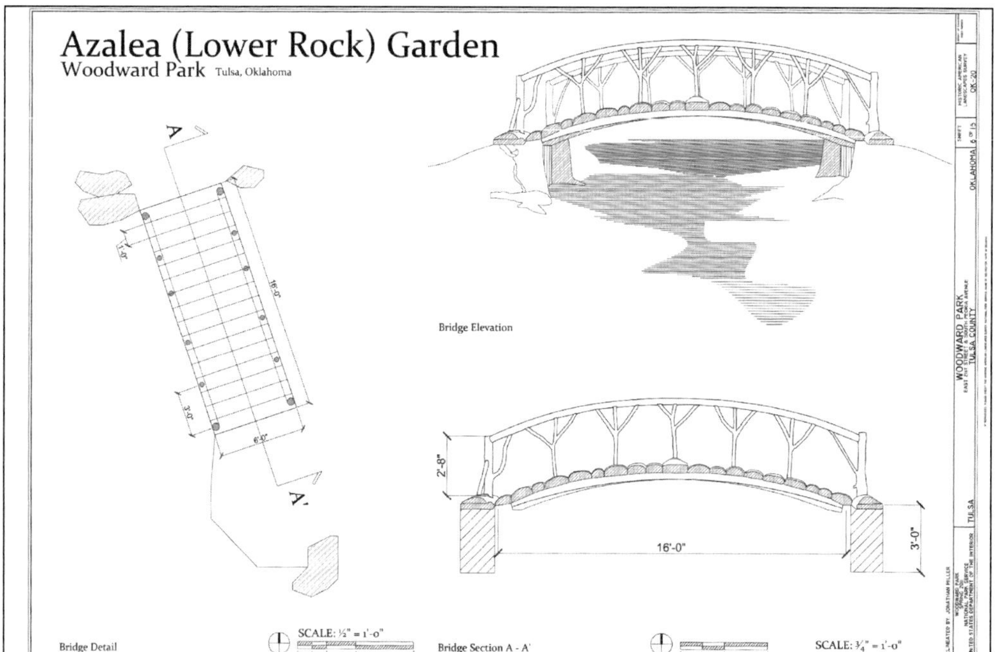

The iconic wood bridge is in the lower azalea garden on the west side of Woodward Park Drive, near the intersection of Twenty-First Street and Terwilleger Boulevard. The as-built drawings of the wooden bridge include a floor plan, elevation, and sketch.

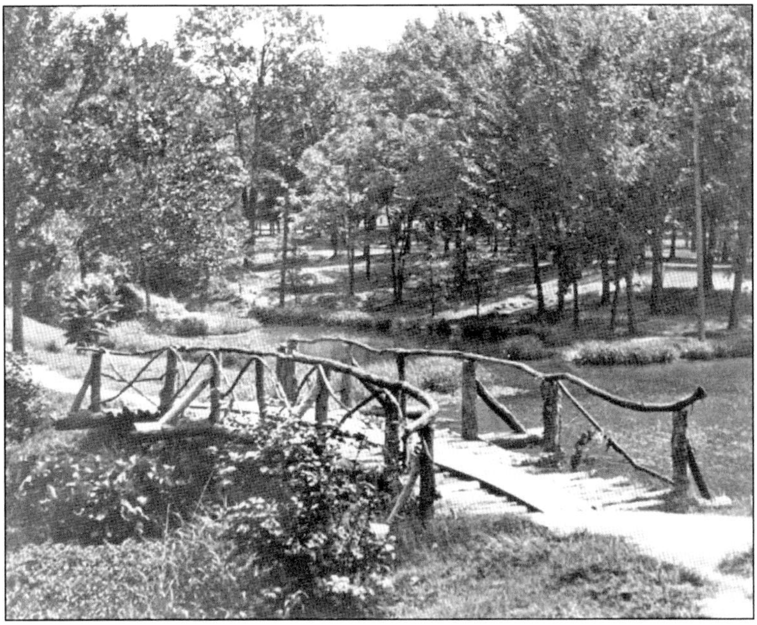

This summertime view shows the landmark wood-rail pedestrian bridge near the entrance to Woodward Park. The bridge is designed in a naturalistic style to blend into the landscape setting of the park. (Courtesy the Beryl Ford Collection/Rotary Club of Tulsa, Tulsa City-County Library and Tulsa Historical Society.)

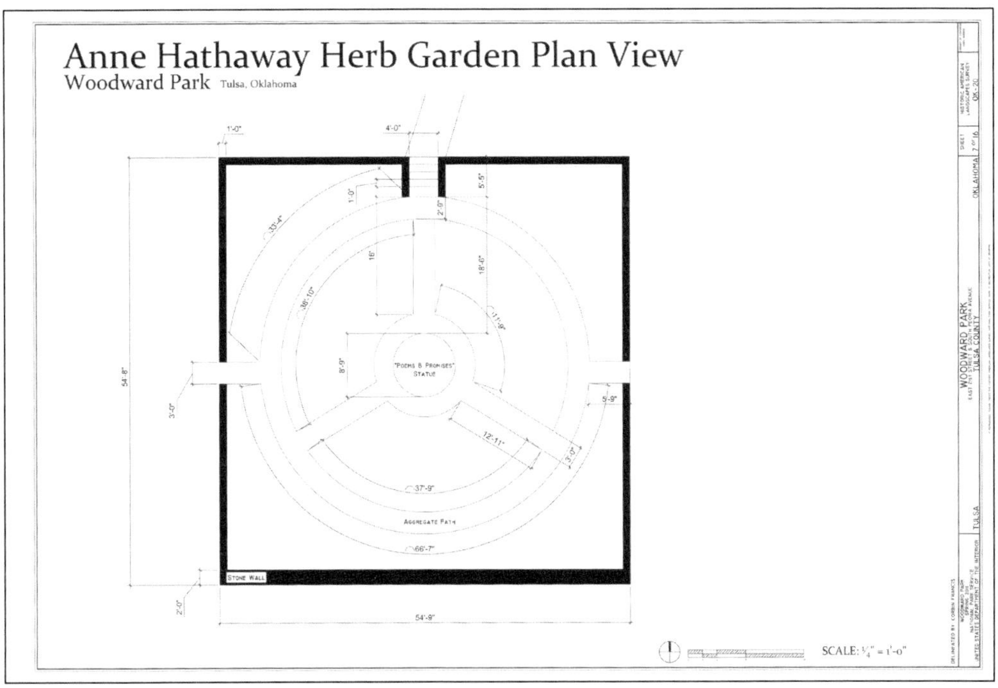

The Anne Hathaway Herb Garden is near the entrance of the park above the rock garden. The as-built measured drawing shows a square, symmetrical site plan with a circular interior walkway and a statue in the center of the garden as a focal point.

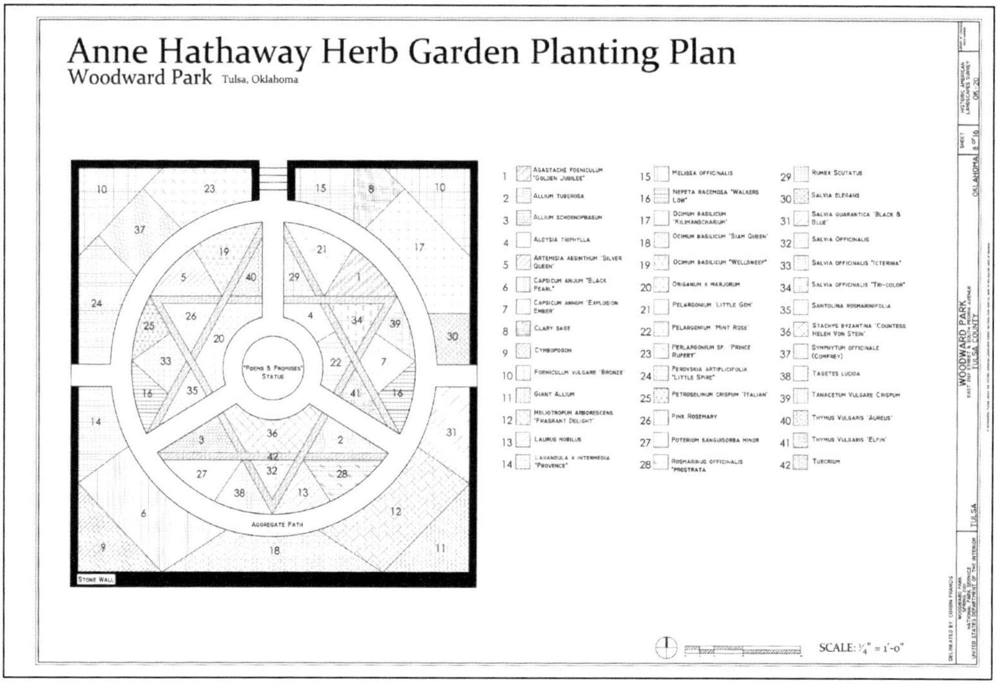

The as-built measured drawing of the Anne Hathaway Herb Garden shows a planting plan for 42 herbs based on a square, symmetrical site plan with an interior circular walkway system, and a statue in the center surrounded by a low 18-inch rock wall.

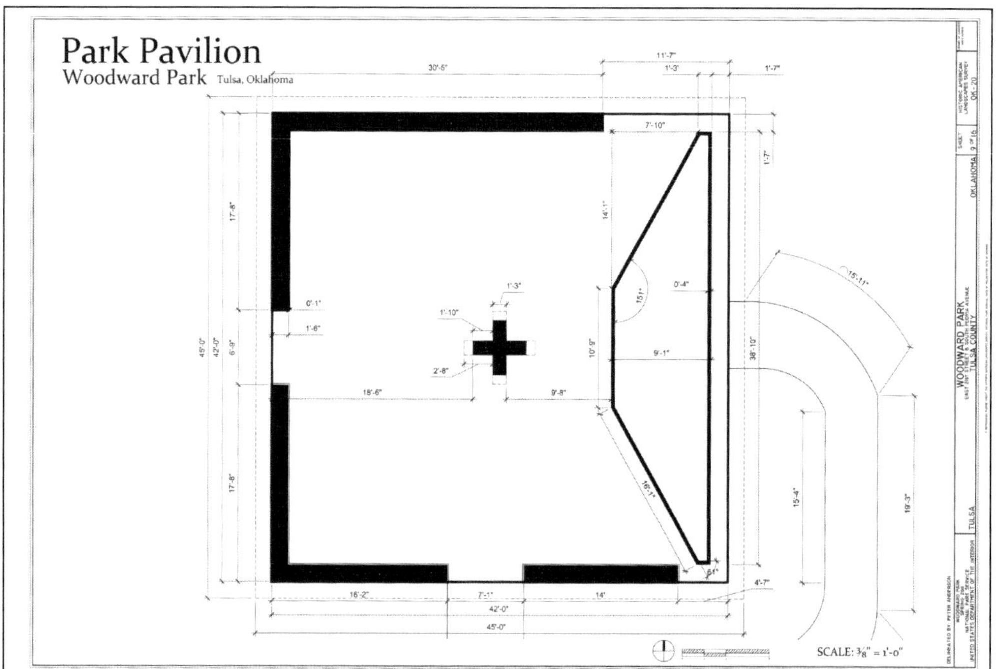

The pavilion is in the center of park on Woodward Park Drive with a walkway on an axis to the entrance to the rose garden. The as-built measured drawing shows a square, symmetrical floor plan for a partially enclosed pavilion with a central column.

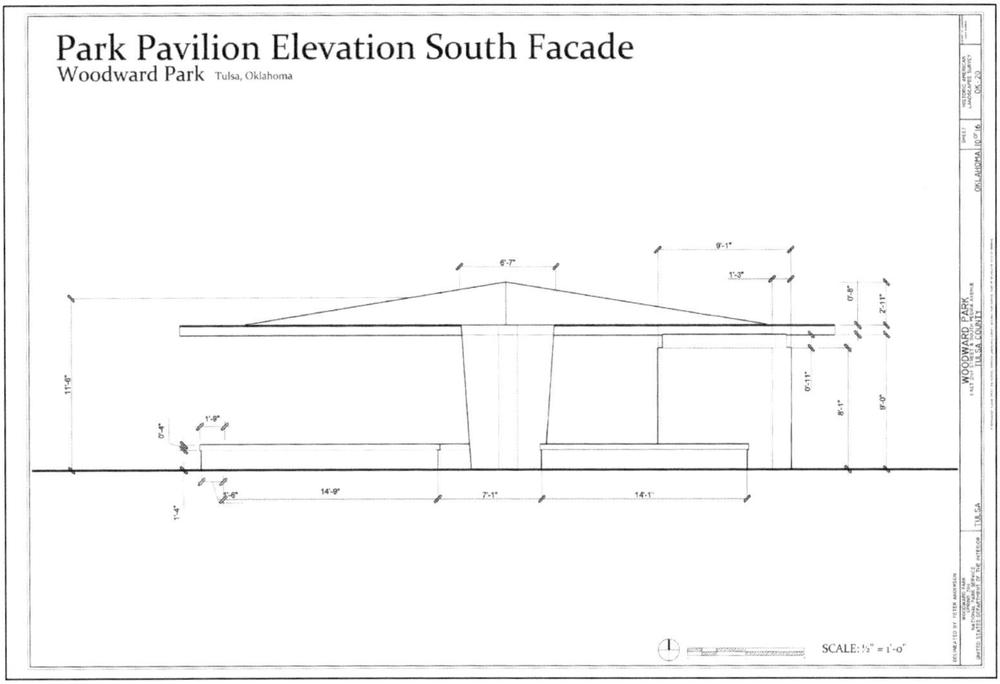

The as-built measured drawing of the pavilion shows the south elevation of a square, symmetrical building with a partially enclosed space and a fireplace in a central column used to support a cantilever roof. A low, 18-inch outside sitting wall inside the roofline defines the size of the pavilion.

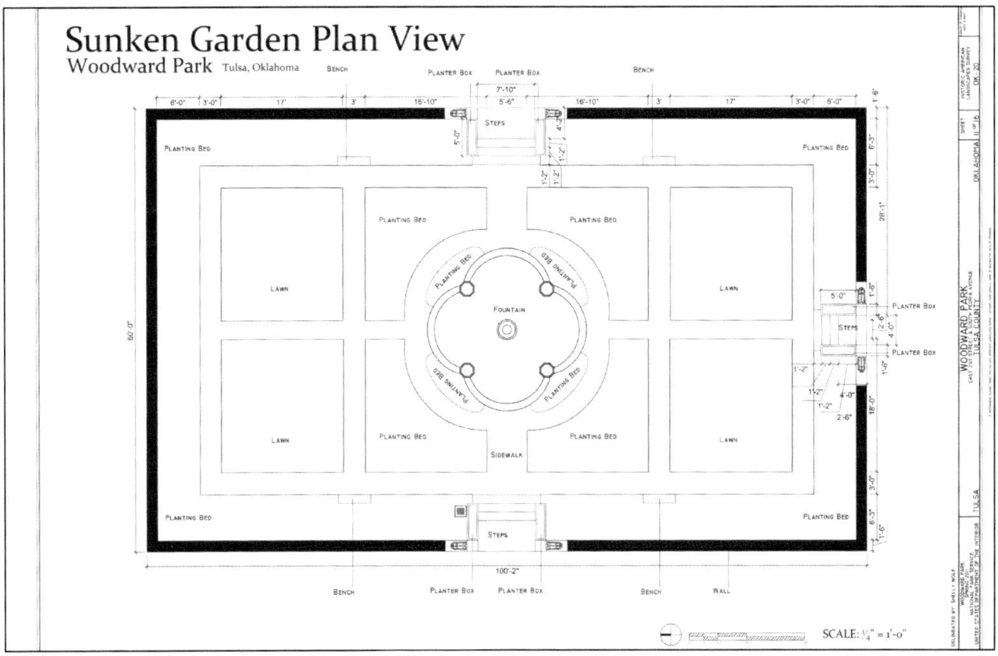

The sunken garden is south of the rose garden near the Tulsa Garden Center, between the carriage house and the conservatory. The as-built measured drawing shows the symmetrical sunken plan with a pool and fountain as the central focal point surrounded by planting beds. (Courtesy Tulsa Historical Society & Museum.)

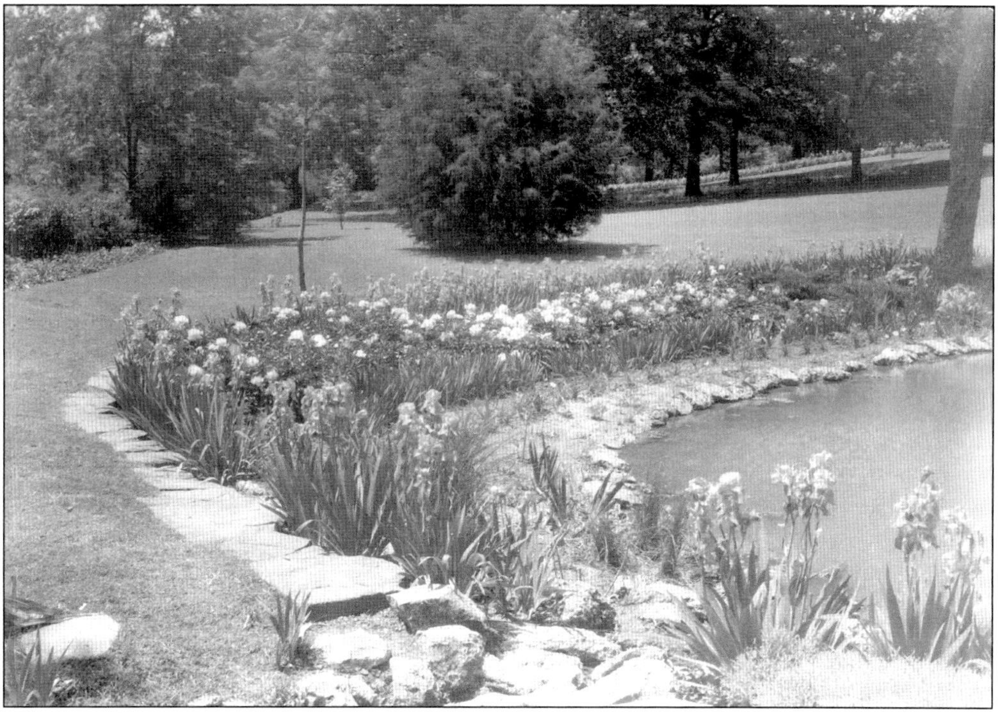

The flowerbed and pond in Woodward Park are not typical of flowerbeds used in parks designed in the naturalistic style. Flowerbeds were a typical design element of the garden landscape design style to add color and variety to the landscape. (Courtesy the Beryl Ford Collection/Rotary Club of Tulsa, Tulsa City-County Library and Tulsa Historical Society.)

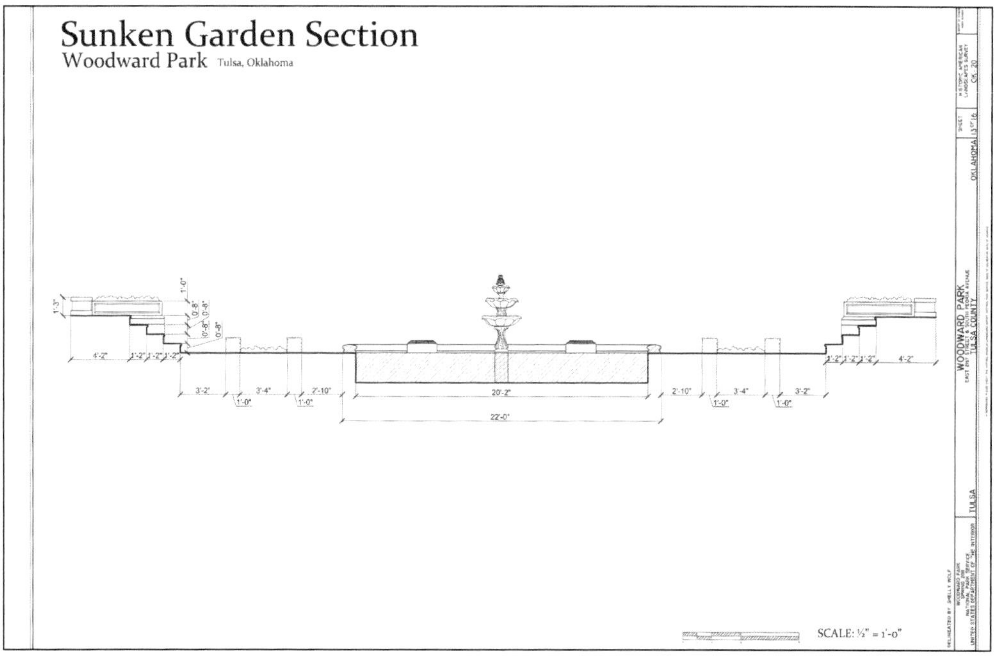

The as-built measured cross section of the sunken garden shows the relationship of the pool and fountain to the entrance steps.

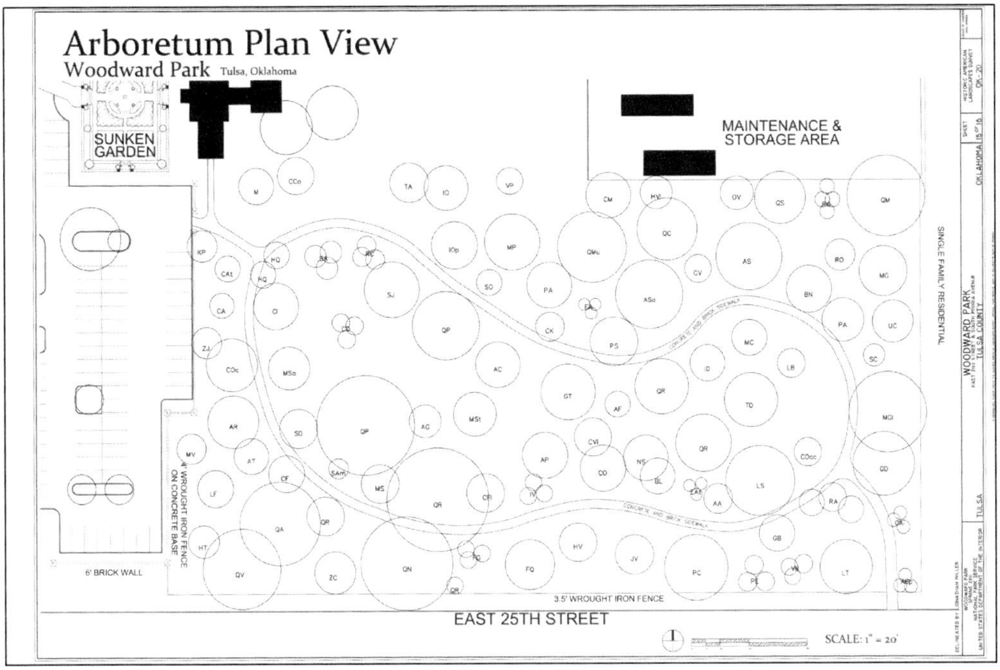

The 2010 as-built measured drawing shows a planting and walkway plan through the arboretum and its relationship to the garden center. The arboretum adjoins the Tulsa Historical Society building and is located alongside the conservatory and sunken garden near the Tulsa Garden Center. It fronts on East Twenty-Fifth Street and South Rockford Avenue.

Arboretum Plant Schedule

Woodward Park Tulsa, Oklahoma

Key	Botanical Name	Common Name
AC	*Acer cappadocicum*	Coliseum Maple
AR	*Acer rubrum*	Rod Maple
ASa	*Acer saccharum* 'Caddo'	Caddo Sugar Maple
AS	*Acer saccharum*	Sugar Maple
AP	*Aesculus pavia*	Red Buckeye
AG	*Amelanchier x grandiflora* 'Autumn Billanoe'	Serviceberry
AF	*Amorpha fruticosa*	Wild Indigo Bush
ASp	*Aralia spinosa*	Devil's Walking Stick
AA	*Aronia arbutifolia* 'Brilliantissima'	Chokeberry
AT	*Asimina triloba*	Paw Paw
BN	*Betula nigra*	River Birch
BL	*Bumelia lanuginose*	Chittamwood
CA	*Callicarpa americana*	Beautyberry
CI	*Carya illinoensis*	Pecan
CO	*Carya ovata*	Shagbark Hickory
CM	*Castanea mollissima*	Chinese Chestnut
CAt	*Cedrus atlantica*	Atlas Cedar
CS	*Celastrus scandens*	Bittersweet
COc	*Celtis occidentalis*	Hackberry
COcc	*Cephalanthus occidentalis*	Buttonbush
CC	*Cercis canadensis*	Redbud
CCa	*Cercis canadensis* 'Alba'	Whitebud
CV	*Chionanthus virginicus*	Fringetree
CK	*Cladrastis kentuckea*	Yellowwood
CAl	*Clethra alnifolia* 'Rosea'	Summersweet Clethra
CD	*Cornus drummondii*	Rough leaf Dogwood
CFl	*Cornus florida* 'Cherokee Chief'	Flowering Dogwood
CFlo	*Cornus florida* 'Cloud 9'	Flowering Dogwood
CF	*Cornus florida*	Flowering Dogwood
CVI	*Crataegus viridis* 'Winter King'	Hawthorne
DV	*Diospyros virginiana*	Persimmon
EA	*Euonymus americanus*	Strawberry Bush
EAt	*Euonymus atropurpureus*	Eastern Wahoo
FG	*Fothergilla gardenii* 'Blue Mist'	Witch Alder
FQ	*Fraxinus quadrangulata*	Blue Ash
GB	*Ginkgo biloba* 'Autumn Gold'	Maidenhair Tree
GT	*Gleditsia triacanthos* 'Shademaster'	Honeylocust
GD	*Gymnocladus dioicus*	Kentucky Coffeetree
HT	*Halesia tetraptera*	Carolina Silverbell
HV	*Hamamelis vernalis* 'Orange Glow'	Vernal Witchhazel
HVi	*Hamamelis virginiana*	Common Witchhazel
HQ	*Hydrangea quercifolia* 'Snowflake'	Oakleaf Hydrangea
ID	*Ilex decidua* 'Warren's Red'	Deciduous Holly
IO	*Ilex opaca*	American Holly
IOp	*Ilex opaca* 'Xanthocarpa'	Yellow-fruited American Holly
IV	*Itea virginica* 'Henry's Garnet'	Virginia Sweetspire
JV	*Juniperus virginiana*	Eastern Red Cedar
KP	*Koelreuteria paniculata*	Goldenraintree
LB	*Lindera benzoin*	Spicebush
LS	*Liquidambar styraciflua*	Sweetgum
LT	*Liriodendron tulipifera*	Tuliptree
LF	*Lonicera fragrantissima*	Winter Honeysuckle
MP	*Maclura pomifera*	Osage Orange
MG	*Magnolia grandiflora* 'Little Gem'	Southern Magnolia
MSt	*Magnolia stellata* 'Dr. Merrill'	Star Magnolia
MS	*Magnolia stellata*	
MV	*Magnolia virginiana*	Sweetbay Magnolia
MSo	*Magnolia x soulangiana* 'Alexandrina'	Saucer Magnolia
M	*Malus sp.*	Flowering Crabapple
MGl	*Metasequoia glyptostroboides*	Dawn Redwood
MC	*Myrica cerifera*	Southern Waxmyrtle
NS	*Nyssa sylvatica*	Black Gum
OV	*Ostrya virginiana*	Hophornbeam
PA	*Picea abies*	Norway Spruce
PE	*Pinus echinata*	Shorleaf Pine
PC	*Pistacia chinensis*	Chinese Pistache
PA	*Prunus angustifolia*	Sand Plum
PS	*Prunus serotina*	Black Cherry
QA	*Quercus alba*	White Oak
QC	*Quercus coccinea*	Scarlet Oak
QF	*Quercus falcate*	Red Oak
QM	*Quercus macrocarpa*	Bur Oak
QMu	*Quercus muehlenbergii*	Chinkapin Oak
QN	*Quercus nigra*	Water Oak
QP	*Quercus palustris*	Pin Oak
QPh	*Quercus phellos*	Willow Oak
QR	*Quercus robur*	English Oak
QS	*Quercus shumardii*	Shumard Oak
QV	*Quercus velutina*	Black Oak
RC	*Rhamnus caroliniana*	Indian Cherry
RA	*Rhus aromatica* 'Gro-low'	Fragrant Sumac
RG	*Rhus glabra* 'Laciniata'	Smooth Sumac
RO	*Ribes odoratum*	Golden Currant
SC	*Sambucus canadensis*	Elderberry
SD	*Sapindus drummondii*	Western Soapberry
SA	*Sassafras albidum*	Sassafras
SJ	*Sophora japonica*	Japanese Pagodatree
SAm	*Styrax americanum*	Snowbell
SO	*Symphoricarpos orbiculatus*	Coralberry
TD	*Taxodium distichum*	Bald Cypress
TA	*Tilia Americana*	Linden
UC	*Ulmus crassifolia*	Cedar Elm
VN	*Viburnum nudum*	Swamp Haw
VP	*Viburnum prunifolium* 'Winterthur'	Black Haw
ZC	*Zanthoxylum clava-hercules*	Prickly Ash
ZJ	*Ziziphus jujube*	Chinese Date

The arboretum provides an opportunity for visitors to study trees and shrubs at various stages of their life cycle. The 2010 as-built drawing shows a list of plants with a key identifying by common or botanical name all the trees and shrubs for visitors to use.

CREEK NATION COUNCIL OAK TREE PARK, TULSA
Type of Project: Park Design
Designer: Tulsa Department of Parks, Staff Landscape Architects Date: 1960s

The Creek Nation Council Oak is the birthplace of Tulsa and an important landmark of the region. The events that have taken place under this post oak have shaped Northeastern Oklahoma's history. Established as a council oak for a segment of the Creek Nation in the area, its importance continued with the oil barons in the 1920s and the citizens of Tulsa today.

The Creek Nation, which currently resides in Oklahoma, once occupied parts of Georgia and Alabama during America's early years. Once referred to as Muscogee Creeks, they were forcibly removed from their homes from 1828 to 1838. In an attempt to appease the Creeks and the white settlers in Georgia and Alabama, the Creeks and other tribes were offered a section of land west of the Mississippi River. These lands, occupied by various tribes, eventually became known as Indian Territory, home to the Five Civilized Tribes.

According to one legend, a leader of a Creek clan traveled up the Arkansas River seeking a place to establish a home for his people; the exact year is unknown. He placed the council fires from his clan at this post oak overlooking the river. The tree became more than a meeting place; it was also the cornerstone of the community. Here is where the square was established, and the busk grounds and stickball field were in an open field just south of the tree. This Creek community produced many important civic leaders in the early years of Tulsa; some became political leaders, ministers, and cattle barons, and one became the first postmaster of Tulsa.

During Tulsa's "Oil Capital" days, the tree was on land owned by Earl Sinclair, which he sold to C.B. Peters in 1921. Both gentlemen revered the tree for its beauty and historical value. The property changed ownership during the 1960s, and at one point during the decade, the tree was almost destroyed to make room for a parking lot. Citizens of Tulsa and the Creek Nation rallied together to save this historic living landmark. Today, it is listed in the National Register of Historic Places as a park under the care of the Tulsa Department of Parks.

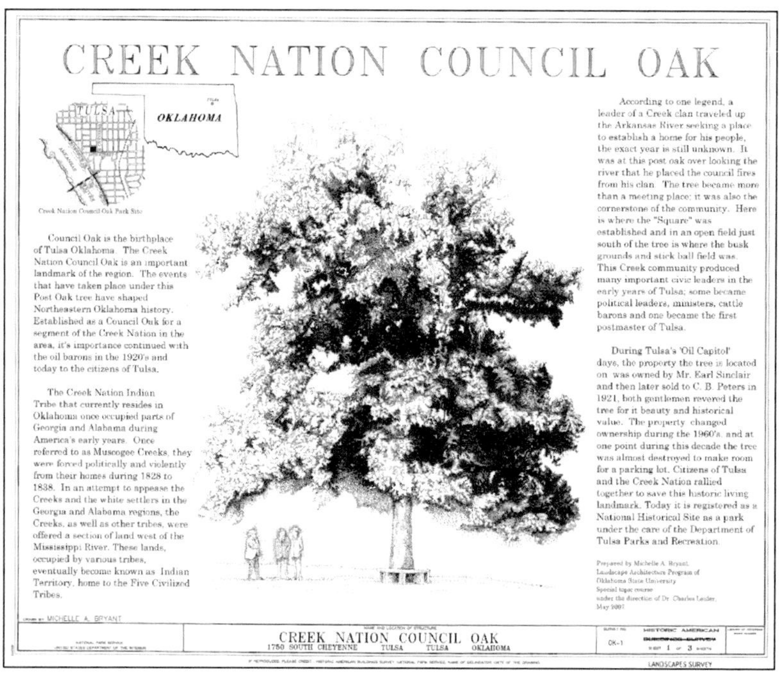

The poster shows maps locating the Creek Nation Council Oak Park in Oklahoma and in Tulsa. The drawing also contains the history of the signing of the treaty under the post oak in the 1830s. A sketch of the tree shows its height and overall size and dominance of the park site.

As Built Planting Plan

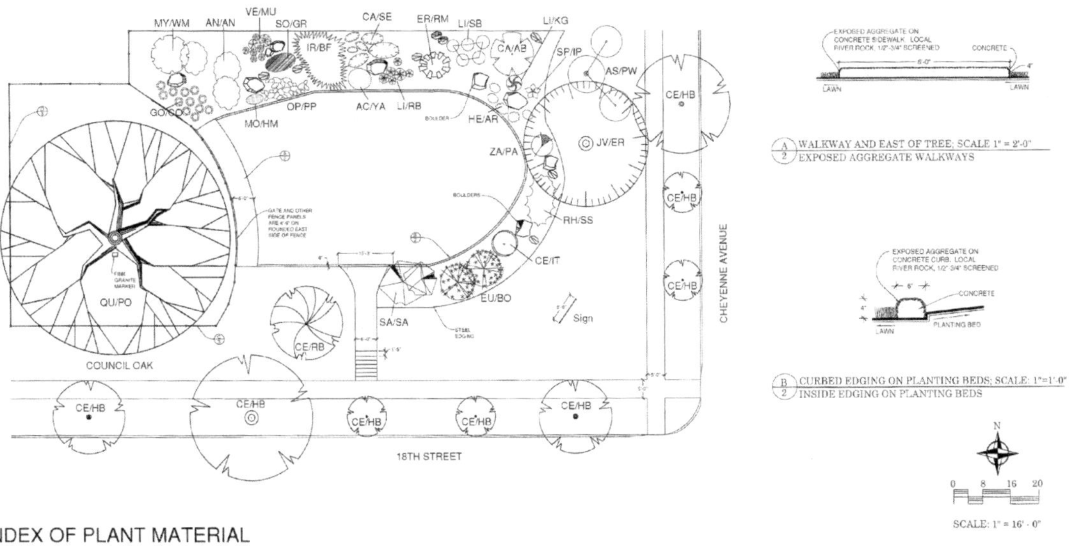

INDEX OF PLANT MATERIAL

KEY	BOTANICAL NAME	COMMON NAME
TREES		
QU/PO	*QUERCUS STELLATA*	POST OAK
JV/ER	*JUNIPERUS VIRGINIANA*	EASTERN REDCEDAR
CE/HB	*CELTIS OCCIDENTALIS*	HACKBERRY
CE/RB	*CERCIS CANADENSIS*	EASTERN REDBUD
SA/SA	*SASSAFRAS ALBIDUM*	SASSAFRAS
AS/PW	*ASIMINA TRILOBA*	PAW PAW

KEY	BOTANICAL NAME	COMMON NAME
SHRUBS		
MY/WM	*MYRICA CERIFERA*	WAX MYRTLE
EU/BO	*EUPATORIUM PERFOLIATUM*	BONESET
CA/AB	*CALLICARPA AMERCANA*	AMERICAN BEAUTYBERRY
CE/IT	*CEONANTHUS AMERCANUS*	INDIAN TEA
RH/SS	*RHUS GLABRA*	SMOOTH SUMAC
AN/AN	*ANGELICA ATROPURPUREA*	ANGELICA
ER/RM	*ERYNGIUM YUCCIFOLIUM*	RATTLESNAKE-MASTER
ZA/PA	*ZANTHOXYLUM AMERCANUM*	PRICKLY ASH
CA/SE	*CASSIA MARILANDICA*	SENNA
VE/MU	*VERBASCUM THAPSUS*	WOOLY MULLEIN
SP/IP	*SPIGELIA MARLANDICA*	INDIAN PINK

KEY	BOTANICAL NAME	COMMON NAME
LI/KG	*LIATRIS PYCNOSTACHYA*	KANSAS GAY FEATHER
LI/SB	*LINDERA BENZOIN*	SPICEBUSH
IR/BF	*IRIS VERSICOLOR*	BLUE FLAG IRIS
SO/GR	*SOLIDAGO CANADENSIS*	GOLDENROD
OP/PP	*OPUNTIA COMRESSA*	PRICKLY PEAR
MO/HM	*MONARDA CERIFERA*	HORSEMINT
LI/RB	*LIATRIS ASPERA*	ROUGH BLAZING STAR
AC/YA	*SCHILLEA MILLEFOLIUM*	YARROW
HE/AR	*HEUCHERA AMERICANA*	ALUMROOT
GO/CO	*GOSSYPIUM AUSTRALE*	NATIVE COTTON

DRAWN BY MICHELLE A. BRYANT

NATIONAL PARK SERVICE
UNITED STATES DEPARTMENT OF THE INTERIOR

NAME AND LOCATION OF STRUCTURE
CREEK NATION COUNCIL OAK
1750 SOUTH CHEYENNE TULSA TULSA OKLAHOMA

SURVEY NO. OK-1
HISTORIC AMERICAN LANDSCAPES SURVEY
SHEET 2 OF 3 SHEETS

IF REPRODUCED, PLEASE CREDIT: HISTORIC AMERICAN BUILDINGS SURVEY, NATIONAL PARK SERVICE, NAME OF DELINEATOR, DATE OF THE DRAWING

The 2010 as-built measured drawing shows a plan for the park designed in the naturalistic style around the post oak with a lawn, small trees, shrubs, and a walkway. The drawing also contains a planting plan with a plant list. The lawn area permits a view of the treaty tree. At the base of the post oak is a pink granite marker identifying the treaty signing.

Fence Detail

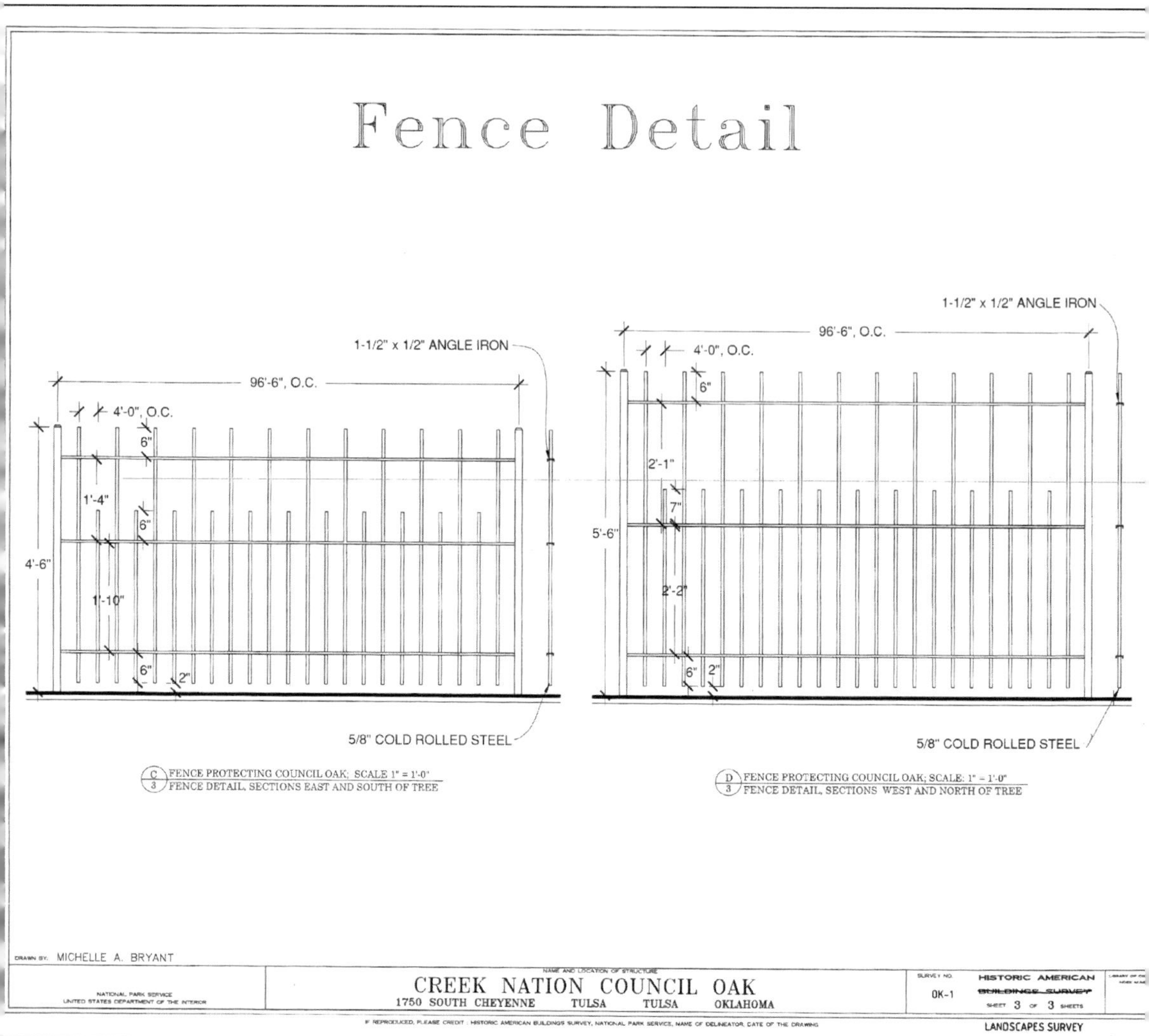

The site is protected by a four-foot spike iron fence that surrounds the park. The post oak treaty tree memorial is in the center of the park. The fence is on the property line around the perimeter of the park with shrubs in the foreground.

Four

Subdivisions and Planned Communities

Swan Lake Park, Tulsa
Type of Project: Subdivision Design
Developer: E.J. Brennan Date: 1917

Swan Lake began as a spring-fed watering hole for Col. Adolphus D. Orcutt's cattle. Colonel Orcutt's eldest son, Samuel Augustus "Gus" Orcutt, and Gus's wife, Annie, were instrumental in developing the Swan Lake area. Annie, who was one-quarter Creek Indian, and her children were allotted 800 acres surrounding the Orcutt watering hole in compliance with the Dawes Allotment Act of 1877. Orcutt Lake, as it came to be known, was a popular gathering spot for Tulsa citizens.

In 1908, Gus Orcutt and a group of developers enlarged the lake and built Tulsa's first amusement park, Orcutt Lake Park, on the north shore. The heyday of the park was from 1908 to 1911. The main entrance marked the end of the trolley line at the foot of St. Louis Avenue just west of the lake. The park included a large dance pavilion with bathhouses underneath (called an airdome), rowboat rentals, midway concessions, a café, a covered swimming pool (called a natatorium), and a $7,600 roller coaster.

The group also began developing a residential neighborhood north of the amusement park. The large lots and homes in the Orcutt Addition were built according to the state's first subdivision regulations. The homes were a variety of styles including Spanish Mission, Tudor Revival, Renaissance Revival, national folk, and eclectic.

E.J. Brennan bought the lake and surrounding land from Orcutt in 1917, and he immediately platted the land surrounding the lake for development that same year. It is considered one of the first residential developments in Oklahoma to use a pond as the centerpiece of its landscape design concept. He named this area Swan Park and renamed Orcutt Lake to Swan Lake, later donating Swan Lake to Tulsa as a public park.

A fountain in the middle of the lake was built in the late 1920s and then rebuilt in 1938 by the WPA. Swan Lake underwent a $1 million renovation in 1986–1987. Living up to its name, Swan Lake is currently home to two rare trumpeter swans as well as an outstanding collection of North American waterfowl that call the lake home.

Study Director: Dr. Charles L. Leider, Landscape Architecture Program
Faculty Advisors: Dr. William Bryans, Department of History; Prof. Nigel Jones, School of Architecture
Study Team Members: Patty Evans, team leader; Frank Hutto; and Leah Wells

Sources:
Tulsa Department of Parks

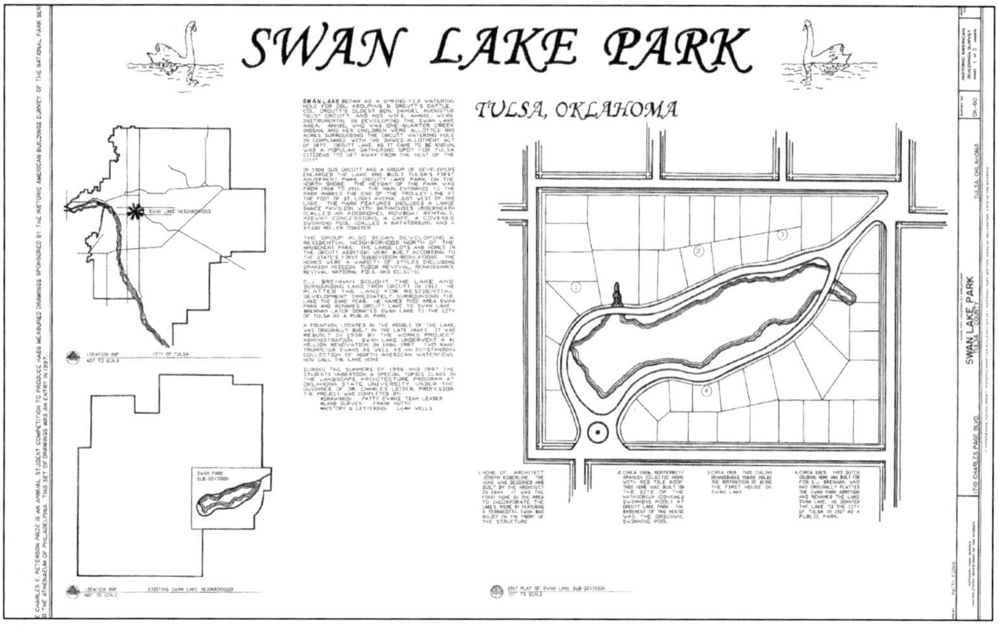

The poster shows the location of the Swan Lake Park in Tulsa and its neighborhood off South Utica Avenue along with a brief history of the property and a site plan of the park in the subdivision. The subdivision represents one of the first efforts in Tulsa and Oklahoma in 1917 to use a pond as focal point for the design for a land development project.

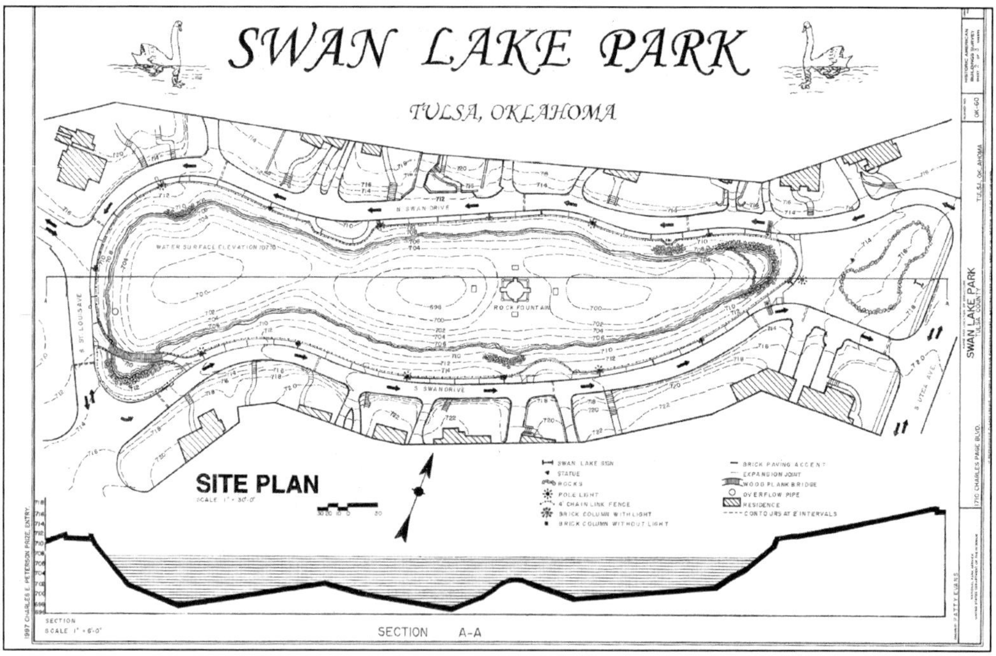

The pond is the centerpiece of the park in the Swan Lake neighborhood, with a perimeter road around the park and lake. The as-built measured drawing shows a profile of the lake's depth. The Swan Lake subdivision was one of the first developments in Oklahoma to introduce the idea of using a pond as a residential amenity. The American Planning Association in 2014 selected it as one of America's best neighborhoods.

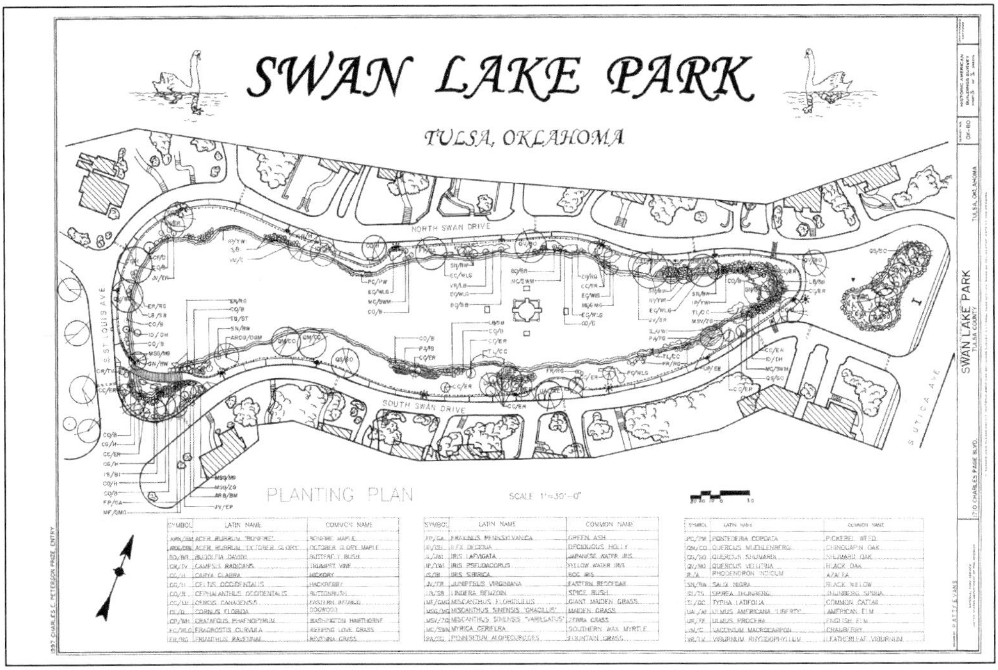

The as-built measured drawing of the planting plan shows that the park has been designed in a naturalistic style. The plan identifies the locations and the names of plants used in the park. A wide variety of trees and shrubs were used. Over 50 percent of the park was left open to provide views of the pond to drivers and the surrounding houses.

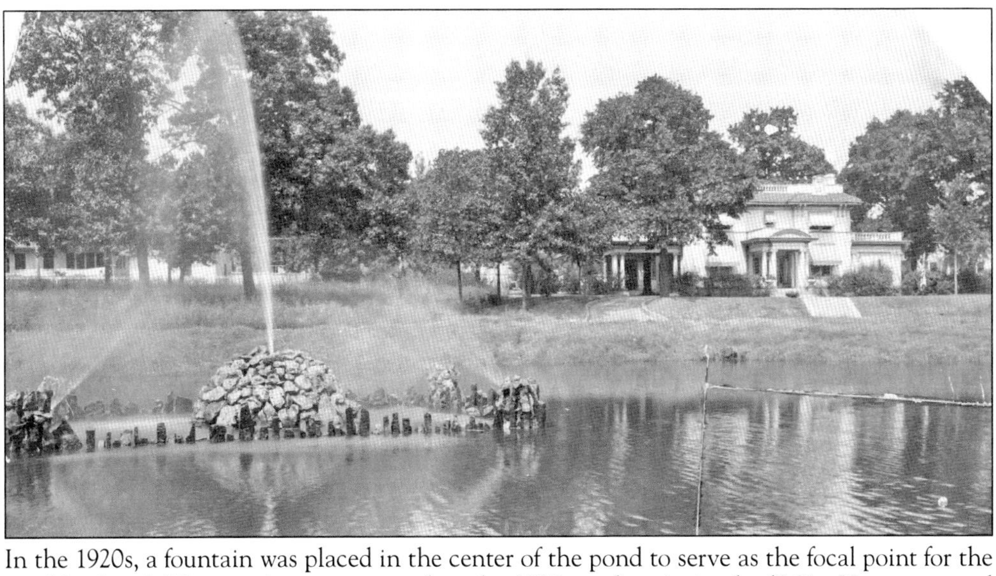

In the 1920s, a fountain was placed in the center of the pond to serve as the focal point for the neighborhood. The pond was renovated in the 1930s and again in the 1960s. Homes around the park enjoy pleasant views of the pond. The park is managed and maintained by the Tulsa Department of Parks. (Courtesy Tulsa Historical Society & Museum.)

Utica Square, Tulsa
Type of Project: Urban Design
Designer: Don Nix and Dale Carter Date: 1951

Utica Square is a suburban shopping center in south Tulsa on the corner of Twenty-First Street and Utica Avenue. It was conceived by developers to accommodate customers so they did not have to travel downtown to shop. At first, developers had difficulty gaining financial backing, since the location was considered on the outskirts of the city. This location turned out to be a viable choice, because Utica Square is now in what is considered midtown Tulsa. After months of consideration and design, construction finally began in 1951, and the shopping center formally opened 15 months later, on May 22, 1952. Utica Square was not only Tulsa's first and finest suburban shopping center, it is also considered one of the country's first. Throughout their planning, the original developers of Utica Square (Don Nix and Dale Carter) had the community in mind. The shopping center was built in a series of small blocks, much like a village or community. This design was meant to be inviting to customers without alienating neighboring residents. Today, the surrounding residences are some of the priciest in Tulsa. The architectural style of Utica Square varies from Georgian to country French and Contemporary. Stringent regulations on storefront designs were enforced to create cohesiveness throughout the shopping center.

The landscape of Utica Square has developed over the years into a simplistic, rectilinear design. Its main features include large and small trees complementing bronze lighting, clocks, and sculptures, a contemporary rectilinear design with well-manicured gardens, changing seasonal color in plantings, and a central garden. When Utica Square was acquired by Helmerich and Payne in 1964, Walter Helmerich commissioned the planting of over 300 trees. In the long run, these trees have created a defining scale with the low commercial buildings. Simply put, Walter Helmerich wanted to beautify Utica Square.

The wealth of trees allowed for a variety ranging from evergreens to deciduous and deciduous flowering. Besides basic street lighting, which primarily surrounds the perimeter of the property, there are ornamental outdoor lamps that portray a late-19th-century English village look. Several bronze clocks are spread throughout the site and remind visitors of times past. Placed sporadically throughout the site are bronze and carved wood sculptures. Each is full scale and placed in locations that provide an emphasis to the overall landscape. All of these features add a sense of sophistication and elegance to the contemporary rectilinear design. This design is further complemented by the use of changing seasonal color in the gardens. This includes different colored begonias, mixed hibiscus, colorful rhododendrons, ornamental grasses, petunias, periwinkles, and many more species. There are extensive plantings throughout the site, but the central garden is what attracts the most attention to the overall landscape. Within the central garden are four ornamental lamps, a carved wood sculpture, and a water feature with a bronze sculpture in the center. The central garden serves as a meeting point for visitors, whether everyday shoppers or tourists.

Study Director: Dr. Charles L. Leider, Landscape Architecture Program
Faculty Advisor: Dr. William Bryans, Department of History
Study Team Member: Tyler Jurney

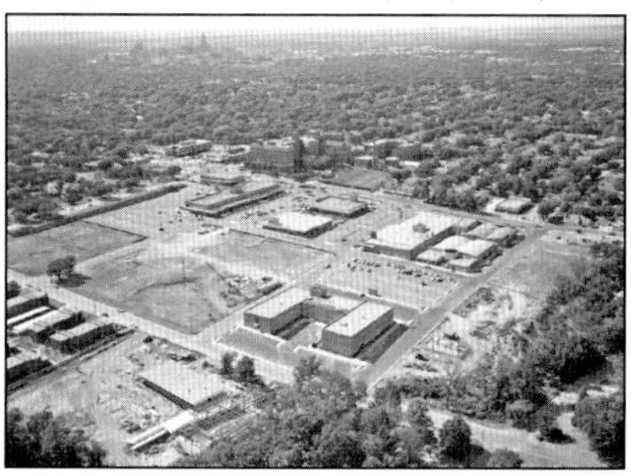

An aerial view of Utica Square in the 1950s looking toward downtown Tulsa shows a bare, undeveloped site compared to the heavy tree cover of the surrounding neighborhood. The site is surrounded by South Utica Avenue on the west, Twenty-First Street on the north, Twenty-Second Street on the south, and South Wheeling Avenue on the east. (Courtesy Tulsa Historical Society & Museum.)

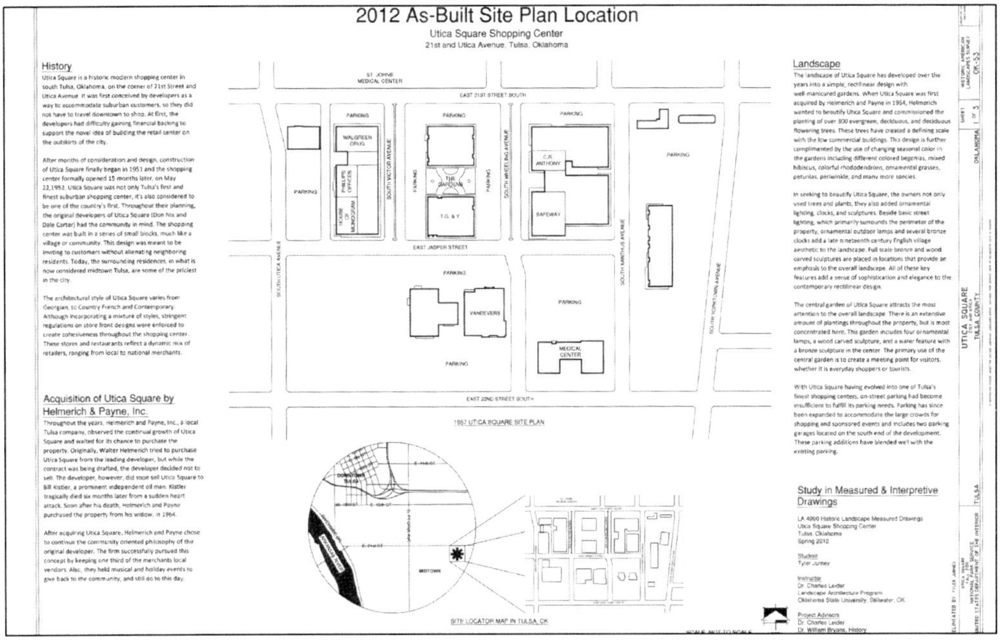

The poster gives the history of the development of Utica Square, with maps showing its location within the city and neighborhood and a 1957 site plan showing the layout of the shopping center fronting on East Twenty-First Street across from St. Johns Medical Center. It was the first green shopping center with internal streets to develop in Oklahoma and introduce a landscape treatment of trees on its internal streets, to create a green canopy, and planting beds throughout the site.

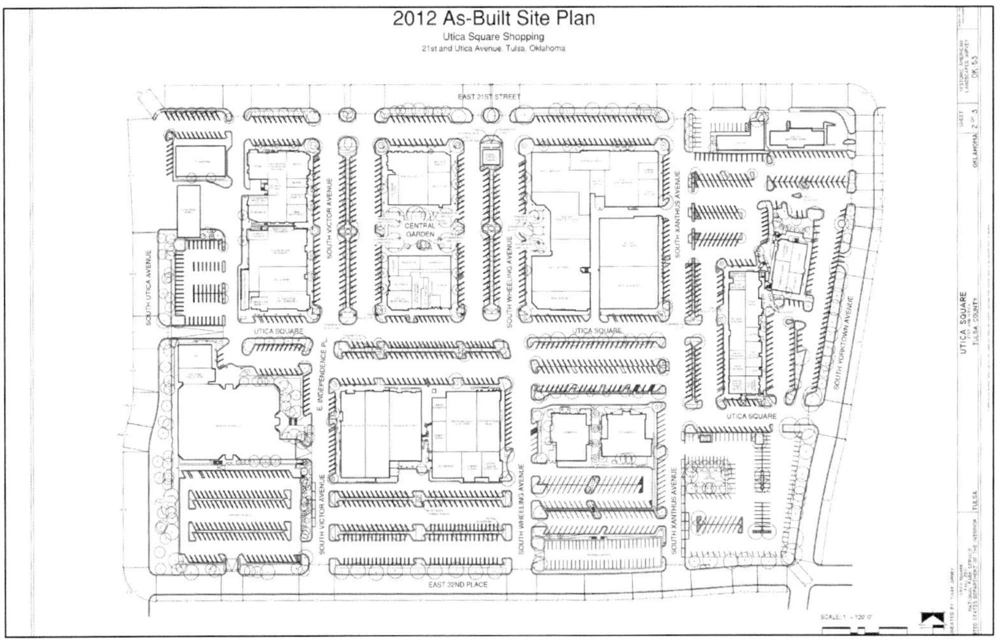

The 2012 as-built measured site plan shows the build-out of the shopping center, with the central green as the focal point of the development. The site featured landscaped parking medians with trees and integrated close-in parking with the internal street system. Shade trees were planted along the sidewalks through the site.

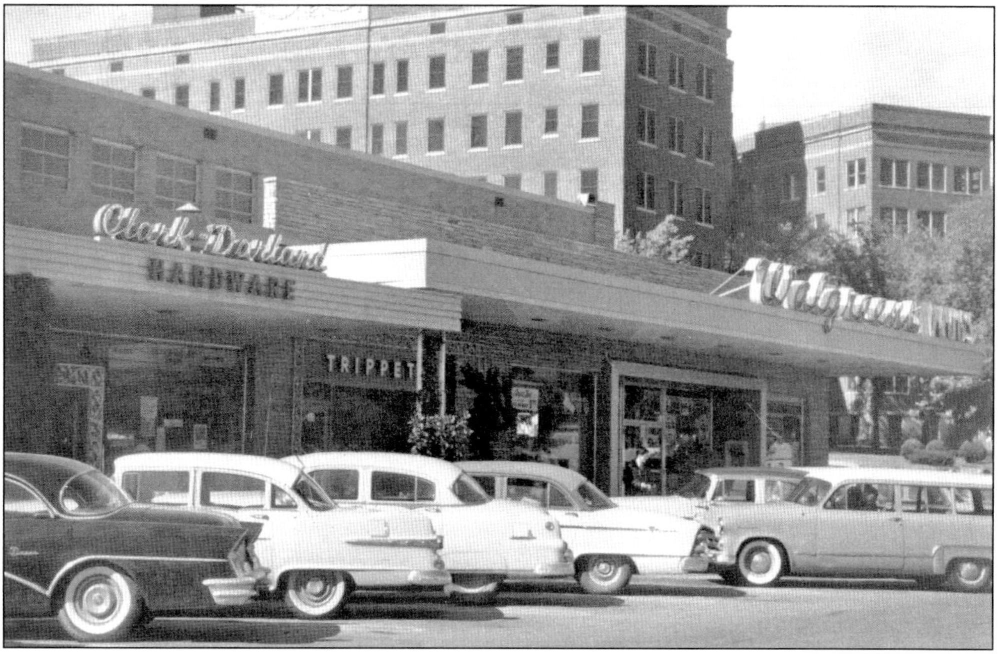

Utica Square was the first shopping center in the 1960s in Tulsa to use on-site storefront parking with covered sidewalks or shade trees and flowers. Access to the shopping center is provided off Twenty-First Street across from St. Johns Medical Center. (Courtesy Tulsa Historical Society & Museum.)

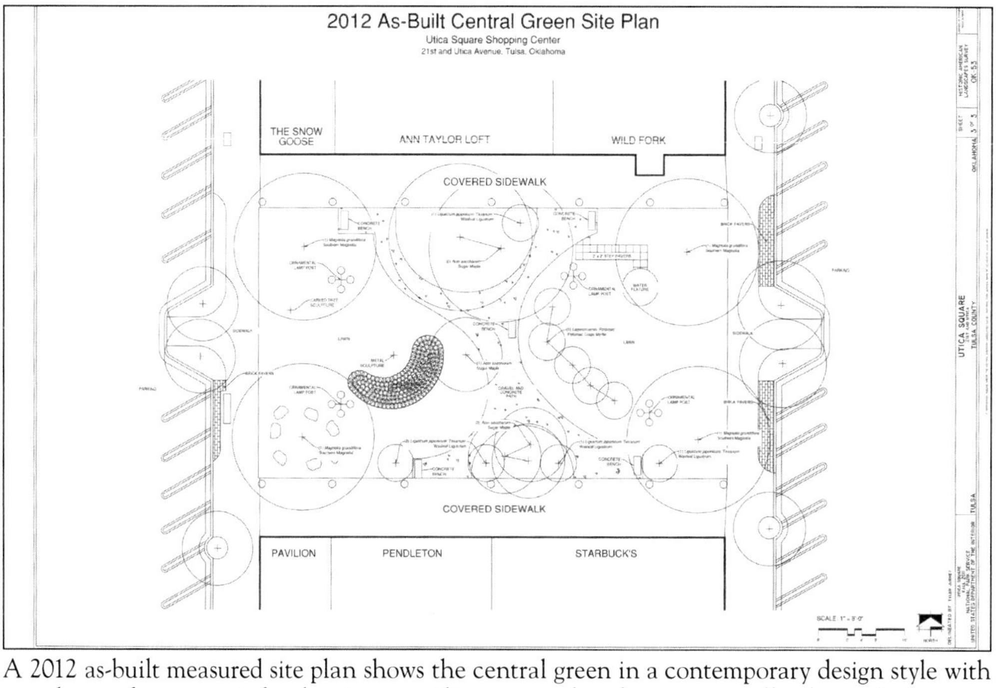

A 2012 as-built measured site plan shows the central green in a contemporary design style with a sculpture feature as it focal point, curvilinear gravel and concrete walks, large shade trees, irregular planting beds, concrete benches, night lighting, and convenient covered walkways in front of the stores.

Five

Vernacular Landscapes

101 Ranch Headquarters Site, Ponca City
Type of Project: Site Plan
Developer: Miller Brothers, Marland, Oklahoma Date: 1929

The 101 Ranch, located a few miles south of Ponca City, encompassed over 110,000 acres at its peak in the late 1920s. It was one of the largest ranches in Oklahoma and the United States. It evolved in several distinct stages, beginning with cattle drives, homesteading in a dugout, ranching, farming, orchards, meatpacking, rodeos, and traveling Wild West shows. The success of the ranch can be contributed to the grazing rights leased from the Ponca Indians.

Its annual round-ups drew people from across the nation to purchase food, enjoy a Wild West show, order a custom saddle, get ice cream from the dairy, stroll the apple orchards, and even see an elephant. Food processing was a significant part of the ranch operation and involved meatpacking, canning, and orchard fruits that went into chutney.

The 101 Ranch headquarters is considered a National Historic Landmark. Today, the visitor will only see a few dilapidated buildings and overgrown foundations. The ranch fell victim to a succession of man-made and natural disasters in the 1920s and through the Great Depression of the 1930s. During this period, the majority of buildings were auctioned for materials. Some buildings escaping destruction included the dairy barns and the general store. Others, like the blacksmith shop, burned when a fire in an adjoining field raged out of control. The immediate danger to the foundations of the remaining buildings, including the White House, is erosion of the site by the main channel of the Salt Fork of the Arkansas River.

The White House was the principal residence of the Miller family at the 101 Ranch. The style of the Greek Revival house was influenced by the owner of the ranch, Joe Miller, and inspired by the plantation architecture of Kentucky, where Joe lived as a young man. Features include an elevated entry and limited ornamentation in prominent locations. The Greek Revival style creates an impression of grandeur, while the porches and overhangs create an imposing presence.

Just as the White House was an integrated design, the entire headquarters site was organized according to function and use. The site contained many different buildings: dairy barns (for 500 Holsteins), meatpacking, tannery, and creamery buildings, a restaurant, a hotel, an office, a grocery store, cider mill, silos, a water tower, a blacksmith shop, a school, a grandstand, a bunkhouse, a foreman's house, houses for key staff members, and summer vacation houses along the river. These structures, located along a central corridor, divided the site into three functional areas—one each for agriculture, livestock, and people.

The Oklahoma State Historic Preservation Office assisted in developing the study approach. Mark Gregory of OSU provided a 1930 aerial photograph that was enlarged and digitized to determine the location of the building footprints and major vegetation. Historic photographs from the Western History Collection were used to identify the plant material.

Study Director: Dr. Charles L. Leider, Landscape Architecture Program
Faculty Advisors: Dr. William Bryans, Department of History; Prof. Nigel Jones, School of Architecture
Study Team Members: Brad Hoffman and Taylor King, team co-leaders; Jerod Costner; Amy Carrel; Budi Laksanna; Steve Leider; Holly Martin; Bill Odle; and Sri Sugeng

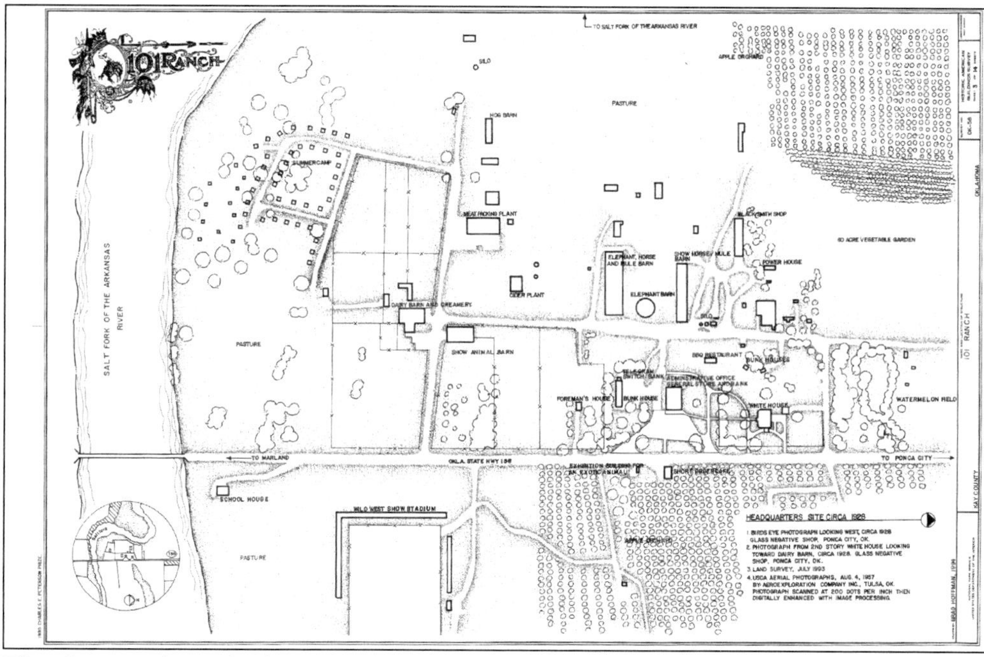

This drawing shows the layout of the 101 Ranch headquarters site at its height in 1929. The ranch at that time included the White House, barns and pens, a bunkhouse/hotel, a two-story store and office building, a café, an exotic animal building, a grandstand with entertainment area, 15 visitor cottages along the South Fork of the Arkansas River, orchards, vegetable fields, and pastureland.

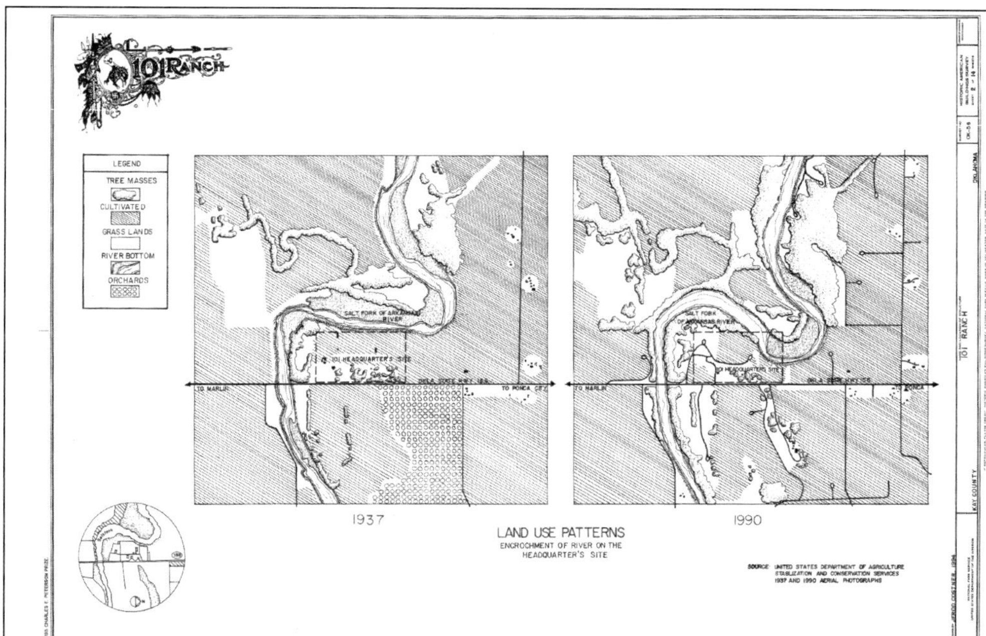

Two maps of the ranch in 1937 and 1993 show the encroachment of the South Fork of the Arkansas River on the headquarters site. The ranch headquarters has been designated a National Historic Landmark by the National Park Service. It is one of the few national landmarks in Oklahoma.

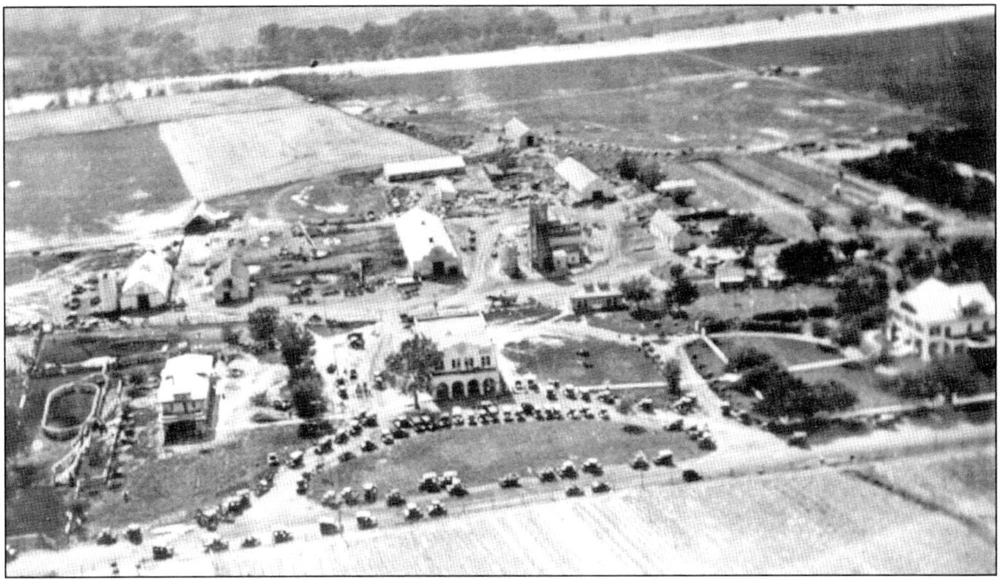

This c. 1929 aerial view of the headquarters site was taken looking west toward the South Fork of the Arkansas River. The site shows the compact development of the headquarters in contrast to the extensive fields surrounding the built-up area of the ranch and the distance of the river from the built-up area. (Courtesy the E.W. Marland Estate Archives.)

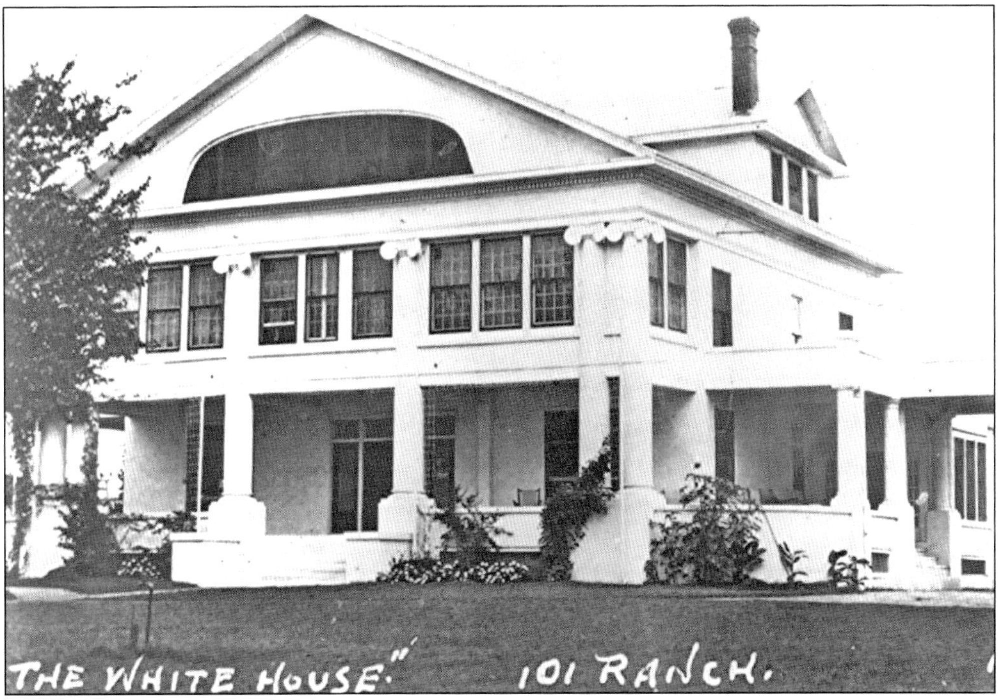

This view of the White House faces south towards the ranch yard in the 1920s. The house was designed in a Greek Revival style influenced by Southern plantations, reflecting the heritage of the Miller family. They came from Kentucky to the Pawnee tribe's assigned land in the Indian Territory after the Civil War to raise cattle on land leased from the tribe. (Courtesy Marland's Grand Home Archives.)

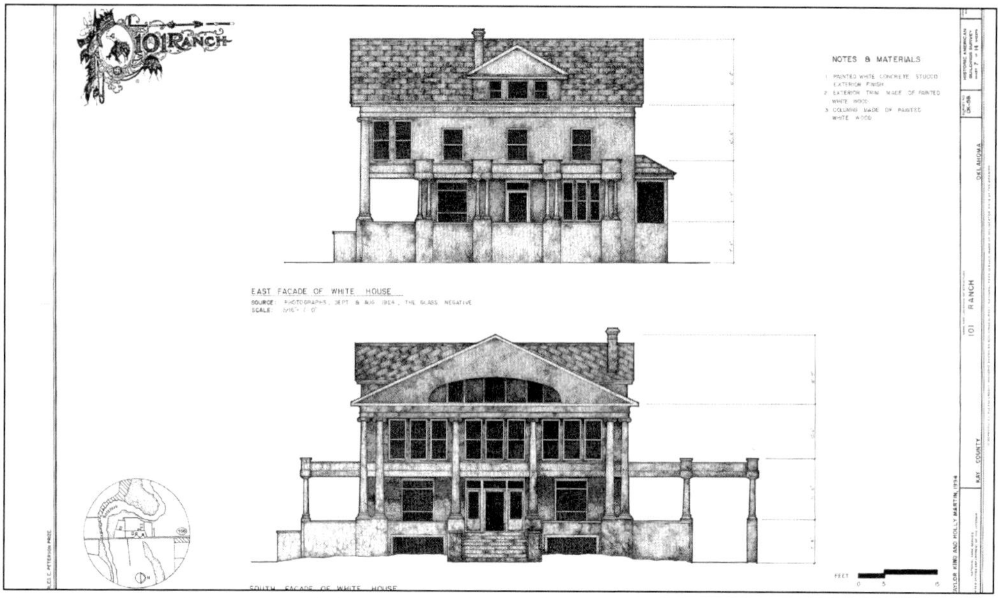

As-built measured drawings of the south and east elevations of the White House in the 1920s show that the house was built of concrete for fire protection, as there was no fire station in the area. The foundation was four feet high to protect against the occasional spring flooding from the river. Covered entrances were provided at the first-floor front and side doors of the house, including the driveway.

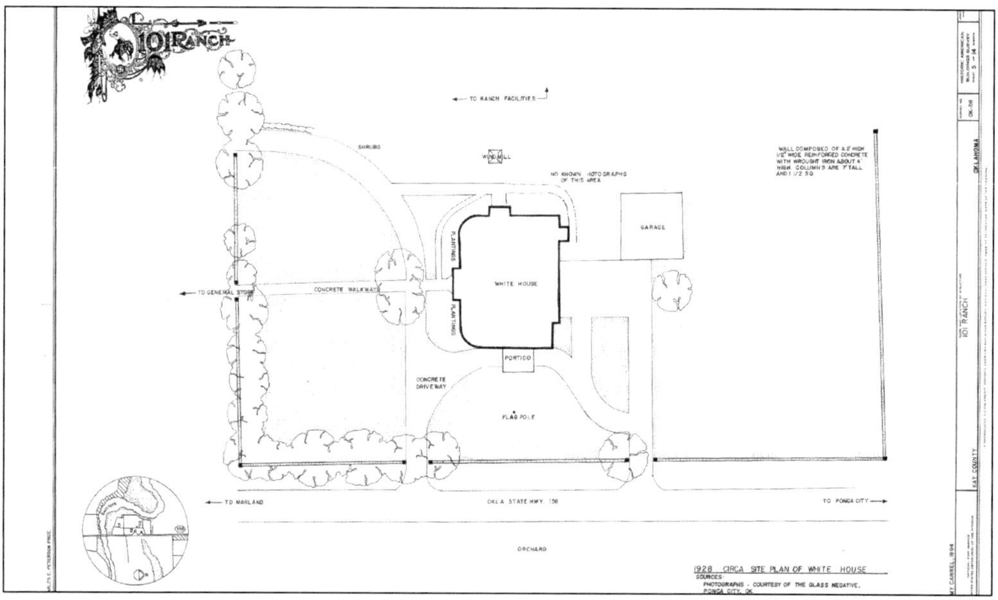

The as-built measured site and planting plan show the White House's landscape was designed in a naturalistic style in the 1920s with a U-shaped curvilinear drive way connecting the front and side doors of house and garage to the highway and the ranch yard. Vegetation was used on the south and east sides to partially screen the house from the highway and general store and café in the commercial area to the south. Trees were used to accent the entrance to the driveway from the highway. Shrubbery was used to soften the foundation of the house and to visually connect the house to the lawn.

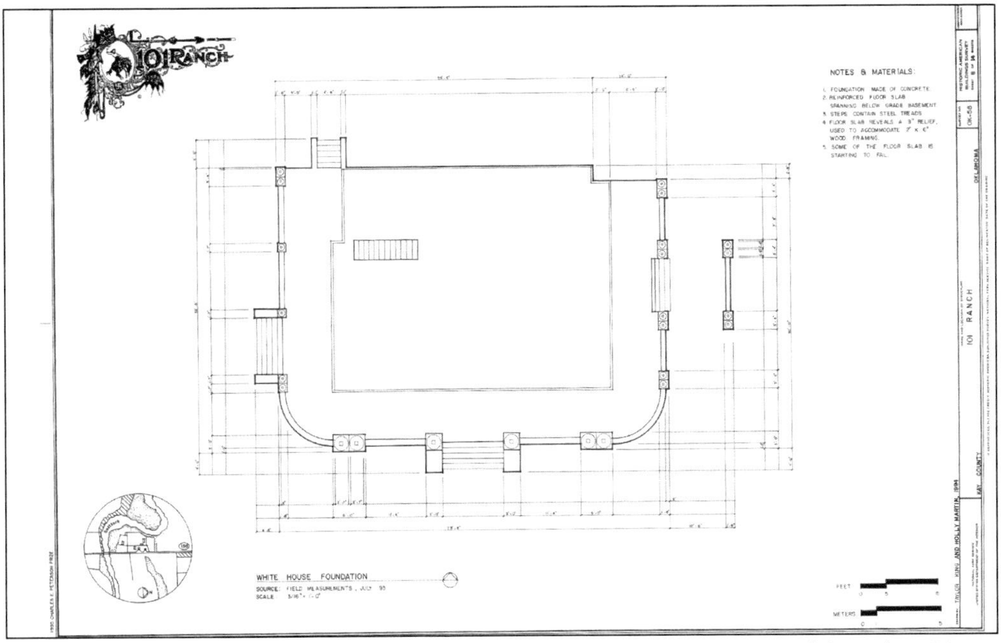

The as-built measured drawing shows the plan of the remaining foundation of the White House in 1933 after it was torn down following the auction of ranch. The foundation reveals that the footings and walls for the house were made of a very durable concrete that supported a full basement and a three-story structure.

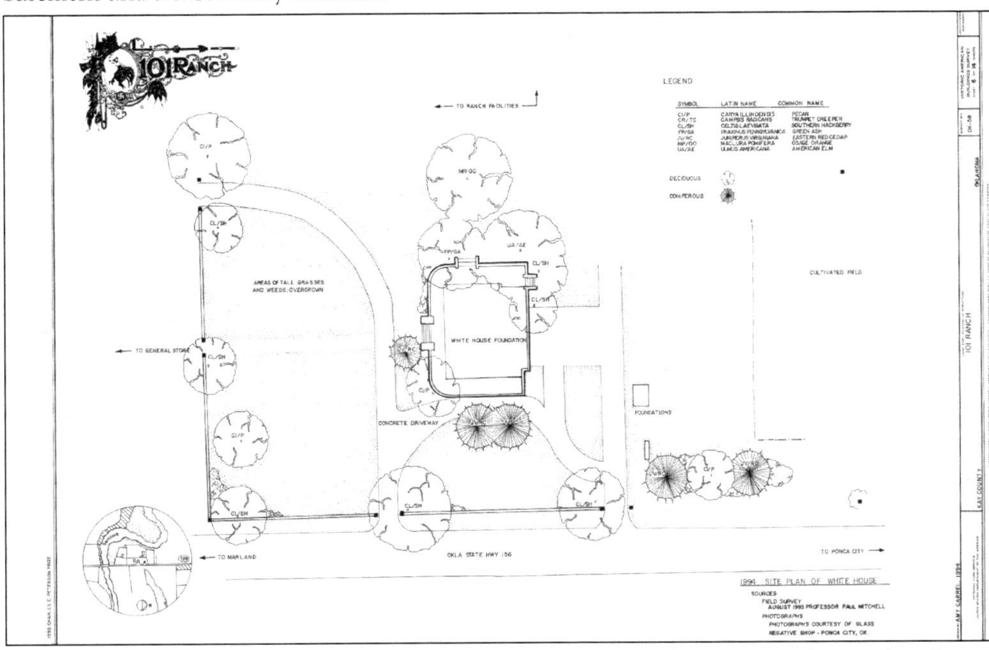

The 1994 as-built measured site and planting plan show the White House after its demolition. The site retained its original naturalistic landscape style and U-shaped driveway. Remnants of the vegetation used to screen the house from the highway, store, and café on the south and east side remain, as do trees used accent the entrance to the driveway. The shrubbery used to soften the foundation of the house and visually connect the house to the lawn has disappeared.

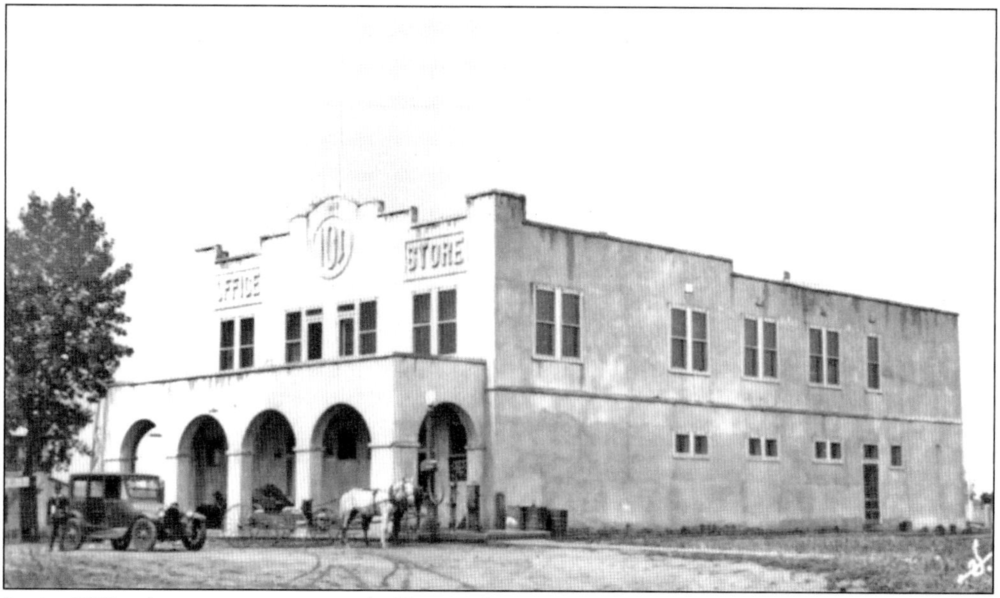

In the 1930s, the two-story store and office, with a one-story arcade in the front and a gas station, was deeply set back from the highway. The first floor was used as general store, while the second floor housed the administrative office of the ranch. A wide, U-shaped driveway with an open lawn from the highway provided access to the building with parking on either side of the entrance drive. (Courtesy Joe Glaser, 101 Old Timers Association.)

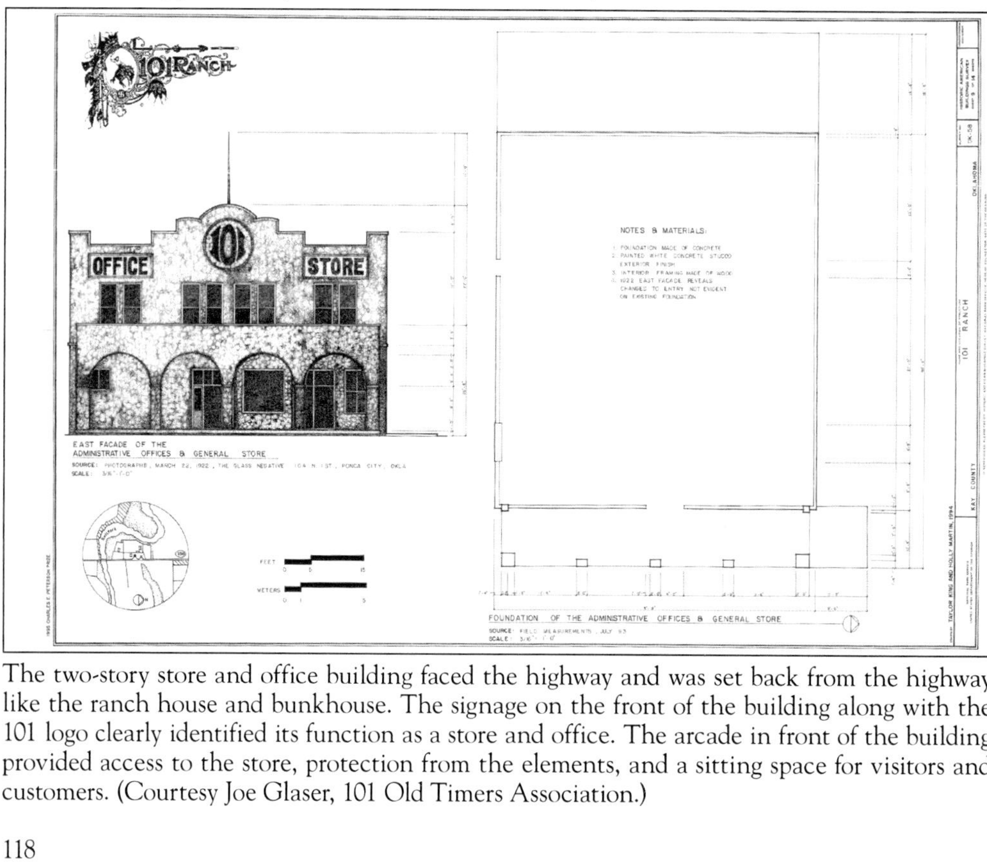

The two-story store and office building faced the highway and was set back from the highway like the ranch house and bunkhouse. The signage on the front of the building along with the 101 logo clearly identified its function as a store and office. The arcade in front of the building provided access to the store, protection from the elements, and a sitting space for visitors and customers. (Courtesy Joe Glaser, 101 Old Timers Association.)

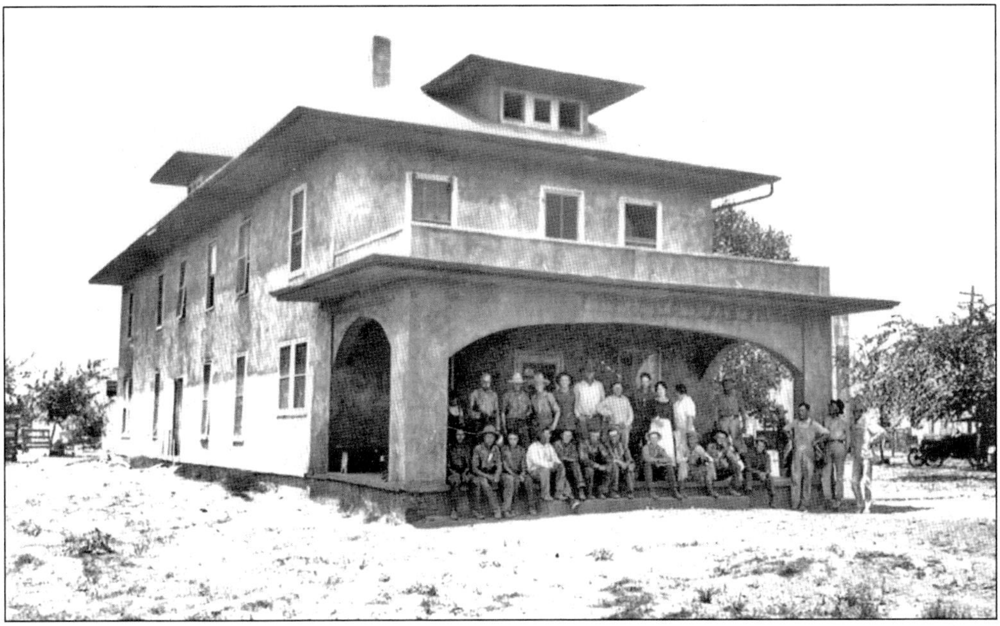

The three-story combination bunkhouse and hotel, as it appeared in 1920s, was south of the store facing the highway and set back in line with the store and ranch house. A front walkway connected all three buildings. The bunkhouse was screened from the store by a small grove of trees. (Courtesy Joe Glaser, 101 Old Timers Association.)

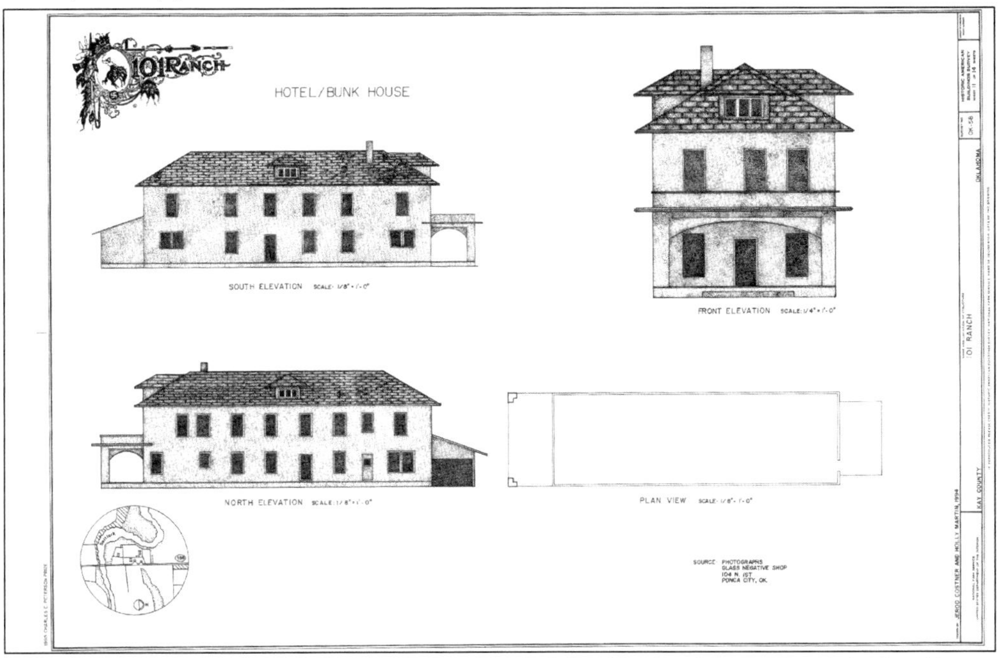

The as-built measured drawings of the elevations of the front and two sides of the bunkhouse show the three-story structure in 1929. The building faced the highway and was on the same setback as the store and ranch house. The front porch provided a sitting space for guests and visitors. A lean-to at the rear of the building provided a storage space. Parking was on the north side of the building.

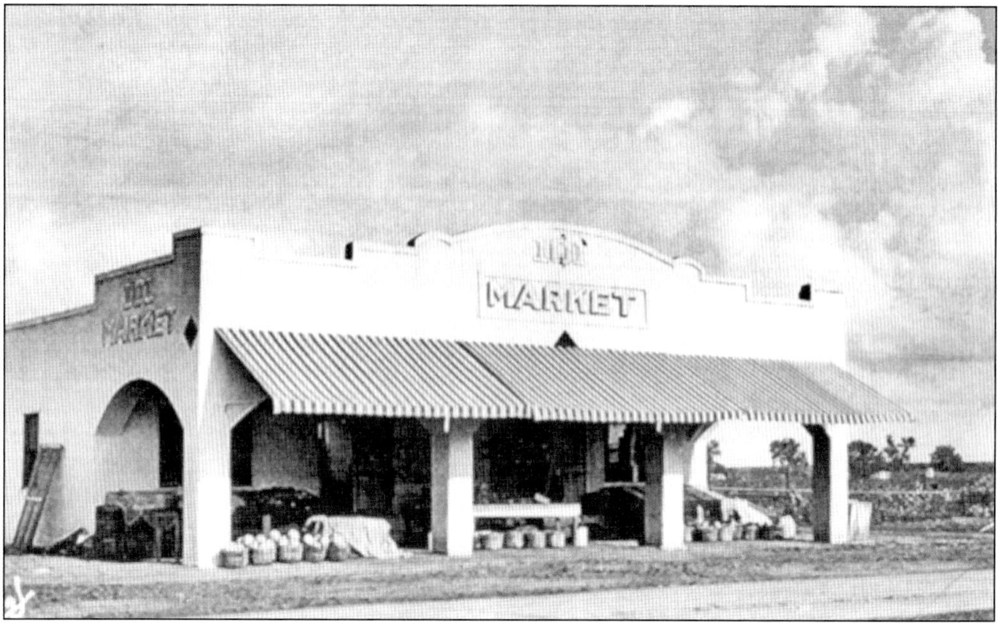

The market was a one-story building that sold ranch-grown vegetables and fruit in the 1920s. It was behind the store along with a circular road with parking. The front of the building contained an arcade and a sun awning for shade. (Courtesy Joe Glaser, 101 Old Timers Association.)

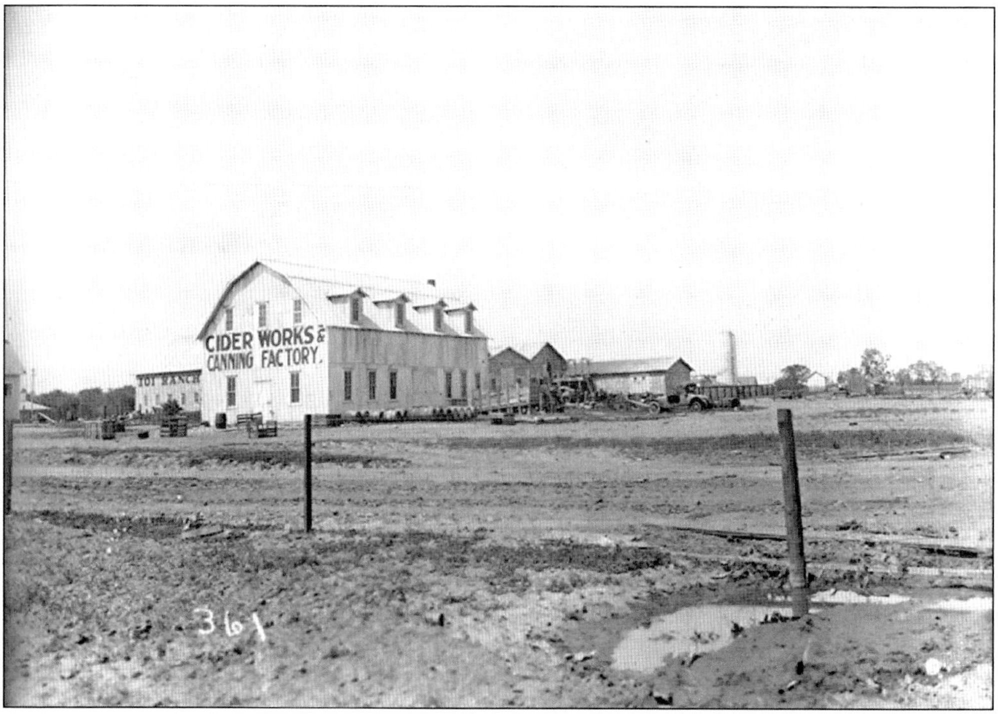

A three-story cider factory and cannery was located in the yard in the 1920s along with other functional buildings. This location provided the building with easy access for unloading produce and shipping finished products through the main entrance past the ranch house to the highway. (Courtesy Joe Glaser, 101 Old Timers Association.)

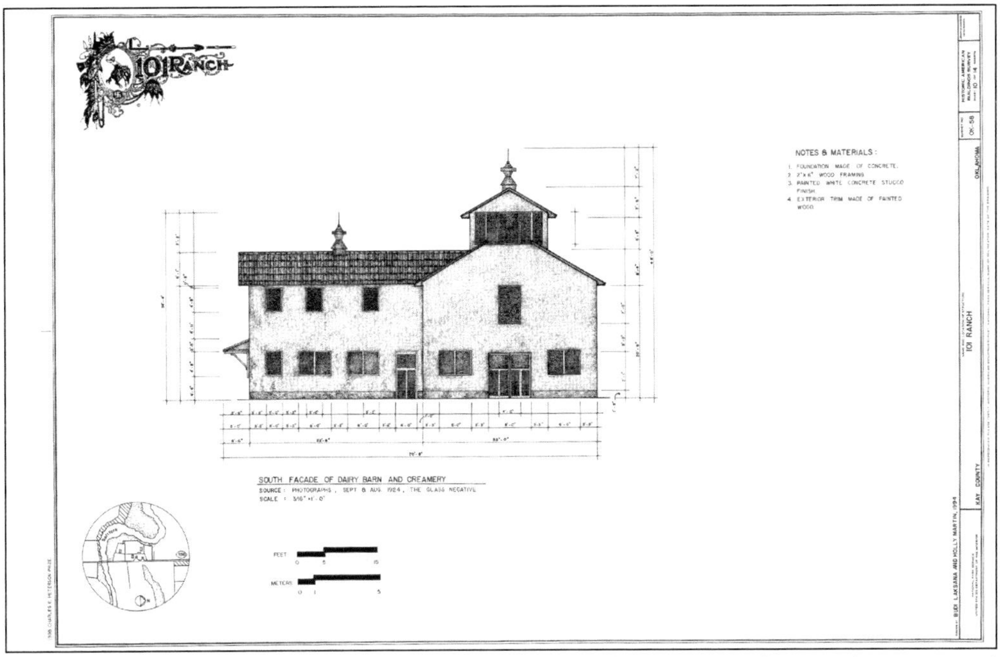

These as-built measured drawings show the dairy barn and creamery with a cupola as it existed in the 1920s and the south elevation of the two-story stucco rectangular frame building. The building was in the yard with other functional buildings. This location provided easy access for trucks through the main entrance road past the ranch house to the highway.

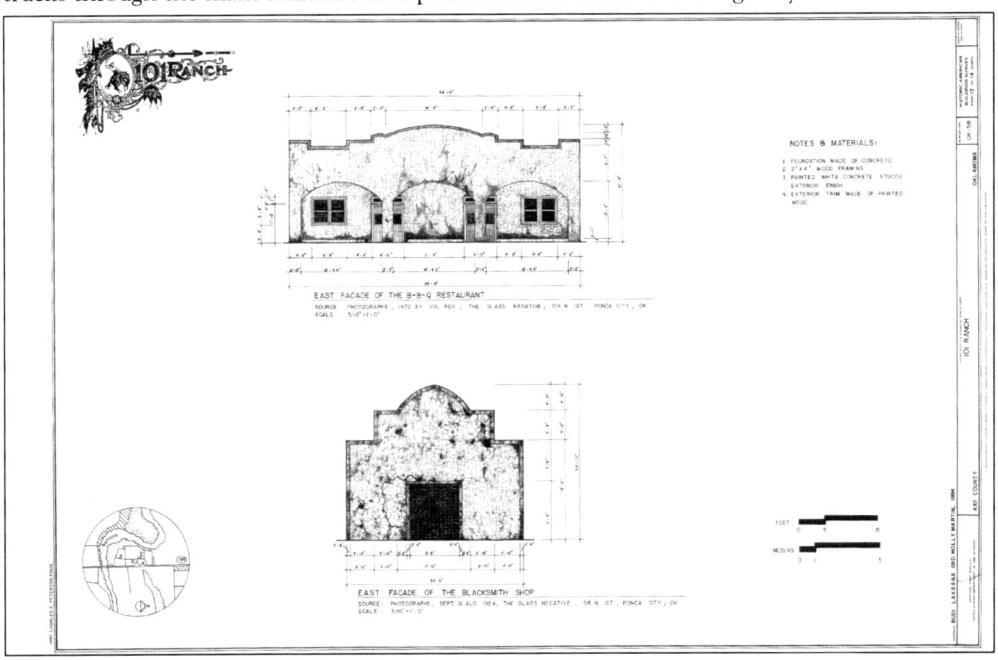

The as-built measured drawings of the elevations in the 1920s show the stucco south facade of the one-story barbecue restaurant and the one-story east stucco facade of the blacksmith shop, which was in the yard behind the store and bunkhouse. This location provided easy access for costumers and workers through walkways and driveways.

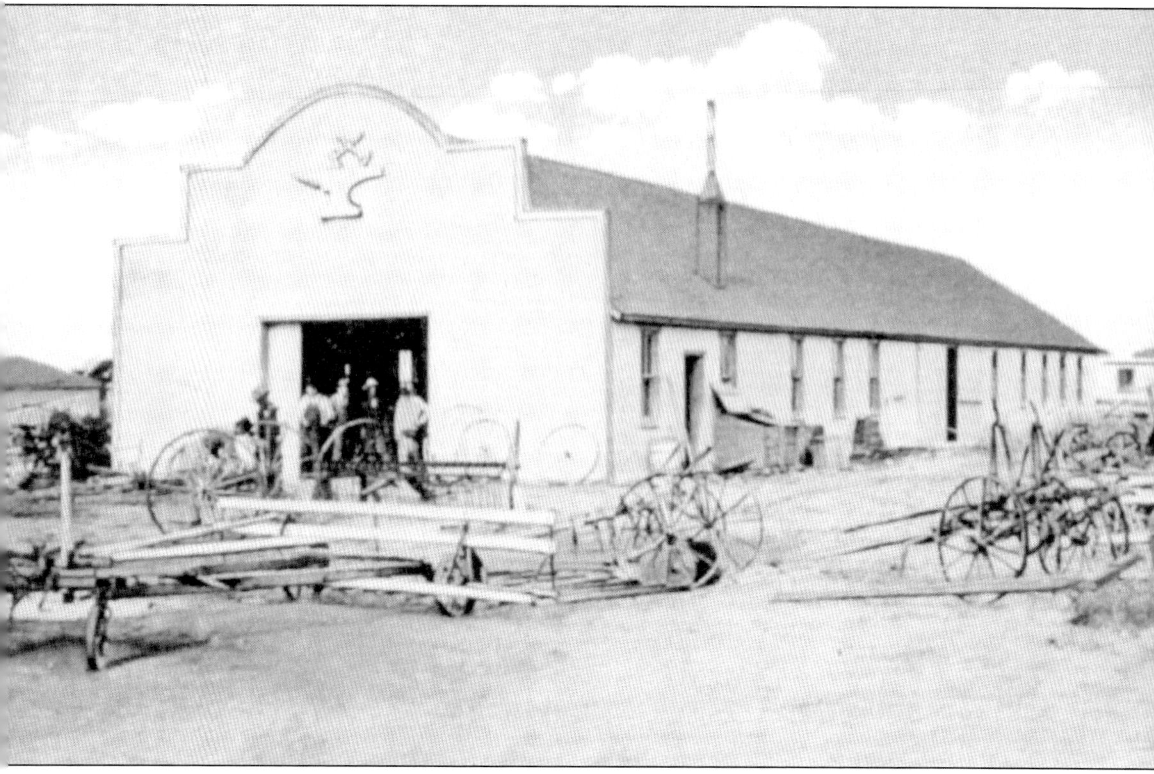

A view shows the single-story rectangular stucco blacksmith shop in the 1920s. It was in the yard close to the horse pens and barn and other functional buildings. This location provided the building with easy access for its services. (Courtesy Joe Glaser, 101 Old Timers Association.)

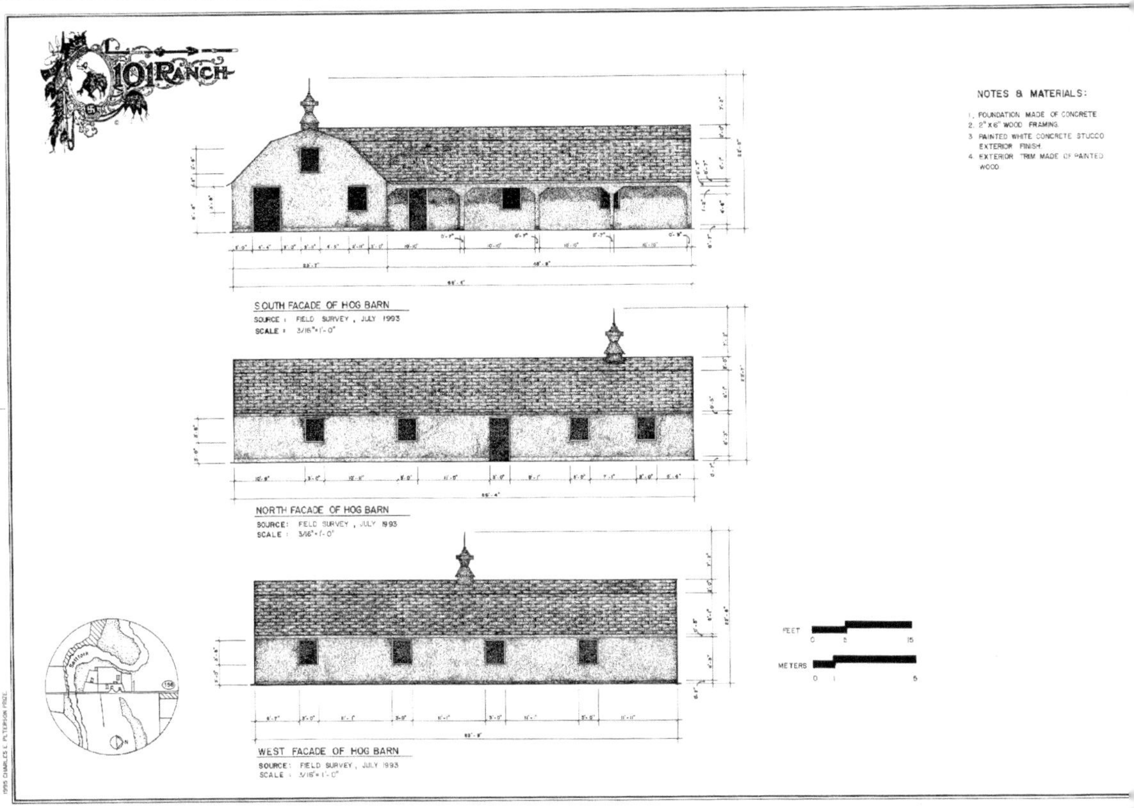

The single-story rectangular stucco hog barn, in this 1993 as-built measured drawing, was one of the few buildings remaining on the headquarters site. Because of odors, it was on the far edge of the yard, away from other inhabited buildings.

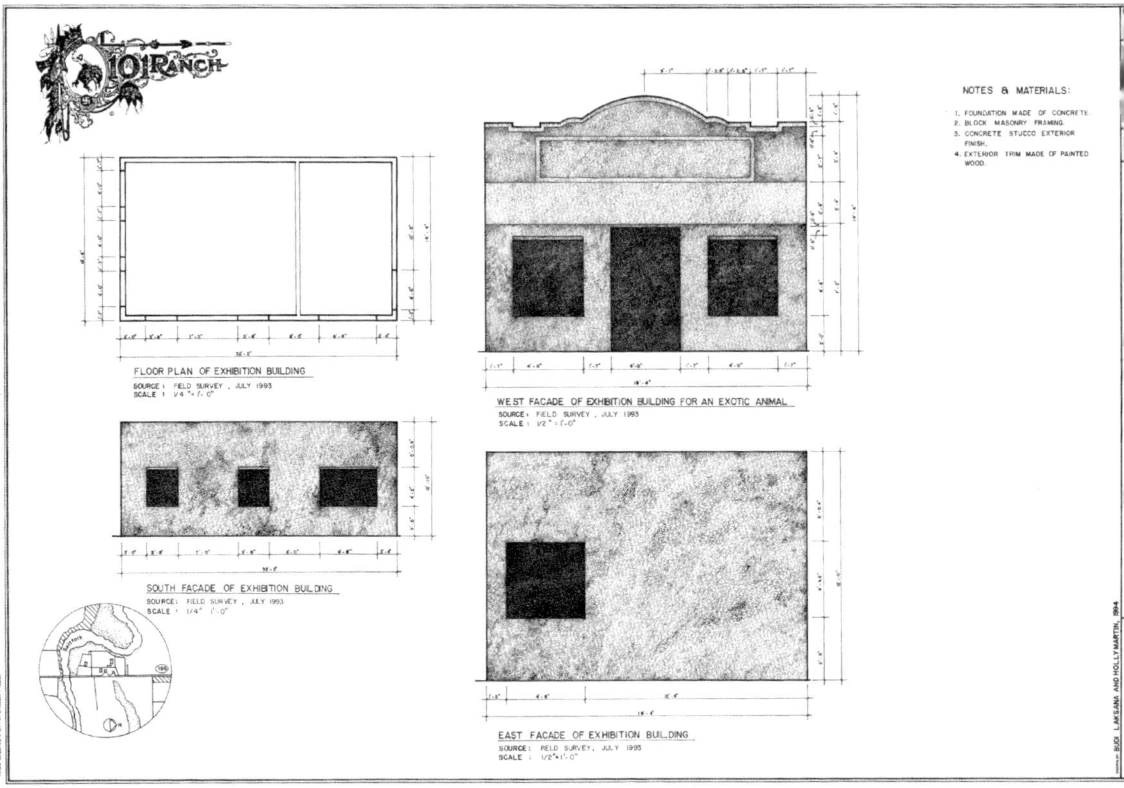

A 1920 as-built measured floor plan and elevations on three sides show the exotic animal building. The building was in the commercial area of the ranch near the store, market, and restaurant. It attracted visitors from all over the region to view the animals.

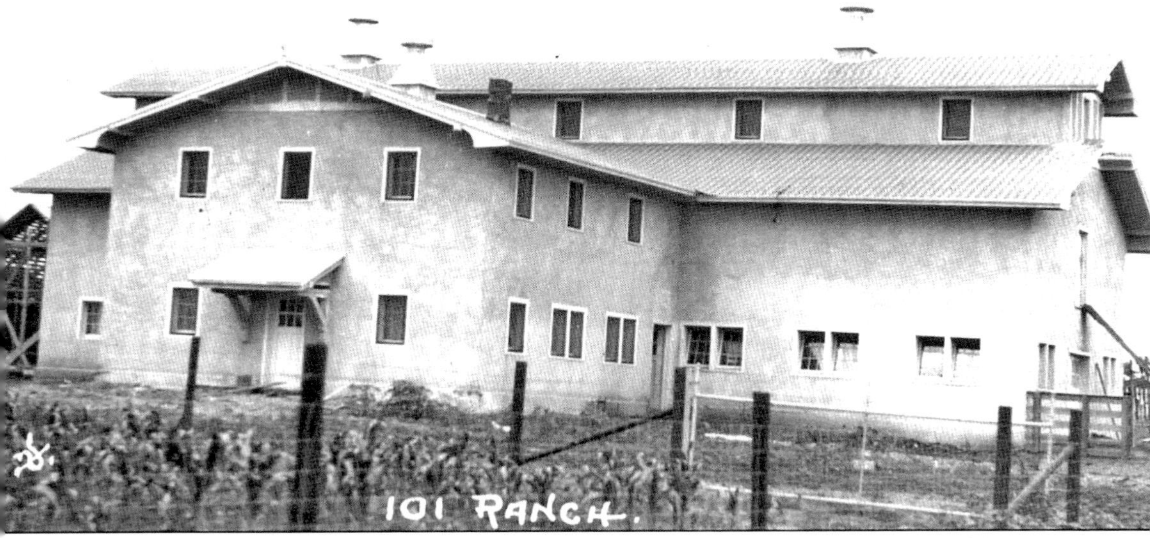

The dairy barn in the 1920s was a combination two- and three-story T-shaped frame building in a fenced-in area for the cows on the west side of the yard with other functional buildings. This location provided the building with easy access for loading milk and supplies. (Courtesy Joe Glaser, 101 Old Timers Association.)

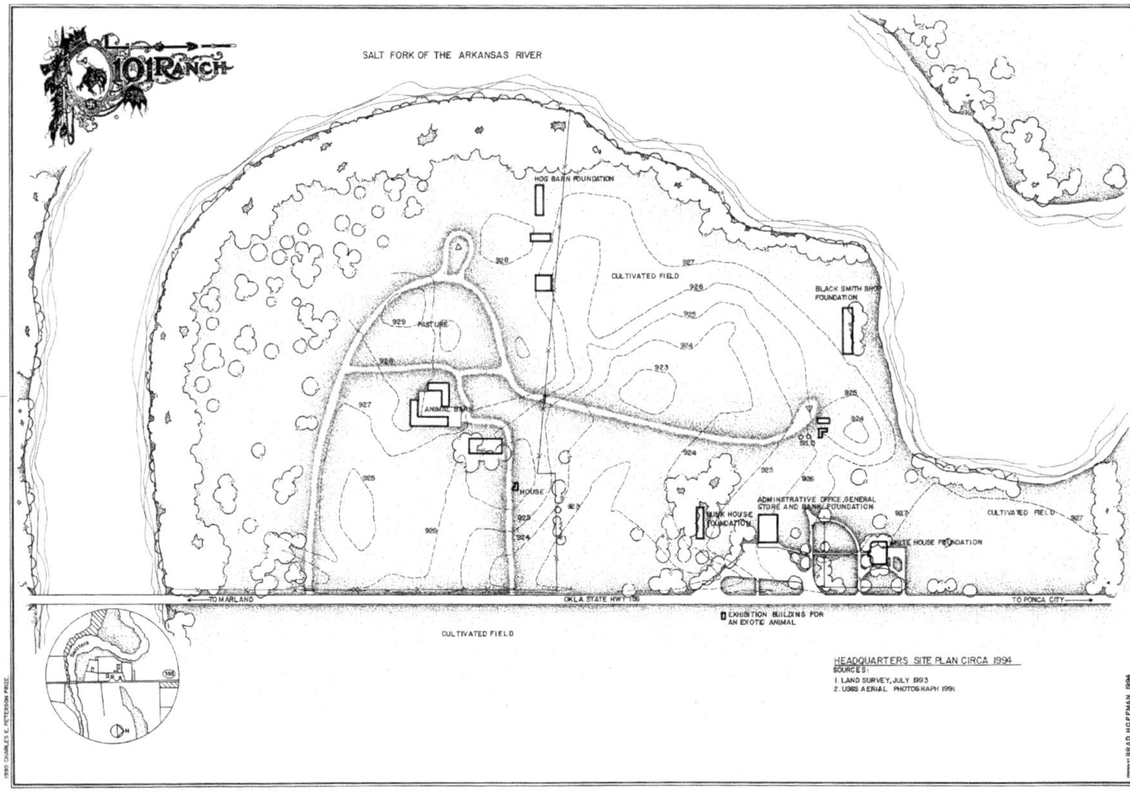

A 1993 as-built measured drawing of the headquarters site shows the encroachment and threat of the river to this national landmark. The hog house was the only remaining building on the site in 1993. The site contains a few foundations of the White House, store and office building, and bunkhouse; it is now an archeological site. A farm with a house and barns was built on the south half of the headquarters site after the land was sold at an auction in the 1930s.

Sources:
Laura Streich, director of the Pioneer Museum
Glass Negative Shop of Ponca City
Oklahoma Historical Society
Western History Collection, University of Oklahoma

Key Citations

Case Studies of Oklahoma Historic Cultural Landscape As-Built Measured and Interpretive Drawings, 1989–2009. US Department of Interior, filed with US Library of Congress (memory.loc.gov/ammem/collections/habs_haer/):

Council Oak Park, Tulsa
Frank Phillips Mansion, Bartlesville
Capitol Hill Park, Guthrie
Honor Heights Park and Union Agency, Muskogee
Tulsa Municipal Rose Garden
Villa Philbrook, Tulsa
101 Ranch, Marland
Cultural Landscape Foundation: Year in Review, 2009

Cultural Landscape Foundation, Washington, DC.
O'Donnell, Patricia M. "IFLA and Cultural Landscapes." *International Federation of Landscape Architects* 81 (March 2009).
Oklahoma Department of Tourism and Recreation. "Self-Guided Regional Driving Tours." www.travelok.com.
Oklahoma State Outdoor Recreation Plan. Oklahoma City: Oklahoma Department of Tourism and Recreation, 1987.
Rossler, Mechtild, and Kerstin Manz. "World Heritage Cultural Landscapes." *International Federation of Landscape Architects* 81 (March 2009).
Survey and Analysis of Historic Designed Landscapes. Student report for Dr. Charles L. Leider, Landscape Architecture Program, Oklahoma State University, 1987.
"World Heritage Site." Wikipedia (accessed June 2010).

Appendix

Survey List of Nominated Historic Landscapes in 1987 by Community

Asher–Sacred Heart Mission
Bartlesville–Frank Phillips Estate, Hillcrest Golf Course
Claremore–Will Rogers Memorial
Enid–Champlin Estate
Fort Gibson–Fort Gibson
Fort Towson–Fort Towson
Guthrie–Scottish Rite Temple
Muskogee–Garfield Buell Estate, Honor Heights Park
Norman–University of Oklahoma
Oklahoma City–Buttram Estate, Oklahoma City Civic Center, Edgemere, Hefner House, Heritage Hills, Fred Jones Estate, Nichols Hills, Overholser Mansion, John Sinopoulo Estate, Spanish Village, State Capitol, Will Rogers Park
Ponca City–Marland Mansion 1, Marland Mansion 2
Stillwater–Thomas Berry Estate, Oklahoma State University
Tulsa–Central Park, Creek Nation Council Oak Park, Thomas Gilcrease Estate, James McBirney Estate, Memorial Park Cemetery, Mohawk Park, Owen Park, Philbrook Art Center, Southern Hills Golf Course, Swan Lake, Terwilleger Heights, Tulsa Garden Center, Tulsa Rose Garden, Woodward Park

Discover Thousands of Local History Books Featuring Millions of Vintage Images

Arcadia Publishing, the leading local history publisher in the United States, is committed to making history accessible and meaningful through publishing books that celebrate and preserve the heritage of America's people and places.

Find more books like this at
www.arcadiapublishing.com

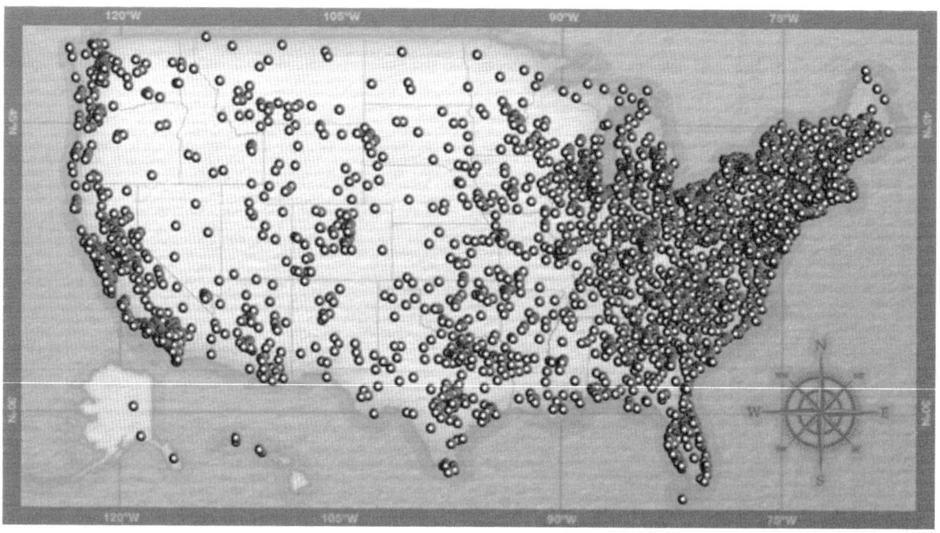

Search for your hometown history, your old stomping grounds, and even your favorite sports team.

Consistent with our mission to preserve history on a local level, this book was printed in South Carolina on American-made paper and manufactured entirely in the United States. Products carrying the accredited Forest Stewardship Council (FSC) label are printed on 100 percent FSC-certified paper.

MADE IN THE USA